The education and care black teachers

Changing identities, changing lives

Audrey Osler

Open University Press
Buckingham • Philadelphia

0335197760

Open University Press
Celtic Court
22 Ballmoor
Buckingham
MK18 1XW

and

1900 Frost Road, Suite 101
Bristol, PA 19007, USA

First Published 1997

Copyright © Audrey Osler, 1997

All rights reserved. Except for the quotation of short passages for the purpose
of criticism and review, no part of this publication may be reproduced, stored in
a retrieval system, or transmitted, in any form or by any means, electronic,
mechanical, photocopying, recording or otherwise, without the prior written
permission of the publisher or a licence from the Copyright Licensing Agency
Limited. Details of such licences (for reprographic reproduction) may be
obtained from the Copyright Licensing Agency Ltd of 90 Tottenham Court
Road, London, W1P 9HE.

A catalogue record of this book is available from the British Library

ISBN   0335 19775 2 (pb)   0335 19776 0 (hb)

Library of Congress Cataloging-in-Publication Data
Osler, Audrey.
    The education and careers of black teachers : changing identities,
changing lives / Audrey Osler.
        p.   cm.
    Includes bibliographical references and index.
    ISBN 0–335-19775–2 (pbk).—ISBN 0–335-19776–0 (hc)
    1. Teachers, Black—Great Britain—Social conditions—Case
studies.   2. Minority teachers—Great Britain—Social conditions—
Case studies.   3. Racism—Great Britain—Case studies.   4. Great
Britain—Race relations—Case studies.   I. Title.
LB1725.G60757   1997   97–9041
371.1′0089′96041—dc21   CIP

Typeset by Graphicraft Typesetters Limited, Hong Kong
Printed in Great Britain by Biddles Ltd, Guildford and King's Lynn

Contents

Acknowledgements

I wish to thank all those colleagues and friends who have supported me in the preparation and writing of this book.

In particular I would like to express a debt of gratitude to all the teachers and students who participated in the research process. I learnt a great deal from you and have been encouraged and inspired by your enthusiasm, hope and determination. Although it would be inappropriate to name you here, I wish to acknowledge your contributions and express my deepest appreciation. I very much enjoyed working with you.

Special thanks to Clive Harber who supervised the thesis on which this book is based, particularly for enabling me to retain my sense of humour throughout. Also to Lynn Davies, Pretap Deshpande, Peter Figueroa, John Hopkin and Robin Richardson for their critical comments, advice and encouragement. To Beverley Burke, Edwina Cooke, Judy Dandy and Surinder Kaur Jalaf for support and assistance with the transcription of tapes. And to Hugh Starkey for acting as my reader.

Researching the life histories of others has made me particularly sensitive to the contributions of many people who have influenced my thinking and sustained and encouraged me at various times in my work over a number of years: Catherine McFarlane, David Ruddell, Vicky Shearn, Jo Shipley, Cas Walker and Heleama Whittaker. Also my parents Esmé and Maurice Osler.

My thanks also to Shona Mullen of the Open University Press for responding so positively and for help and advice in shaping the book.

The author and publishers wish to thank the editors of the *European Journal of Intercultural Studies* for their agreement to our use of material in Chapter 10 adapted from Audrey Osler, Education for democracy and equality: the experiences, values and attitudes of ethnic minority student teachers. *European Journal of Intercultural Studies*, 5(1): 23–37. Also, the editors of *Teachers and Teaching* for material from Audrey Osler, Black teachers and citizenship: researching differing identities. *Teachers and Teaching*, 3(1): 47–60.

Abbreviations and acronyms

A level	GCE Advanced Level
ARTEN	Anti-Racist Teacher Education Network: a voluntary network of teacher educators which aims to promote equality
BEd	Bachelor of Education: a four-year Honours degree resulting in Qualified Teacher Status
CRE	Commission for Racial Equality: a government-funded body, concerned with the implementation of the Race Relations Act 1976
CSE	Certificate of Secondary Education
DES	Department of Education and Science
DfE	Department for Education
DfEE	Department for Education and Employment
EAL	English as an Additional Language
ERA	Education Reform Act 1988
ESL	English as a Second Language
ESG	Educational Support Grant
FE	Further Education
GCE	General Certificate of Education
GCSE	General Certificate of Secondary Education
GRIST	Grant Related In-service Training
HEFCE	Higher Education Funding Council for England
HMI	Her Majesty's Inspectorate
Higher	Scottish Certificate of Education higher level examination, providing access to higher education: equivalent to A level
ITE	initial teacher education, including BEd and PGCE
LEA	Local Education Authority
NAME	National Anti-Racist Movement in Education, a voluntary body
NCC	National Curriculum Council
Ofsted	Office for Standards in Education

O level	GCE O level
PGCE	Postgraduate Certificate of Education: one-year course for graduates leading to Qualified Teacher Status
PSE	Personal and Social Education
TTA	Teacher Training Agency
TVEI	Technical and Vocational Education Initiative

Teachers' pay

Teachers' pay scales in England and Wales have changed a number of times in recent years. At the time of the interviews teachers were paid according to a common pay scale and received 'incentive allowances' A, B, C, D and E in return for taking on particular responsibilities. These allowances corresponded with the former pay scales 1, 2, 3, 4 and Senior Teacher. Teachers are currently paid on a Common Pay Spine with additional incentive points for specific responsibilities.

A number of teachers in this study were employed in Section 11 posts. Section 11 refers to special funding arrangements made under Section 11 of the Local Government Act 1966 for the needs of ethnic minority children.

Introduction

I have written this book out of a concern to make visible the experiences of black and ethnic minority teachers in Britain. The research project on which it is based was undertaken in order to give black[1] teachers an opportunity to speak for themselves; to provide black perspectives on the processes of schooling; and to find out what it feels like to be a black teacher within the context of a society and an education system which is structured not only by class and by gender, but also by 'race'.[2]

Over the last decade or so there has been a growing interest in teachers' lives and careers. Many of these studies have sought to understand how teachers perceive their work (Connell 1985; Apple 1986; Ozga 1988; Hargreaves 1994) and how they develop their particular professional identities and careers (Ball and Goodson 1985; Sikes et al. 1985; Nias 1989). There is a developing recognition of the impact of teachers' own biographies on their education and training (for example, Thomas 1995) and on curriculum development and reform. Whilst some writers note the absence of black and ethnic minority people from their research (Ball 1987; Nias 1989), others fail to provide any information on 'race' and ethnicity. Although Casey (1993) addresses the experiences of African-American women teachers and Ghuman (1995) the experiences of British Asian teachers, the lives and work of black and ethnic minority teachers on the whole remain invisible.

Concerns have been raised about 'images of' studies of black and ethnic minority communities (Dyer 1988; Troyna 1994) which in their attempt to compensate for the missing variable of 'race', may run the risk of 'ethnicism' by presenting the communities in question as 'other' against a white norm. Troyna argues that such studies

> have a tendency to degenerate into essentialism and reductionism. This means that racism – in institutional, systematic, interpersonal or ideological forms – is adduced as a monocausal model or explanation for, say, the low representation of ethnic minorities in the teaching profession

... Yet ... racism articulates with gender, class and age in complex, sometimes contradictory and often nonsynchronous ways.

(Troyna 1994: 331)

This study seeks to avoid this dilemma by using a life-history approach to research black teachers' experiences and allowing the concerns of those teachers to strongly influence its framework. By drawing on life histories it is possible to place issues of gender and social class as well as 'race' at the heart of the analysis. Since the lives of black and ethnic minorities are not confined to issues of racism, but are multidimensional, then by drawing from those accounts it is possible to consider how racism operates without separating it artificially from other structural constraints. While not denying the power of racism, or its impact on the life chances of black people, it is possible to explore how individuals make decisions which, although they may be *influenced* by structural racism, are not inevitably *determined* by it.

My interest in this area developed as I reflected on my own career in teaching and the impact which 'race' issues have had upon it. I began teaching in the late 1970s in a predominantly white secondary school in a neighbourhood on the fringe of South-East London where it turned out that the National Front were active. Many of the parents of the children whom I taught had moved out of London from multi-ethnic areas to the suburbs, and saw their move as a step up the social ladder. The school was a new purpose-built 11–18 comprehensive with a relatively young and enthusiastic staff; in my first year I was one of some ten newly qualified teachers. Despite the generally liberal attitudes of a large number of the teachers, none of us was adequately prepared to deal with the racist remarks and graffiti which were often encountered in school, and one commonly adopted strategy was to ignore the problem.

There was little in my own Postgraduate Certificate of Education (PGCE) course that I could draw upon which seemed directly relevant to the situation: although a lot of work had been done on developing pupils' understanding of bias and stereotyping in the history methods course, applying these principles in the context of the racist attitudes which I encountered in my first appointment felt like an overwhelming task. There were only two or three black children in the school at any one time, and these children generally transferred to other schools quite quickly. A black woman who worked as a supply teacher was regularly subjected to racist abuse, often from pupils she did not teach, in encounters in the corridors or playground. My personal background of growing up in a 'mixed race' family seemed far removed from the experiences of the pupils I was teaching, and the only other permanent black member of staff, a male physical education and drama teacher, told me that when he encountered racist behaviour in pupils he dealt with it by threat or use of physical violence on the sports field, an option which we both knew was not open to me.

After teaching for two years I registered on a part-time basis for an Advanced Diploma in Education at a London college, and began studying issues relating to 'race' and education. I also attended courses on multicultural education organised by the local education authority, in the hope that I would get some ideas and support in tackling the problems of racism in school, but was disappointed to discover that other teachers on these courses, who were generally from multicultural schools, had different priorities and were more concerned to develop ways of teaching which incorporated the cultures of the black children they were teaching than with developing strategies to challenge racism.

Although the school management was happy to support my attendance at such courses, and within the humanities department in which I was based there was ample opportunity for curriculum development, it was clear that the school as a whole did not identify issues of racism as a priority. Indeed, the headteacher advised me that if I did not raise them I might pass as white! Consequently, I began looking for a promoted post outside the school and was eventually appointed to a new multicultural unit in Birmingham, where the strategy was to introduce multicultural and anti-racist teaching into schools by working alongside teachers following a collaborative model and to support this work by running in-service courses.

This period in Birmingham was an important and influential one in my own personal and professional development. For the first time I had the opportunity of working as part of a team of like-minded colleagues, and although we did not always agree about the strategies we should adopt, it was a very stimulating environment in which to work. I had, perhaps naively, imagined that teachers working in a large multicultural city would have developed their thinking further than those at my former school, and that the experience of working with black and ethnic minority children would have encouraged a stronger commitment to anti-racism. I was soon disabused of this and encountered teachers who showed none of the liberal tendencies of my old colleagues; some teachers in one multi-ethnic school where I worked even felt free to express racist comments in the staff room. Nevertheless, I was able to find both black and white colleagues who were committed to challenging racism in schools and to learn a lot about my own teaching through having access to the classrooms of many colleagues. I was also able to join a support group of black women teachers and to gain some experience of working in primary schools.

The pressure of constantly working to challenge racism, together with the growing uncertainties about Section 11 funding, led me, after nearly four years, to look for alternative employment. As a result of a year's secondment to a small non-governmental organisation, I was able to develop my skills in in-service training. I wished to build upon this experience and to continue to work for racial equality and justice without what I by then perceived to be the hindrance of a job which carried a multicultural label. For the next three years I was responsible for running a broad programme of in-service training as head of a teachers' centre in Hertfordshire, in the area where I had been schooled.

Following the publication of the Swann Report, my new local education authority appointed an adviser for multicultural education and in 1987–88 began a training programme on multicultural education for headteachers. Although in one sense I was back home, it was strange to see the relatively small impact of this dimension of the curriculum on many local schools; my sense of familiarity when I visited my own old school was not just due to the physical surroundings but seemed to relate to the curriculum content and general ethos which appeared to be similar to that of own schooling some 15 years earlier. As head of a teachers' centre I found myself in a high-profile position within the locality, and some of my ideas and beliefs, which seemed unexceptional in Birmingham, appeared radical or even alien in my home town.

During this three-year period, while I held responsibility for the continuing professional development programme of teachers in both primary and secondary schools, I became increasingly interested in the structural position of black teachers and of women teachers within the education system. About this time the Commission for Racial Equality (CRE) survey (1988a) of ethnic minority teachers in eight local authorities was published, revealing that black teachers often encountered a ceiling, beyond which it was extremely difficult to progress. My own appointment, at senior teacher level, was then the most senior post held by a black or ethnic minority person within the advisory service. At the teachers' centre we were developing professional and personal development courses for women teachers which were attracting applicants from across the authority and so I began, tentatively, to develop networks with black women teachers and to exchange information about career and work experiences. However, it was becoming clear that, with the introduction of local financial management of schools, the local authority might be unable to support the continuation of teachers' centres and so I sought opportunities to move into teacher education. In 1990 I took up a post as lecturer in education at the University of Birmingham. This post carried a special responsibility for staff development in equal opportunities.

My own career path has not been carefully planned, yet at all stages it would appear to have been influenced by issues relating to 'race'. While this can be explained in part by personal choices and commitment, at certain times other factors such as identity and the experience of working in a racially structured society, have helped shape and influence the available options. In studying the lives and careers of other black and ethnic minority teachers, I am setting out to try to increase my understanding of the influences which have led them into teaching and to identify those factors which have shaped their careers. My own life history and career path have thus played an important part in the initial motivation and conception of this book.

This book is based on a research project which draws on the narratives of black and ethnic minority students, teachers and senior managers in education. In Part One, entitled 'Making Sense of the Past; Re-interpreting the Present' I focus on racism within British society and within the education system, setting a context within which the teachers' and students' narratives of their lives can be understood and interpreted. One purpose of this part is to acknowledge some of the structural constraints which operate on the lives of individuals and the broad context in which they make choices about their work. Another is to explore the specific policy contexts within which teachers are currently operating and to identify opportunities which might be developed to promote greater social justice in education. Policy development and research have often failed to consider the complexities of the lived experiences of black and ethnic minority people and so for this reason I draw on biographical material as well as research to allow their voices direct expression. Part One concludes with a discussion of the research project from which the data in Parts Two and Three of the book are drawn.

Black and ethnic minority teachers' own understandings and interpretations of their lives have been largely unrecorded and, it might be argued, suppressed by research agendas which have assumed that intending and practising teachers are white. In Part Two, entitled 'Changing Lives' I examine the life histories of experienced black teachers, drawing particularly on the narratives of six individuals and identifying broad themes which emerge. These themes are then discussed drawing on data from the wider sample. The key focus is the development of teacher identities, i.e. the formation of professional identities and the ways these relate to teachers' political and community identities as black people. Structural racism provides us with some understanding of the underrepresentation of people from black and ethnic minority communities within the education service but established theories of racism do not adequately address the experiences of those who reach senior positions. Part Two therefore examines the narratives of black senior managers (headteachers, advisers and inspectors) to consider not only how racism interacts with gender, class and other factors in complex and contradictory ways but how individuals work to achieve 'career success' and to challenge racism in their own lives and in the lives of their students.

Part Three of the book, 'Daring to Teach', examines the attitudes of young black and ethnic minority people, sixth-formers and graduates, to teaching as a career, relating their decisions about their careers and futures to their understandings of their own developing identities. I consider the perceptions of those who have largely succeeded within the education system, examining their own schooling, their experiences of higher education and their views of teachers and teaching. The section includes the narratives of students who have made an initial commitment to teaching as a career and who are following teacher education courses, focusing on their experiences on these courses.

Structural theories of racism do not adequately explain how individuals are able to negotiate or effectively challenge racism or develop strategies to minimise its impact on their lives and on the lives of their fellow teachers and students, while at the same time often recognising its structural and all-pervasive nature. In the final part, Part Four, 'Changing the Future', I therefore draw upon the experiences of black and ethnic minority teachers and students to consider the value and limitations of structural theories in relation to individual agency. The book concludes with recommendations for policy and practice to promote greater social justice in schools and in teacher education.

Notes

1 The teachers and most of the students who were participants in this study all accepted the term 'black', to a greater or lesser extent, as one of many self-descriptors and this is a point which is developed in the text. Consequently I also use it to refer to the research participants. In a book where one of the main themes is identities, it is important to stress at the outset that self-definition is an important principle. I recognise that not all members of Asian communities, for example, feel equally comfortable with the descriptor 'black' and that various communities may encounter different forms of racism and inequality. For this reason I generally adopt the more inclusive term 'black and ethnic minority' when seeking a general descriptor.
2 Throughout the text I have placed the word 'race' in inverted commas as a reminder that it is a category with no scientific or biological validity. Nevertheless, it is an important social category, in that the status of individuals and groups, their access to resources and power may be expressed in 'racial' terms.

Part one _____

Making sense of the past; reinterpreting the present

One

Racism, education and inequality in Britain

Introduction

Our life stories are in a continual process of composition and re-composition. We interpret and reinterpret various aspects of our personal histories according to our developing understanding of the broader historical context in which these events occurred. Current events, for example, a film, a conversation or something we read or hear on the radio may give a new significance to past events in our lives.

This chapter sets the scene for teachers' life stories, providing a social, political and theoretical context for the new data and analysis which is presented in Parts Two and Three of this book. A central aim is to review what is known about the effects of racism on the lives of black and ethnic minority people in Britain. The chapter examines British immigration and anti-discrimination legislation since the Second World War and considers its impact on society generally and on education policy in particular. It then reviews the evidence for continuing racial inequalities in education.

Immigration and anti-discrimination legislation

The Nationality Act 1948 gave UK citizenship to citizens of Britain's colonies and former colonies. Workers were actively recruited in the colonies to meet labour shortages in certain sectors of British industry, particularly transport, the health service and manufacturing. Although most white people believed that the West Indian settlers were largely unskilled manual workers, of those coming to the UK only 5 per cent of the women and 13 per cent of the men were unskilled. Nevertheless, many were obliged to accept jobs which white workers did not want; in the late 1950s, half the West Indian men in London were working in jobs below their levels of skills and qualifications (Fryer 1984). Teachers from this study recall hardships and disappointments which they or their parents faced on arrival:

One of the first things they did was to reject my educational qualifications when I came here. Even though the papers were set in England
and sent out to Jamaica for me to sit and sent back here to be marked
and so forth. So I had to go back [to college to re-sit the examinations].
                                                  (Frank, secondary headteacher)

My father was educated and he could speak English fluently. He did an
MA in India and he came over, I think, with the intention of carrying
on with his studying and doing some kind of professional training. And
he ended up working in the usual factories and foundries of Smethwick.
                                                                  (Balbir, teacher)

There were no jobs [in teaching]. The people wouldn't give you a job
in industry as well. They'd just look at you and say, 'No vacancies'.
                                                  (Kuldip, primary headteacher)

Although the 1950s and 1960s marked a time of full employment, migrant
workers were vulnerable to exploitation; racism effectively operated to de-
skill and segregate many of them into low-paid work (Sivanandan 1982).

In 1962, the Conservative Government responded to lobbying from within
the party and a growing incidence of racist attacks on black and ethnic
minorities by introducing legislation which identified the problem, not as
white racism, but as the black presence itself. The Commonwealth Immigrants Act 1962 was designed to reduce the annual number of new arrivals
in Britain by restricting entry to those with employment vouchers. Black
and ethnic minority citizens were now identified as 'immigrants' which
effectively made their citizenship second class, with the legal double jeop-
ardy of deportation if convicted of an offence within five years of arrival.
It was a widely held and 'common sense' view that the fewer black and
ethnic minority people there were in the country, the better it would be
for the country's 'race relations'. This view had been expressed from the
earliest stages of the post-war migration process and can be traced in debates
within the Cabinet and in a number of government departments from 1948
onwards (Solomos 1988).

Although Labour politicians criticised the 1962 legislation, with Labour
leader Hugh Gaitskell describing it as 'miserable, shameful, shabby' (Fryer
1984: 381), in 1965 the Labour Government issued a White Paper on
Commonwealth immigration which was also based on the assumption that
the problem was one of numbers. It introduced an annual limitation on
employment vouchers to 8500, which were largely issued to skilled workers
and professional people. While the major political parties and popular debate
identified black and ethnic minorities as a problem, such communities across
the country were subjected to a wave of racial violence as the media reported anti-immigration speeches and campaigns. In 1965, the same Labour
Government passed the Race Relations Act which outlawed 'incitement to

racial hatred' (inaugurated by the prosecution of Malcolm X) and forbade discrimination in 'places of public resort' – discrimination in housing, education, employment and a wide range of institutions went unchecked.

Early in 1968, the Commonwealth Immigrants Act was hurriedly pushed through parliament to prevent free entry into Britain of Kenyan Asians who were British passport-holders. This Act included a clause which divided Commonwealth citizens into two groups: 'patrials', those who had a parent or grandparent 'born, naturalised or adopted in the UK', and non-patrials, those who did not. The former group maintained their right of free entry. In effect, rights were generally lost or maintained according to skin colour. The previous autumn Enoch Powell had whipped up popular fears about the numbers of potential Kenyan Asians who might wish to settle in Britain; following this piece of legislation his speeches, calling for 'repatriation' of black people, further inflamed popular racism and racist violence.

The Race Relations Act 1968 was introduced as a more wide-ranging piece of anti-discrimination law once the limitations of the 1965 Act became clear. The law was extended to include employment, housing, education, the provision of services and the publication or display of discriminatory advertisements or notices. Many of its proponents argued that its importance lay not only in its implementation, but in what they believed would be its educative effect on public opinion. Yet its impact on public attitudes was arguably minimal, with public attention focusing on the arguments of its opponents that it would give special privileges to black people.

In many ways the Race Relations Act 1968 contradicted the general trend of official government policies towards black and ethnic minority people during the decade. The problem was now defined as one of numbers and racial discrimination was written into the immigration laws (Dummett 1973). As we shall see, education policy was also to reflect the viewpoint that the *numbers* of black pupils constituted a problem. In 1991, almost 30 years after the first legal controls on black immigration, the black and ethnic minority presence in Britain continued to be presented as a problem of numbers. Justifying the need for the government's Asylum Bill, designed to impose restrictions on the rights of those seeking entry to Britain as refugees, Foreign Secretary Douglas Hurd told Amnesty International that although he 'understood and shared Amnesty's concern' to ensure that 'Britain respects its obligations to the refugee', this had to be reconciled 'with a truth dinned into me through the years when I was Home Secretary, namely that the good relations between communities in this country depend to a very large extent on a firm and fair system of immigration control' (*The Guardian*, 26 November 1991).

The Immigration Act 1971, which came into force in 1973, brought an end to virtually all primary immigration and further restricted the entry of dependants. Migrant workers were allowed to enter only to do a specific job, for a period no longer than 12 months in the first instance. Police and immigration officers could now arrest suspected illegal immigrants without a warrant. Black and ethnic minority people living in Britain were thus subject to further controls including arrest as suspected illegal immigrants, detention without trial, separation of families, and personal indignities and humiliations such as the vaginal examination of women on arrival in Britain. This legislation did not bring about the improvement in 'race relations' forecast by politicians who continued to view the size of the black and ethnic minority population as the problem. The effects were quite the opposite: the fact that racism was built into the law encouraged and supported popular expressions of prejudice and racial violence.

The ways in which the media has helped create and maintain this climate of racist opinion have been well charted (for example, Gordon and Rosenberg 1989; Twitchin 1990). It is not just the overtly racist headlines and cartoons which contribute to this; Stuart Hall (1981: 37) draws attention to the ways in which the coverage of race relations problems on liberal television documentaries was 'impregnated with unconscious racism' since it is 'precisely predicated on racist premises'. More recently, a study of popular television found that ethnic stereotypes continue to have an impact on young white students' perceptions, black actors are only occasionally being cast in non-racially defined parts and television continues to maintain the 'comfortable prejudices' of many white people (Ross 1992).

From the early 1970s immigration has been controlled by a range of administrative rules which have been formulated in such a way as to allow room for discretion on the part of immigration officers, so that would-be immigrants have found themselves subject to practices beyond the rule of law. The Nationality Act 1981, which was intended to re-define British citizenship, introduced three classes of citizenship but its main effect has been to reinforce the earlier restrictions placed on immigration. One very significant consequence of the Act is that UK citizenship is no longer automatically gained by birth in Britain.

In the mid-1970s, the returning Labour Government introduced two important pieces of anti-discrimination legislation. The Race Relations Act 1976 introduced provisions which took account of indirect discrimination and gave power to the new Commission for Racial Equality to investigate discriminatory employment policies and practices. It also strengthened the Public Order Act 1936, making it an offence to publish or distribute material likely to encourage racial hatred. Parekh (1991) outlines some of its limitations which include failure to prohibit certain forms of discrimination, insufficient powers given to the CRE to enforce the Act's provisions, demands for impossibly high standards of proof, and exclusion of a range of government activities from the Commission's jurisdiction. Despite these, and the rather restrictive ways in which the courts have interpreted some of the Act's clauses, in contrast to their more liberal interpretation of the Sex Discrimination Act 1975, Parekh argues that the contribution of the law in improving race relations has been considerable, creating 'a climate in which blacks felt confident and welcome'.

One of the Commission's duties is to review the 1976 Act and make recommendations to the Secretary of State for its amendment. In 1991 the Commission issued a consultative paper putting forward proposals to simplify investigations, widen their scope, set up a discrimination section within the industrial tribunals system, extend legal aid to discrimination cases, require employers to introduce ethnic record-keeping and monitoring, and extend the Race Relations Act to all government activities, including the immigration, police and prison services. In the second review of the Race Relations Act 1976 (CRE 1992b) the Commission concludes that its broad framework is sound but that the Government must make reforms; without the introduction of such reforms, people remain unprotected by the law in many cases of racial discrimination.

One legal reform which has been proposed is the recognition of racial violence as a separate offence. Racially motivated attacks have a political dimension, they are a denial of a particular group's equal citizenship rights; each individual attack threatens a wider group of people perceived to be of the same ethnic group. Although a report commissioned by the All-Party Parliamentary Group on Race and Community has highlighted a need for further public and parliamentary debate on such questions (Parekh 1994), and a strong case has been presented for the introduction of a new law to guarantee the equal rights of black and ethnic minority citizens, the Conservative Government continued to deny the need to recognise racial violence as a separate offence.

Racial harassment and violence

A study of recorded racial attacks from different parts of the country concluded that few neighbourhoods could be considered totally safe for black people (Gordon 1986). The problem is not confined to particular areas; for example arson attacks have occurred in rural areas and in middle-class suburbs. Parekh (1994) provides us with some disturbing statistics: the last two years saw 14 racially motivated murders of African Caribbeans and Asians, and the British Crime Survey estimates 130 000 racially motivated incidents (including assaults, vandalism and threats) to have occurred in 1991. He reminds us that racial incidents have an impact on whole families and calculates that since African Caribbean and Asian families have on average just under three children, as many as 650 000 people suffered directly from the effects of racial incidents. In other words, in one single year, just under one-third of the total ethnic minority population experienced directly the distress of racial motivated incidents.

The scale of the problem continues to be underreported, since people either fear reprisals or lack confidence in the agencies which are meant to help them (CRE 1987), expecting, for example, police bias or inaction:

Last week some friends of ours had some bother and she didn't want
to phone the police; she asked my dad to, because my dad's got sort of
a snobby accent. My dad phoned the solicitor, but whenever the police
come, whenever it's an Asian person, the police really take their time
and when they do come there's tons and tons of them. But when it's
whites the police come, sort of quicker, but there's less of them.

(Nazrah, aged 15, quoted in Osler 1989: 49)

This problem is compounded by agencies who do not acknowledge or record
cases because officials do not recognise racial harassment as an issue or lack
a consistent policy for record-keeping. Nevertheless, available statistics suggest that South Asians appear to be particularly vulnerable (Virdee 1995).

Employment

In the areas where black and ethnic minority people live, unemployment is
likely to be much higher than elsewhere. For example, at the time of the
1991 Census, black and ethnic minority communities made up 21.5 per cent
of Birmingham's total population and 56 per cent of the population in the
Handsworth area; unemployment was 28.8 per cent in Handsworth ward
and 25.2 per cent in Soho ward, compared with an average of 14.6 per cent
for Birmingham as a whole (Birmingham City Council, no date).

The Labour Force Survey analysis indicates that by around 1989, the
experiences of various minority groups had begun to diverge. Certain groups,
African-Asian and Indian men in particular, have come to occupy a labour
market position which is only slightly below that of white men. Participation rates remain low among Pakistani and Bangladeshi women and fewer
ethnic minority men than white men in all age groups are in employment
(Jones 1993). Some Pakistani and Bangladeshi women may be 'economically inactive' because they are unable to find employment rather than
through choice. The 1991 Census confirms that although there are substantial differentials in economic activity rates between various ethnic minorities, unemployment rates are higher for both women and men amongst
ethnic minorities than for white people. Bangladeshis have the highest
unemployment rates, followed by black (African and African Caribbean)
ethnic groups and Pakistanis (Owen 1994). Among young men this is
explained in terms of larger numbers remaining in full-time education but
in other age groups it may actually disguise a much higher unemployment
rate (Jones 1993).

Young people from ethnic minorities are more likely to stay in education,
with only half of 16–24-year-olds participating in the labour market. Chinese and Black-African communities contain a very high proportion of students, 86 and 81.6 per cent respectively. Among young people aged 16–24
years the Chinese experience unemployment rates most similar to those for

white people (at just under 15 per cent), with Indians displaying the next lowest unemployment rates, at over one-fifth. In this age group, unemployment is highest among Pakistani and black (African and African Caribbean) people; at 35.8 and 32.4 per cent, respectively, this is more than double the unemployment rate (14.6 per cent) among white young people. In all ethnic groups, there is higher youth unemployment among males than females.

There have been relatively few studies of the recent experiences of black and ethnic minority young people in the labour market. Cross *et al.* (1990) found that black and ethnic minorities, particularly Asian boys and African Caribbean girls, have more ambition than their white peers to secure jobs with training, skills and prospects. The routes taken by black and ethnic minority young people into the labour market differ considerably from that of white young people; for example, Asians had a very low participation rate in the Youth Training Scheme. Drew found that when educational attainment and various alternative pathways into the labour market were taken into account, ethnic origin is the single most important factor in becoming established in a job: at age 19 years, African Caribbean and Asian young people are less likely than white to have achieved this (Drew 1995). Thus there is strong evidence for continuing racial discrimination in the youth labour market.

Educational policy responses to black and ethnic minority children

Educational policy development needs to be seen in the broader political context, and links can be identified between the educational responses to black and ethnic minority children in school, the development of immigration law, and laws and policies designed either to reduce or dissolve racial tension or promote racial equality. Black and ethnic minority children have long been perceived as a 'problem' in British schools and the educational response to this perception can be traced through policy approaches since the 1960s. It has been suggested at various times during this period that African Caribbean and Asian students' language structures or skills are inadequate for successful learning, that they suffer from culture shock, intergenerational family conflicts, repressive or inadequate parenting, and identity crises. The problem has been seen to lie within the students themselves, in their numbers in schools, in their supposed family and cultural characteristics, and in their responses to schooling. The assumption has often been that they face a dilemma in coping with the demands of a progressive and forward-thinking society and school system, coming as they do from cultures and families which are considered to be inadequate or backward. There has been reluctance to explore the notion that the problem might lie within the education system rather than within family cultures. Only occasionally has it been acknowledged that the experiences of black and ethnic minority children in British schools might highlight the failure or underachievement of the system; such failure or underachievement has usually been rather conveniently located either in the individual student, the family or community.

Educational policies, 1958–1980s

A number of writers (Carby 1982; Mullard 1982; Troyna 1982; Troyna and Williams 1986) have traced ideological and policy developments during the 1960s and 1970s from assimilation through to integration and cultural pluralism. In the early 1980s, the focus of the debate changed and some local authorities introduced specifically anti-racist perspectives and policies.

The 1958 anti-black riots in Nottingham and Notting Hill marked a significant turning point in official policy responses to black and ethnic minority people. As we have seen, the Commonwealth Immigrants Act 1962 and subsequent immigration legislation was justified by arguments which identified ethnic minorities as a problem. Stuart Hall (1978) identifies this point as one from which the 'new and indigenous racism of the post-war period' developed. Policy-making on 'race' and education acknowledged and accepted white hostility to black immigrants and focused on racial and cultural differences.

Government arguments concerning the need to exercise control over numbers of immigrants were closely reflected in educational policies from the 1950s to the mid-1960s. Assimilationist education policies aimed to achieve better 'race relations' through the schooling of the next generation of black and ethnic minority people. These children were to be provided with a different set of values from their parents and thus avoid the racist hostility their parents had experienced. Carby, for example, quotes a 1964 Commonwealth Immigrants Advisory Council (1982: 185) report:

> ... a national system of education must aim at producing citizens who can take their place in a society properly equipped to exercise rights and perform duties which are the same as other citizens ... a national system cannot be expected to perpetuate the different values of immigrant groups.

In 1965, the Department of Education and Science (DES) published a circular endorsing the practice of forced dispersal of ethnic minorities from their local schools, a policy ostensibly designed to increase their contact with white students and the 'majority culture'. In fact, the circular itself (circular 7/65, quoted in Troyna and Williams 1986: 19) stated the issue as being one of numbers of black and ethnic minority students:

> Experience suggests however that apart from unusual difficulties (such as a high proportion of non-English speakers), up to a fifth of immigrant

children in any one group fit in with reasonable ease, but that, if the proportion goes over about one-third either in the school as a whole or in any one class, serious strains arise.

Language was a key issue in assimilationist theory. The purpose of learning English was not just to communicate efficiently in school and the wider community but was seen as 'the key to cultural and social assimilation' and the means by which ethnic minorities could overcome the 'inadequacies of [their] language' (Troyna and Williams 1986: 15). Those children who arrived speaking Punjabi, Urdu or a Caribbean Creole were not acknowledged as having particular linguistic skills but were judged as not speaking English properly or even as 'non-speakers'.

Policy responses to pupils of South Asian and African Caribbean descent were very different; children arriving from the Indian sub-continent were usually placed in separate centres or classes in which they were taught English (often without any assessment of whether or not they were able to speak English) whilst African Caribbean children were placed directly into mainstream schools, where, if they were seen to fail or judged to behave badly, they were transferred to special schools or placed in low streams. This process of labelling restricted access to the mainstream curriculum and to examination opportunities. Although challenged from within the black community (see for example, Coard 1971) such practices continued in a number of local education authorities into the 1980s.

From the late 1960s, multicultural or cultural pluralist models of education were beginning to emerge; greater attention was given to social and cultural diversity. While many teachers who were committed to the idea of equality of opportunity broadened the curriculum so that children's cultures might be acknowledged and celebrated, much of what was introduced the 1970s under the guise of 'multicultural education' was arguably extremely patronising of black and ethnic minority people and was designed to have a palliative effect.

Until the late 1970s, little thought appears to have been given to the potential benefits of multicultural education for white children. The terms of reference of the Rampton/Swann Committee, set up in 1979, were 'to review in relation to schools the educational needs and attainments of children from ethnic minority groups' and to 'give early and particular attention to the educational needs and attainments of pupils of West Indian origin'. The first purpose of multicultural education was therefore to address black achievement, although many teachers did not necessarily see multiculturalism in these terms, concerned as they were with issues of motivation, discipline and control (Stone 1981).

It is important to consider the context in which multicultural education policies and practice were developed. From the late 1960s, black and ethnic minority communities were experiencing increasing levels of racist violence and hostility, encapsulated in Enoch Powell's populist speeches on race.

Western Europe's economic crisis of the mid-1970s had a disproportionate effect on black and ethnic minority people in Britain, so that by the early 1980s the unemployment rate among African Caribbean school-leavers was four times the national average.

The impact of racism on pupils and teachers

Despite evidence of the damaging effects of racism on the lives of black and ethnic minority pupils (Milner 1975) and strategies proposed for challenging racism in schools (Jeffcoate 1979), by the mid-1980s few schools had developed a curriculum which drew on the experiences of a range of cultures, and still less addressed the issues of racism and structural inequalities in society. Moreover, many parents and communities were rightly suspicious of an education which in practice often presented a differentiated package to their children, purporting to give them a sense of identity and self-pride, whilst effectively denying them access to examinations, to certain types of employment and to higher education (Stone 1981).

Within the African Caribbean community there was widespread recognition of the ways in which education was failing black children. Marina Maxwell, a teacher who came to Britain from the Caribbean, was perhaps the first black person to speak out publicly against racism in education. In an article published in 1968, she drew attention to racism in teacher attitudes and the curriculum, and to the inadequacies of teacher education. Challenging the prevailing theories explaining the problems of black children in terms of pupil insecurity, low self-esteem and inadequate parenting, she placed the responsibility firmly within the British education system, concluding: 'Give a migrant child two weeks in this atmosphere and you have a "problem nigger"' (Maxwell 1968, quoted in Klein 1993). Her viewpoint was endorsed by other black writers:

> By institutionalising the prejudices and the undermining assumptions we face in our everyday lives, the schools have kept our children at the very bottom of the ladder of employability and laid the blame on us. The schools' ability to churn out cheap, unskilled factory fodder . . . may have served the economic needs of this society; it has not met the aspirations of a community which has always equated education with liberation from poverty.
>
> (Bryan *et al.* 1985)

Teachers, working in a climate where both government ministers and local education officers saw black and ethnic minority children as an 'educational problem' and a threat to the educational standards of the white community, often accepted the 'common sense' thinking of the times when they placed these children in low streams and provided them with unchallenging work.

Deficit models of black and ethnic minority families were widely held, and these further reinforced low teacher expectations.

Low expectations of black and ethnic minority children and teachers' prior assumptions about their behaviour will be communicated to them, often in unintentional ways, and this is likely to influence subsequent behaviour and educational achievements. Children may react by denying aspects of themselves, their families and cultural identities. Such reactions have been explained in terms of children's 'low self-image' (Milner 1975) but this explanation is inadequate since it focuses the problem (and therefore the solution) as lying with the child who has been labelled. Attention is removed from the labeller, the teacher, and the racist context in which the school operates. This may help explain why relatively little attention has been given to teacher education and training or to the processes of institutional change.

The ways in which racist messages are transmitted through the curriculum have since been explored in some detail. Studies of racial bias in children's books and learning materials (Zimet 1976; Dixon 1977; Stinton 1979; Preiswerk 1980; Klein 1985) and of the ways in which television contributes to the reinforcement of racist attitudes and practices within British society (Twitchin 1990; Ross 1992) serve to remind us that both pupils and teachers have regularly been presented with racist ideas and images. Such images have a powerful influence on young readers and contribute to the miseducation of white children by failing to confront and challenge racist and other anti-democratic values.

A review of the research into the political understanding of 16–19-year-olds found that the overwhelming majority of the sample were politically illiterate, and that an overt expression of racist values was commonplace among white youth:

> Perhaps the most salient [theme], commented upon time and time again by the different research teams, is the political innocence, naivety and ignorance of young people ... Stemming perhaps from such political ignorance is the overt racism which the research projects commonly reveal to be endemic among white youth in Britain. Political ignorance and racism are hardly the hallmarks of a healthy multiracial democracy.
>
> (McGurk 1987: 6)

The myth of underachievement

Until the mid-1980s, research in 'race' and education largely focused on the attainment of pupils from ethnic minority groups and their alleged 'underachievement'. Official reports from the late 1960s highlighted the low levels of attainment of ethnic minority pupils, particularly African Caribbean children, reinforcing the notion of ethnic minority underachievement in the minds of teachers. They have no doubt served to influence teacher expectation of these children, as became apparent with the publication of the Eggleston Report (Eggleston *et al.* 1986). Interpretation of statistical evidence on pupil achievement needs to acknowledge the complexity of these issues since 'the greatest danger lies in the possibility that ill-conceived and poorly formulated studies will perpetuate the notion of black educational underachievement as a given rather than as a problematic' (Troyna 1984: 164).

Another difficulty, when considering the phenomenon of 'black underachievement', is to see 'black pupils', 'African Caribbean pupils' or 'Asian pupils' as monolithic categories. It is clearly important to consider the social class composition of different ethnic groups, to recognise that children from African and Caribbean, or Bangladeshi, Indian, and Pakistani backgrounds may fare very differently within the education system, and to consider gender as a factor in achievement.

Skellington and Morris (1992) produced evidence from an investigation of pupil achievement in inner London which indicated that pupils of Indian descent were performing better than pupils of Pakistani descent, who in turn were achieving higher examination results than those of Bangladeshi descent at 16 years. A report published by the Government's Office for Standards in Education (Ofsted) highlighted improving levels of attainment among ethnic minority pupils in many areas, but noted the growing gap between the highest and lowest achieving ethnic groups in many local education authorities (LEAs), with African Caribbean boys, in particular, not sharing in increasing rates of achievement and a sharp rise in the number of exclusions from school affecting a disproportionate number of African Caribbean pupils (Gillborn and Gipps 1996). Yet patterns of achievement differ between LEAs: for example, a pilot teacher assessment of basic skills carried out in Birmingham primary schools in 1993 showed that African Caribbean children were out-performing their peers at age 5 years and the city's National Curriculum tests for 1992 and 1994 confirmed that they are ahead at age 7 years (Hofkins 1994). Sadly this lead is lost among those at secondary school as evidenced by GCSE results.

Clearly it is important not to present black underachievement as given or inevitable but to investigate the factors which support or undermine children's learning. There is some evidence to suggest that the targeting of resources, for example, to support the learning of bilingual pupils, has been shown to bring about positive results, as in Tower Hamlets in London, where targeted language support for Bangladeshi pupils had a significant impact on examination results at GCSE (Gillborn and Gipps 1996). Nevertheless, Troyna and Williams (1986: 25–6) have argued that it is 'racism and not formal educational qualifications [which] is the main determinant of life chances for black students in the UK, a fact heavily stressed in the research reports but which continues to be ignored in the formulation of educational policies'. Formal qualifications do, however, greatly influence life chances, and certainly access to higher education.

One important variable in pupils' achievement levels may be the effectiveness of particular schools. In a study of 18 comprehensive schools, Smith and Tomlinson found that black and ethnic minority pupils made greater progress in some schools than in others. They found wide variations in pupil progress between schools and concluded that schools 'that are good for white pupils tended to be about equally good for black pupils' (Smith and Tomlinson 1989: 305). A follow-up study revealed that more black and ethnic minority pupils went to the less effective schools, but the researchers argued that 'It did not make sense to talk of schools which were universally effective or ineffective; there was no single dimension of school effectiveness' (Drew and Gray 1991: 168).

Anti-racism and challenges to anti-racism

Although the Rampton Report (DES 1981) acknowledged racism as the major factor contributing to African Caribbean children's underachievement, the 1985 Swann Report seemed to play down the factor of racism. Nevertheless, it highlighted a number of features of a 'good education' for all pupils, including:

- the use of teaching materials which are multicultural in content and global in perspective;
- the provision of opportunities for pupils to identify and challenge racism;
- the inclusion of effective political education, with scope to consider how power is exercised and by whom;
- and the identification and removal of practices and procedures which directly or indirectly work against pupils from any ethnic group.

It stressed that these issues should be addressed in all contexts and be given particular emphasis in predominantly or all-white areas (DES 1985). Although its proposals were modest, few were accepted by the then Secretary of State for Education. Nevertheless, a number of LEAs responded quite positively to them.

During the 1980s, there was growing recognition of the need to challenge racism within the education system. A number of educational policy-makers at local authority level began to acknowledge that the celebration of cultural diversity was an inadequate response to the very real problems of structural inequality. Some LEAs began to develop policies which reflected this change and those of Berkshire (1979) and the Inner London Education Authority (1977) were particularly notable in influencing other LEAs. The focus of educational research began to shift away from an examination of the alleged underachievement or failure of black pupils towards an examination of the quality of educational provision.

With hindsight, it is possible to identify certain of the anti-racist initiatives developed at this time as inadequate. To believe that race awareness programmes could readily educate away racist attitudes and structures might now be seen as naive. Within the black communities, it was observed that a number of white people were learning and using the discourse of anti-racism, yet continuing to reinforce structural inequality within their organisations. Nevertheless the anti-racist commitment of groups of teachers, expressed locally through Section 11 funded initiatives and through the work of organisations such as Development Education Centres, and nationally through networks such as NAME (National Anti-Racist Movement in Education) and ARTEN (Anti-Racist Teacher Education Network) and through teacher unions, played an important role during the 1980s in redefining or redirecting multicultural education to emphasise the goals of 'race' equality and social justice.

In 1986, the report of a government-funded project *Education for Some* marked a turning point from looking at black and ethnic minority people as the problem to examining educational provision and vocational opportunities for young people from ethnic minority groups. It examined provision of education and careers guidance by schools, careers officers, youth training and work experience schemes, employers, LEAs and the DES and uncovered evidence of racism at all levels, both personal and institutional. Although students, generally speaking, did not perceive their teachers to be racist and the teachers did not see themselves as such, decisions made on behalf of these students were found to be racist in effect, as they were damaging of their life chances (Eggleston *et al.* 1986). The research highlighted a form of institutional racism which could be identified by outcome. It also made a significant contribution to anti-racist education in its recommendations, which included both general guidance on the planning and implementation of the curriculum in schools and specific recommendations for further education (FE), the careers service, LEAs, and the then Manpower Services Commission (later the Training Agency).

The political right attacked anti-racism in education and presented it at one level as a distraction from what was emphasised as central, the acquisition of basic skills, and at another level as a dangerous tendency which would not only undermine 'standards' but which would also threaten British values and undermine British culture. These ideas were particularly influential and can be found both in the speeches of government ministers and in a number of specially produced pamphlets and books. In one such collection of papers *The Wayward Curriculum: a cause for parents' concern?* the status of 'established subjects' such as mathematics, English, and history, are presented as under threat as standards are eroded through the introduction of new, dubious teaching methods and the 'relativisation of values'. At the same time, 'newer subjects' such as sociology, politics and political education are presented as dangerous and/or inappropriate for school pupils. The introduction claims: 'The anti-racist movement finds it has lost sight of the simple truth that racial prejudice is wrong and adopted a confused bigotry of its own, involving hatred of white people and traditional culture (O'Keeffe 1986: 13). Another contributor (Partington 1986: 70–71) claims that:

> ... at the grassroots in most areas and in the commanding heights in others, a steady and successful campaign has been carried out to subvert the teaching of history and to preach contempt and hatred for the central political and cultural traditions both of Britain and of the western civilisation of which it is a part.

The former Prime Minister, Margaret Thatcher, aligned herself with such concerns and sentiments when she was quoted in a BBC Panorama programme *The Class Revolution* as saying: 'We want our children to learn to add, subtract and not to learn anti-racist maths – whatever that may be'. A government programme of monetarism, large-scale privatisation and a dismantling of the welfare state, developed during the 1980s, was matched by increasing levels of unemployment, the decaying of inner cities and a growth in racism. The decade saw an increased emphasis on individualism and a narrow interpretation of Britishness and British culture, one which is exclusive rather than inclusive of minority groups.

Various national newspapers published attacks on anti-racism and other initiatives to promote equity within the education system which have reached a much wider public audience. Often it has been the LEAs who have supported such initiatives which have been the focus of attack (Richardson 1992). The murder in the playground of Burnage High School of a Manchester schoolboy, Ahmed Iqbal Ullah, in 1986, might have been the occasion for a review of policies which were failing to address issues of equality; instead, the report into the murder was used by the media as another means of discrediting anti-racist policies in education. In fact the Burnage Report (Macdonald 1989) was not a condemnation of anti-racism, although it did criticise the management style within the school and an approach which 'effectively excludes white students and parents from the process of anti-racism and absolves them from responsibility for any anti-racist education' (Macdonald *et al.* 1989: 402).

The ideology behind the Education Reform Act 1988 is one which emphasised competition; it introduced open enrolment, requiring schools to accept pupils up to capacity. In spite of record numbers of pupils taking and passing public examinations (HMI 1988), the Act was presented as addressing falling standards through assessment of pupil, teacher and school performance. The Education Act 1993 introduced statutory requirements for the publication of league tables of schools by examination results. These are justified in terms of 'parental choice' but nevertheless have the effect of setting up schools in competition with each other for a limited supply of resources. The introduction of grant-maintained schools and City Technology Colleges, also justified in terms of parental choice, further increased inequalities in the resourcing of schools. It is likely that these inequalities will be most keenly experienced in the inner cities where a substantial proportion of the black and ethnic minority population lives since schools in these areas are often experiencing the effects of years of underresourcing, and parents are less likely to be able to supplement inadequate provision from their own incomes or be in a position to pay for their children's travel to alternative schools. Since a school's income is directly related to the number of children on roll, inner-city schools with falling rolls experience further cuts in funding.

In a local newspaper report on the results of the first national tests for 7-year-olds in 1991, four West Midlands LEAs are highlighted as being near the bottom of an LEA league table, with 'Deprivation and a high ethnic population' offered as explanations. One local politician was quoted as explaining the results in terms of numbers of black students and this theme is developed in an editorial comment:

> It is self evident that large numbers of ethnic minority children in areas such as Birmingham, Sandwell, Walsall and Dudley must have a bearing on regional results. If a child is brought up in a home where the language mainly spoken is one other than English he [*sic*] has to be at a learning disadvantage compared with those who hear only English from birth. No one wishes to blame or pillory such children for a situation not of their own making.

The editorial then discusses an LEA decision to allow Sikh boys to wear the kirpan, or ceremonial knife, at school, observing: 'It ignores the realities of playground politics. It only needs one youth, perhaps feeling threatened, to draw his Kirpan in anger, and a race riot could ensue' (*Birmingham Evening Mail*, 19 December 1991). In this 1991 report, ethnic minority students are still viewed as a problem in terms of numbers, and seen to be suffering from a 'learning disadvantage' as a result of their home culture. While the children are not blamed directly, their presence in schools is used in the first instance to explain poor results. In the editorial, Sikh students are presented as the cause of potential racial violence – the very presence of ethnic minority students may lead to a race riot. There is no suggestion of racist attitudes or behaviours within the white community or any acknowledgement of the level of racist violence which many black people and ethnic minority are subjected to as part of their everyday lives.

Summary

British immigration policy, which has identified black and ethnic minorities as a problem and large numbers of such people as a threat to peace and stability, has had a significant impact on society, reinforcing popular racism and setting a context for educational policy development during the 1960s and 1970s. During the 1980s, concerns within the black and ethnic communities and changing attitudes in some local authorities led to the development of policies which sought to challenge racism within the education system but these initiatives were fiercely opposed by the political right. In the 1990s it is still possible to find 'race relations' defined in terms of restrictions on the numbers of black people and for such attitudes to be reflected in judgements about the quality of schools.

Two

Racial justice and current policy frameworks

Introduction

As we have seen, attempts to challenge racism in education have often been politically controversial and have received little, if any, support from central government. Despite this lack of support, local authorities and schools have traditionally enjoyed a high degree of autonomy to develop policies and practice for greater social justice. The Education Reform Act 1988 (ERA) and the Education Act 1993 reduced the influence of LEAs and restricted the opportunities for teachers to engage in curriculum development. Nevertheless, in the late 1990s there may again be scope for schools and teachers to challenge inequality and social exclusion. Although the issues of 'race' and racism continue to play little part in current policy debates on education, there remain tensions and contradictions in official approaches which may be exploited by those who wish to promote equity and social justice.

The publication of the Ofsted report of research into the achievement of ethnic minorities in education (Gillborn and Gipps 1996) reinforced the conviction that school effectiveness depends on improving the achievement of all pupils. It revealed that although there has been a general improvement in achievement, for example at GCSE, not all groups of pupils have shared equally in this. Generally the greatest improvements have been made by the ethnic groups that already were faring best locally. In the London borough of Brent, the LEA with the largest proportion of pupils from ethnic minority backgrounds, those classified as 'Asian' were the most successful group and also enjoyed the greatest increased success in the years 1991 to 1993. The GCSE exam results of the least successful, African Caribbeans, showed the least improvement over the same period. The GCSE results from Birmingham, the LEA with the largest numbers of ethnic minority pupils, showed a similar pattern, with an increasing gap in 1994 between the highest achieving white pupils and the lowest achieving African Caribbean pupils.

Despite official awareness of these growing disparities and continuing concern from within black and ethnic minority communities, the funding mechanism for the educational support of ethnic minorities, Section 11, is due to end in 1998 with no indication on how it will be replaced. Richardson (1996a) and Peters (1996) have produced suggestions on a future scheme for funding racial equality in education, stressing the need to invest in the professional development of teachers and to provide effective support to all pupils from black and ethnic minority pupils to enable full participation in society.

Just as educational research agendas now commonly recognise the links between 'race' and ethnicity and other factors such as gender, sexuality and social background, policy development also increasingly recognises the links between such areas in equalising opportunities. The issue of school exclusions is a clear example of one where 'race' equality issues need to be addressed alongside questions of gender, and curriculum access for those with special educational needs. In 1995–96, permanent exclusions from school continued to rise (*The Times Educational Supplement*, 8 November 1996). African Caribbean boys are grossly overrepresented in these statistics (Cooper *et al.* 1991; Bourne *et al.* 1994; DfE 1993; Parsons 1995; Stirling 1996). These children are thus denied access to the curriculum; Parsons (1995) estimates that only 27 per cent of primary pupils and 15 per cent of secondary pupils may return to mainstream schooling following permanent exclusion. There is a growing concern within the African Caribbean community about what is seen as a crisis in education.

There are indications that, at local authority level, issues of social inclusion and justice are now perhaps being given priority in education. In Birmingham, a report from the Chief Education Officer to the City Council Education Committee notes that although there has been previous guidance in education on specific aspects of equality, past policy development has focused on specific areas such special educational needs or education for a multicultural society. A more cohesive approach is recommended in line with the city's *Education Development Strategy to 2000*:

> There should not be barriers – whether, for example, of race, of religion, of poverty or wealth, of institutional practice, or gender or of disability – to any individual citizen or groups of citizens within the population taking advantage of their educational entitlement.

Accordingly, the report proposes a relaunch and refocus of equal opportunities work, bringing together expertise from various quarters 'to disseminate good practice and ensure that progress is maintained through management priority as well as the work of committed individuals' (Birmingham City Council, 12 November 1996). This inclusive approach to equality issues in education has also been characterised as one based on shared common values and international human rights standards (Osler and Starkey 1996).

Issues of 'race' and equality need to be placed again on the policy agendas of schools, LEAs and teacher education institutions if we are to avoid injustice and permanent social exclusion. It is in such a context that schools,

LEAs, non-governmental organisations (NGOs) and teacher unions concerned to promote racial justice are working. It is also the context in which the teachers, headteachers and LEA advisers and inspectors whose narratives are presented in Part Two of this book are working. This chapter briefly reviews curriculum access and one initiative to promote equality through the curriculum. It then examines the Ofsted framework for the inspection of schools as one instrument for addressing issues of equality.

Curriculum and curriculum access

Teachers in predominantly white schools had only just begun to address issues of 'race' equality and social justice and their curriculum implications in response to the Swann Report when advent of the National Curriculum required schools to devote themselves to change on an unprecedented scale. Despite the reference in the 1988 ERA to entitlement for all children and the stress on breadth, balance, continuity and progression, the National Curriculum, put together largely as a collection of separate subject documents and strongly influenced by the political right, was heavily criticised as a 'nationalistic' curriculum (Davies *et al.* 1990; David 1993) and quickly proved itself to be unwieldy, overladen and content heavy. The DES document *From Policy to Practice* (1989: 3.8) stated that: 'The whole curriculum for all pupils will certainly need to include at appropriate (and in some cases all) stages: . . . a coverage across the curriculum of gender and multi-cultural issues'. There is some evidence that schools and teachers in those LEAs with a history of greater commitment to equal opportunities perceived gender equality issues as having moved down the agenda in response to educational reform, whereas in other LEAs which had taken few equality initiatives new evaluation and reporting requirements raised the profile of these issues. Two-thirds of LEAs claimed Ofsted inspection criteria had raised the profile of equal opportunities (Arnot *et al.* 1996).

Opportunities to promote cultural diversity and challenge racism in schools are likely to be dependent on teacher commitment, professional expertise and upon receiving support at the institutional level. If teachers are to challenge racism effectively they need to be working within a context in which racism is acknowledged. Newer teachers, trained since the introduction of a National Curriculum and without practical experience of curriculum development at school level, are likely to be particularly disadvantaged.

The failure of the National Curriculum Council (NCC) to publish the report of its Task Group on multicultural education in 1990–91 reflected the strength of right-wing opposition to multicultural education, yet Tomlinson argues that it is still possible to incorporate a multicultural dimension: 'No one group, however powerful, can design or influence a National Curriculum in a democracy without being influenced by alternative conceptions, values, interests and ideologies' (Tomlinson 1993: 27). The non-publication of the NCC report on multicultural education led to the establishment of an alternative group coordinated by the Runnymede Trust, which published a practical guide for ensuring 'race' equality entitled *Equality Assurance* (1993). It has been reprinted a number of times and the popularity of such a guide suggests that many teachers and schools remain committed to the goal of racial justice in education at a time when they are under pressure to implement numerous reforms and when there is little or no support from central government to achieve such a goal.

One key concern within the black and ethnic minority communities is how national assessment procedures introduced alongside the National Curriculum will affect their children. There was considerable anger and frustration within these communities over lack of consultation in the introduction of the ERA (Tomlinson 1987); the absence of such consultation and the implied lack of concern is particularly noteworthy in the arrangements for assessment. Although there is a danger that national tests may contain cultural, gender and class bias, and serve to label children and reinforce negative teacher expectations (Davies *et al.* 1990) a number of commentators concerned with racial equality have argued that such assessment may challenge certain teachers' negative judgements of black children. The publication of achievement statistics place social and racial inequality in the public sphere. While they may be used by individual parents to select a school they also provide those with an egalitarian agenda with important evidence in their struggle for racial justice.

The national legislative context

A number of pieces of national legislation have direct implications for racial equality in schools. As well as the 1988 ERA referred to above, which has implications for curriculum, the Children Act 1991 asserts the principle of the 'best interests of the child' in decision-making and stresses the importance of working with the family. In this respect it is in harmony with the 1989 United Nations Convention on the Rights of the Child which has extensive implications for social justice in education (Osler 1994d; Osler and Starkey 1996). The Children Act expects local authorities to take account of the religions, ethnic origins and cultural and linguistic backgrounds of children in their communities, and by inference the same requirements might be expected of governing bodies. The Race Relations Act 1976, which is discussed in Chapter 1, outlaws indirect as well as direct discrimination. Schools and governing bodies therefore have a legal requirement to overcome forms of indirect discrimination which can occur in areas such as exclusions, assessment, employment and admissions. This means that particular requirements which, although applied to all racial groups, may exclude members of a particular group, may be unlawful. For example, dress regulations, which cannot be justified on educational grounds, would be indirectly discriminatory. Under Section 71 of the Race Relations Act, governors might encourage applications from a particular racial group which has been underrepresented for the work in question; this would be true for black and ethnic minority teachers at all levels. Many DfEE circulars are legally binding, and it is worth noting that DES Circular 12/91 on school teacher appraisal not only makes reference to equal opportunities and the duty not to discriminate but also argues that: 'Appraisers should . . . actively encourage all school teachers, including women teachers and teachers from the ethnic minorities, who have management potential to consider applying for management posts' (DES 1991).

Policy development and racial equality

Schools, LEAs and other agencies wishing to promote greater social justice need to examine their policies and practice to ensure that these do not reinforce racial inequality and thereby institutionalise racism. The following checklist highlights ways in which inequality can be perpetuated; it builds upon the work of researchers who examined the relationship between racial inequalities and policies and practices (Ben-Tovim *et al.* 1986).

1 *Policies and practices which fail to address racial injustice*
   - When a child complains of racial abuse how does the school respond? Are the racial elements of the case acknowledged? Is racial harassment explicitly dealt with in policies on equal opportunities or behaviour?
   - What policies exist within the teacher union to deal with cases of racial harassment? In cases where one union member is making a complaint against another what mechanisms exist for ensuring that action is not taken against a complainant?
   - What resources have been allocated to dealing with racial harassment?
2 *Policies and practices which create and maintain racial inequalities, formulated without taking black people into account (institutionalised racism through custom and tradition)*
   - Are jobs advertised in the black and ethnic minority press?
   - Does the school have an employment policy linked to targets to reflect pupil community, in terms of 'race'?
   - Do advertisements highlight the cultural diversity of a school/LEA as one of its positive features?
   - Is there internal recruitment? If so, what steps are taken (for example, job descriptions, interviewing, monitoring of 'acting' posts) to ensure that equality of opportunity is maintained?
   - Word-of-mouth recruitment can deny access to particular groups: what steps have been taken to ensure that support staff or supply teachers are not recruited exclusively in this way, for example, in emergencies?
3 *Abuse of the cultural differences of racial minorities: failure to provide information in the appropriate languages, or the application of ethnic stereotypes*

- Does the school have a language policy which includes guidance on provision of information to parents and prospective parents in appropriate languages?
- Are any assumptions made about particular groups of students, for example, the family obligations of Asian girls, which might limit access to careers advice or extracurricular activities?

4 *Policies and practices which assume negative racial stereotypes contribute to racial inequality and contribute to institutionalised racism*

- Such practices are not merely the results of the racism of individuals but may represent an integral part of the professional culture, they have become part of the professional's view of the client-group, and provide a means by which discriminatory practices are applied.
- How are rewards and punishments monitored in school? Is there any indication, for example, overrepresentation in short-term or permanent exclusions, that negative stereotyping may be influencing decisions by staff, senior management or governors?
- Are assumptions made about the appropriateness of particular sanctions according to gender or perceived ethnicity?

The Ofsted inspection framework and racial justice

The 1995 Ofsted guidance on school inspections may prove to be a useful instrument in promoting equality initiatives, given the prominence given by central government to inspections as a means of raising standards. Although inspection may only confirm what the senior management of a school already know concerning strengths and weaknesses, references to equality within the Ofsted guidance may usefully be exploited by those committed to challenging racism. The handbooks for nursery and primary, secondary and special schools (Ofsted 1995: 10–11) all state that:

> Throughout the inspection, the requirements of the schedule should be applied in relation to *all* pupils in the school. Inspectors must ensure that the full range of age, gender, attainment, special educational need, ethnicity and background is taken into account, including provision for, and attainment of, pupils for whom English is an additional language.

> The team must also include one or more inspectors charged with inspecting or co-ordinating the inspection of: equal opportunities issues; and, where relevant, the education of pupils for whom English is an additional language.

Table 2.1 addresses key issues relating to equality and racial justice highlighted in the Ofsted handbooks: *Guidance on the Inspection of Schools* (nursery and primary, secondary and special). The left-hand column highlights the formal Ofsted requirement, the measure against which schools are inspected.

Table 2.1 The Ofsted inspection framework, equality and racial justice

Inspection requirement	Implications for practice: Stage 1	Implications for practice: Stage 2
3.1 Characteristics of the school • Include a description of school composition in terms of pupils' attainment on entry, gender, ethnicity and background.	• Equal opportunities record-keeping includes details of ethnic group composition, pupil languages and language-related issues.	• Report attainment levels in comparison with national norms. • Economic indicators, e.g. free school meals, not accepted as reason for low attainment.
4.1 Attainment and progress • Report on what pupils achieve by 5 years in nursery or reception classes, by the end of each key stage, and by 19 years with reference to attainment. • Highlight any significant variations in attainment among pupils of different gender, ethnicity or background. • Report whether attainment and progress of minority groups is comparable with others.	• Equal opportunities monitoring and analysis carried out by senior management. • Needs assessed against appropriate economic indicators. • Principal results of monitoring are routinely reported to governing body. • Language policy emphasises that proficiency in Standard English is essential for academic success; such proficiency need not be achieved through devaluing or removing forms of language used in the home and community.	• Results of analysis shared with all staff; targets agreed and set for whole school, departments and classes. • Governors discuss results and request progress reports. • Introduce appropriate schemes in response to needs, e.g. homework club, book-loan scheme. • Investigate research into successful interventions in other schools.
4.2 Attitudes, behaviour and personal development • Evaluate and report on pupils' response to the teaching and other provision made by the school, highlighting strengths and weaknesses, as shown by the quality of relationships in	• Staff report on pupil response to teaching. • Staff examine behavioural and equal opportunities to ensure harassment and bullying are addressed and monitored.	• Survey pupils to establish viewpoints on good teaching/lessons. • Survey parents to establish viewpoints on behaviour and pupil responsibility.

- the school including the degree of racial harmony.
- Assess how pupils, including those of different ethnic groups, relate to one another.
- Report any inappropriate behaviour including harassment and bullying, towards particular groups of pupils.
- Note the level of respect between pupils and teachers and other adults in school, and whether pupils are encouraged to articulate their own views and beliefs.
- Are pupils interested in views and ideas different from their own? Do they recognise and understand a diversity of beliefs, attitudes, and social and cultural traditions?

5.1 *Teaching*

- Highlight the extent to which teaching meets the needs of all pupils.
- Focus on any pupils for whom English is an additional language.

- Monitor disciplinary procedures and effects, including exclusions from school.
- Do stereotypical assumptions in the classroom lead to an overfocus or an underfocus in any particular groups, e.g. extra control over 'boisterous' African Caribbean boys or acceptance of 'natural' bad behaviour; lack of attention for 'passive' Asian girls?
- Staff/pupils address equality issues through assemblies.

- Employ a variety of pupil groupings for differentiation.
- Provide support and resources for pupils in early stages of learning English as an additional language.
- Build upon students' prior knowledge and values in Personal and Social Education.
- Bilingual learners have structured opportunities to interact with pupils for whom English is the first language.

- Individual governors participate in assemblies, Personal and Social Education, to contribute to pupils' personal development.
- Parents linked to tutor groups to support groups of pupils with study skills, etc.

- Recognise and provide for variety of cognitive and language development paths in learning, e.g. groupings by first language, prior knowledge, particular skills, access to bilingual dictionaries and glossaries.
- Identify particular learning needs of advanced bilingual learners.
- Build upon pupils' prior knowledge and values in all curriculum areas, including science and maths.

Table 2.1 (Cont'd)

Inspection requirement	Implications for practice: Stage 1	Implications for practice: Stage 2
5.2 *Curriculum and assessment* • Evaluate and report on the planning and content of the curriculum and its contribution to the educational standards achieved by all pupils. • Evaluate how curriculum planning and implementation takes account of age, capacity, gender, ethnicity, background, competence in English as an additional language and special educational need. • Evaluate procedures for assessing pupils' attainment. • Does the curriculum provide equality of access and opportunity for pupils to learn and to make progress? • Consider the impact of the organisation of pupils into class and teaching groups on equality of access and opportunity. • Judge whether careers guidance is objective and free from gender and other stereotyping.	• Evaluate curriculum accessibility for all: What is the curriculum presented? Where flexibility exists what is taught? • Develop programmes which recognise cultural diversity and acknowledge pupils' experiences. • Senior management and governors promote equal curriculum access for all pupils. • Monitor pupil placement into teaching groups, assessment and examination results and pupil destinations by ethnicity, gender. • Ensure that assessment policies include formative use of assessment which is understood by pupils. • Introduce careers education at an early stage, i.e. in primary school and lower secondary school; enhance pupil aspirations.	• Distinguish between language support and other special needs and provide appropriate support. • Ensure parents understand assessment policies and are advised on formative use of assessment. • Invite women and men from a range of ethnic backgrounds to talk about experiences in non-traditional careers. • Staff teams review own practice to promote greater curriculum access. • Provide direct teaching about 'race' and gender equality.
5.3 *Pupils' spiritual, moral and social development* • Evaluate and report on the strengths and weaknesses of the school's provision for the spiritual, moral, social and cultural development, through the curriculum and life of the school, the example set for pupils by adults in the school.	• Staff review and report on opportunities for introducing spiritual/ moral/social/cultural issues in each curriculum area. • Senior management review opportunities for pupil participation and responsibility at whole school level.	• Review of pupil participation and responsibility with pupils. Pupils invited to suggest how this might be increased. • Pupils and their parents consulted on the development of more inclusive collective worship.

- Evaluate the quality of collective worship.
- Does the school provide pupils with knowledge and understanding of values and beliefs and enable them to reflect on their experiences to promote spiritual awareness and self-knowledge?
- Does the school teach principles which distinguish right from wrong?
- Does the school encourage pupils to relate positively to each other?
- Are pupils encouraged to take responsibility, participate fully in the school community and develop an understanding of citizenship?
- Are pupils taught to appreciate their own cultural traditions and the diversity and richness of other cultures?

5.4 Support, guidance and pupils' welfare

- Evaluate and report on the school's provision for pupils' educational and personal support and guidance of pupils and its contribution to educational standards.
- Does the school have effective measures to eliminate oppressive behaviour including all forms of harassment and bullying?
- Does the school recognise and record incidents of harassment and bullying that occur, and what steps are taken to prevent repetition?

- Staff share experiences of pupil participation and responsibility at classroom level.
- Senior management review ways in which collective worship is inclusive of pupils' cultural traditions.

- Staff review effectiveness of pastoral care system for all groups of pupils.
- Develop mentoring and other individual support programmes.
- Review equal opportunities policies, record-keeping and practices; assess effectiveness of policies and practices with reference to pupil attainment.

- Structural opportunities developed for pupil participation and decision-making, e.g. through school and/or class councils. How might resource allocation be linked to pupil priorities?
- Curricular and extra-curricular opportunities developed for pupils to experience citizenship and to explore its meaning at local/national/European/global levels.
- Staff recognise importance of multiple/hybrid identities and encourage pupils to explore and extend own identities through range of role models and broad-based curriculum.

- Consult with pupils and parents on appropriate support and guidance systems.
- Research and act on pupils' views on measures to respond to and prevent harassment and bullying.

Table 2.1 (Cont'd)

Inspection requirement	Implications for practice: Stage 1	Implications for practice: Stage 2
5.5 Partnership with parents and the community • Evaluate and report on the effectiveness of the school's partnership with parents. • Establish whether the school does all it can to gain the involvement of all parents.	• Discuss expectations of pupils with parents, concerning homework, discipline and other shared responsibilities. • Produce written communications to parents in a clear, accessible form, e.g. add a statement to letters in all relevant languages giving a telephone number for those who need to clarify/discuss contents. • Establish whether parents' meetings are arranged at convenient times. • Monitor involvement of parents by ethnicity and gender. • Does prospectus present ethnic diversity as an asset?	• Assess the impact of parental partnerships on achievement; consult with parents on this (and be prepared to act). • Who in the community is drawn on? Is the local community a learning resource or just a stream of visitors in and out of school? • Discuss values with parents, e.g. tensions between individual liberty and group responsibility.
6.1 Leadership and management • Evaluate and report on how well the governors, headteacher and staff with management responsibilities contribute to the quality of education and standards achieved by all pupils. • To what extent is there a positive ethos, which reflects the school's commitment to high achievement, an effective learning environment, good relationships and equality of opportunity for all pupils?	• Does school management have systematic means of evaluating what is happening at classroom level, as part of school evaluation procedures? • How does management respond to good practice, e.g. how would it support an individual teacher working to develop self-directed learning in a school with a control ethos? • How does management respond to poor practice?	• How does school leadership reflect commitment to equal opportunities in relationships between management and teachers? • Are there mechanisms for keeping equality and justice on the agenda in policies and practices relating to all aspects of school life, e.g. a requirement to report on equal opportunities implications in headteachers' reports to governors and governors reports to parents?

- How does the leadership of the school contribute to attitudes, relationships and the provision of equal opportunities?

6.2 *Staffing, accommodation and learning resources*

- Evaluate and report on the adequacy of staffing, accommodation and learning resources.
- Establish whether teaching and support staff who work with pupils for whom English is an additional language, are experienced and qualified for such work.
- Assess the effectiveness of the staff development and in-service training programme in motivating staff and in meeting individual and corporate needs.

- Provide in-service training for teams, departments or whole staff on curriculum access.
- Develop recruitment policy and practice which ensures that staff at all levels, including senior management, provide relevant role models for all pupils.
- What are the staff development priorities, do they reflect equal opportunities concerns?
- Do advertisements for all posts stress equal opportunities commitment of school and present multicultural make-up of school in a positive way?
- Is staffroom culture open and positive to equality issues?
- Are governors receiving training on fair employment practices and procedures?

- Ensure that all staff have access to professional development according to individual development plans for equality.
- How are decisions made concerning those who are sent on particular courses, e.g. do members of underrepresented groups have access to management training?
- Staff responsibilities monitored to ensure women/men, ethnic minorities not allocated stereotypical or marginal roles.
- Appoint bilingual teachers and assistants as appropriate, to support bilingual learners using their home language.
- Specialist language teachers share expertise with colleagues, particularly through collaborative teaching.

6.3 *Efficiency*

- Evaluate and report on efficiency and effectiveness with which the resources are managed.
- Pay particular attention to the deployment of additional teaching and support staff for pupils for whom English is an additional language, including any staff financed through special grants.

- Are staff allocated to pupils according to tradition or by objective needs?
- How are objective needs assessed when supporting pupils with additional learning needs?
- Are staff opinions sought when assessing needs? Are records of pupil attainments and progress referred to?

- Reallocate resources to meet needs of those disadvantaged by current arrangements.
- Are pupils invited to identify their own learning needs as part of the process of allocating resources?
- Are resources used strategically to increase teachers' skills, e.g. through collaborative planning?

The centre and right-hand columns represent possible responses by schools and examine implications for good practice in two stages. Stage 1 broadly represents initiatives in schools with a developing equal opportunities culture, those who have developed a policy and are now taking initial steps towards equalising opportunities. Stage 2 addresses schools which have already developed their practice to promote racial justice and suggests initiatives at a more advanced level. Interestingly, the Ofsted guidance on equal opportunities is placed within the section on leadership and management, so acknowledging such issues as a responsibility of heads and governors and as a whole school concern.

Summary

Recent legislation has both introduced a highly prescriptive curriculum and at the same time given schools greater autonomy in certain areas of decision-making; it would seem that schools are left with a responsibility to ensure racial equality in education but are operating within a political context where structural inequality is often denied and even perpetuated. Nevertheless, issues of equality of opportunity and access remain on the agendas of a number of local authorities and have been given a significant place within the Ofsted inspection framework, providing us with a useful measure against which standards might be set.

Three

The educational experiences of black and ethnic minority people

Introduction

While teachers, school and local authorities have taken important initiatives to challenge racism, these measures have often been implemented without sufficient consultation of black and ethnic minority communities or assessment of their needs. Policies and research have often failed to consider the complexities of the lived experience of black and ethnic minority people. This chapter examines some of the pathways that black and ethnic minority students have taken through the education system, both within schools and within higher education, an area which has often been overlooked. It includes black and ethnic minority people's experiences as teachers and parents as well as students and draws on both biographical accounts and available research.

In bringing together biographical accounts and setting them alongside the research literature on black people in the education system, I wish to explore not only how racism and other structural constraints might operate on people's lives, but also to consider the relationship between these structural factors and the personal decisions that individuals from black and ethnic minority communities make about their lives. An acknowledgement of the structural context does not imply an acceptance of black and ethnic minority people as helpless victims of racism. This chapter considers evidence of the personal decisions and actions that individuals take, seeking to set them within a broader context, and recognising that they are not likely to be independent of structural constraints. If we are to effectively challenge racism it is important to understand the complex ways in which racism and interpersonal behaviour are related.

Pupils in school

I vividly remember the day I made up my mind to go to Cambridge University. It was summer, a school outing, and we went there by coach. . . . I had the confidence that only unbounded ignorance can give. I had no idea what a leap it represented in class terms. In truth I had only a dim idea of how the British class system worked. To grow up Black in Britain is to grow up an outsider, and in any case, this was the sixties with its cult of egalitarianism. . . . I did not appreciate why it should be particularly remarkable that a Black girl should go to Cambridge. I took no advice, confided in no one and, blissfully ignorant of the fact that it couldn't be done, went ahead and did it.

(Diane Abbott MP)

Diane Abbott's (1989) account of how she challenged the more modest expectations of her parents and the scepticism of her grammar school teachers by applying for and gaining a place at Cambridge University is a story of success achieved against the odds. Her story reflects determination, confidence and optimism despite the incredulity, disinterest and indifference shown by her teachers. Her account of her educational success is all the more striking when it is placed in the context of the accounts of classroom life presented by a number of researchers working in both primary (Wright 1992; Epstein 1993; Connolly 1995) and secondary schools (Wright 1986; Mac an Ghaill 1988; Gillborn 1990; Mirza 1992). Such research commonly reveals contradictions between the experiences of many black and ethnic minority pupils, which include heightened control, low teacher expectations and pupil frustration, distress and resentment, and schools' stated equal opportunities objectives and policies.

In another autobiographical account two sisters, Isha McKenzie-Mavinga and Thelma Perkins, set out to discover something of the father they cannot remember, as part of establishing their own cultural heritage. Born to a Jewish mother and Trinidadian father, family stresses lead to both girls being placed in care for periods of time. They provide vivid accounts of their schooling, as 'mixed race' children growing up in predominantly white schools, in Birmingham and London during the 1950s and early 1960s. The following extracts from their stories demonstrate how 'race', gender and class interact in complex ways, and how perceived ethnicity may influence interpersonal relationships between children and between teachers and pupils. In the first account the elder sister, Thelma, describes starting secondary school in Birmingham in 1954:

I was enrolled in the local girls' secondary modern, Highgate School on Upper Highgate Street. I was the only black girl, I was as middle class as the teachers who taught us and my accent was definitely not Birmingham. I was at a distinct disadvantage when school drama productions were being cast: I was always the witch or the black king in the nativity play . . .

My attitude towards learning defied any of the stereotypes about black pupils that later emerged, as I was a voracious reader – which was uncommon enough in most pupils at that school – and I was therefore given access to my teacher's personal books . . .

[She recalls a second school] It was here, for the first time that I could remember, that I was hit for doing nothing wrong . . . My mother never did anything about it, although today she would probably have seen the teacher in court.

Once again I was the only black girl in the school. The only one who read whenever she got the chance and the only one who was not apparently from a working-class background. Once again I made only a few friends . . .

(McKenzie-Mavinga and Perkins 1991: 23–25)

Thelma may have defied the stereotypes that were later to be applied to black pupils, but it is clear from her account that a black girl with middle-class tastes and accent, acquired during her time at a Kent children's home, was not easily accommodated in the white working-class school, by either teachers or other pupils. Her younger sister, Isha, brought up in care amongst white children and staff, had to struggle at secondary school to establish herself among black girls born in the Caribbean. These girls, who were her role models, eventually accepted her. Isha describes her secondary schooling in London:

I took the eleven plus examination, was graded as a borderline pass . . . and I ended up at King Alfred's School for Girls in Catford. It was there in 1961, that I attached myself to a group of girls from the Caribbean. I spent the first few months being seen as a nice black girl by my white friends, while trying to qualify as a member of the black group. I was, however, a highly suspicious candidate with my light skin, and underwent vigorous questioning about my origins. I always replied airily, 'Oh, I'm a West Indian American' . . . In the end they would always want to know if I was a 'half-caste', and I learned that this was applied to me because I had a light skin and a white parent. Yes, I would say, I admit to being a 'half-caste'. I did not know whether or not I was supposed to be proud of this definition: it seemed like an important definition and therefore I stuck with it.

. . . I kept up with my friends and excelled in most subjects including bad behaviour, although I managed to escape expulsion because I was a special case living in care. I was deeply disturbed when teachers cornered black pupils and told them not to behave as they did in Jamaica because they were now in Britain and must do as the British did. The white girls gossiped that my friends ate 'Kit-e-kat' and took all the jobs. A girl in the home had called me a black monkey.

(McKenzie-Mavinga and Perkins 1991: 38–40)

Isha's story reflects the tensions faced by a black child living in a white children's home where racial stereotyping and racist myths went unchallenged among the children. Her disturbance at her teachers' attitudes towards black pupils clearly had an impact, if not on her academic achievements then certainly on her general response to schooling. One regional study found that children living in children's homes are 80 times more likely to be excluded from school (Maginnis 1993) and figures from the Department for Education and Employment (DfEE) indicate that one-third of children excluded from secondary school are in local authority care (Doe 1996).

Most of the early studies into ethnic minority achievement paid little attention to issues related to gender. Young African Caribbean women's achievements and relative 'success' in education have largely been ignored. Nevertheless, despite their achievements and their ambitions young black women are, at their point of entry into the labour market, failing 'to secure the economic status and occupational prestige they deserve' (Mirza 1992: 189). The attitudes of teachers, career advisers and potential employers may be of greater significance in securing employment which reflects examination success than the actual examination results themselves.

A study of the transition of a group of young Birmingham women from school to work and further education, found that racism was a pervasive influence on the lives of both black and white young women, and that teachers adopted different strategies for managing Asian and African Caribbean girls:

> The personal racism of young white women and men was overlaid by the racist assumptions of white teachers, employers and careers advisers. Black cultures and family forms were seen as deviant and abnormal, and identified as one of the main causes of young black women's problems in school and the job market. White teachers and employers adopted a 'divide and rule' tactic which played young Asian women off against their Afro-Caribbean peers.
>
> (Griffin 1985: 186)

Thelma Perkins, who eventually trained first as a nurse and then as a teacher, highlights the narrow ways in which black people were perceived within the employment market in her account of an encounter with her first employer in 1957:

> I left school and began work as the first black clerical employee of the Birmingham Co-operative Society; I was a punch key operator. After six months I was called into the managing director's office and asked if I was happy and got on well with my colleagues. I was informed that they never employed a Jamaican before! My father was from Trinidad but I did not bother to enlighten him.
>
> (McKenzie-Mavinga and Perkins 1991: 26)

While young black people are likely to experience racism in schooling and in the job market, and in dealings with teachers, careers advisers and employers, the form this takes and its impact is likely to be influenced by such factors as gender and perceived ethnicity.

A number of studies have explored teacher–pupil relationships, the particular experiences of African Caribbean and Asian boys and girls within schools, and the various strategies girls and boys adopt when teacher injustice or inequality is perceived (Gillborn 1988; Mac an Ghaill 1988; Mirza 1992). These studies do not really account for different teacher attitudes towards black boys and girls, nor do they explore the impact of these attitudes on 'achievement' or 'underachievement' except in terms of pupil behaviour. An extensive review of the research into the performance of African Caribbean children in schools concluded that the notion of poor self-esteem and self-identity was critical to an understanding of these children's apparent lack of success (Taylor 1981). Much of this early research is now questioned, both in its use of unreliable data and in its failure to acknowledge the impact of institutional racism on the lives of black pupils, but the question still remains as to how black and ethnic minority pupils respond to institutional racism and low expectations of teachers. The potential for teacher attitude or behaviour to influence or damage individual or group self-concept is likely to vary according to circumstance:

> It would . . . be unwarranted to assume that a subordinated group would necessarily have a thoroughly negative group-self-image . . . the subordinate group's image of itself . . . will also depend on the dynamics within the group . . . Of course, the inter- and the intra-group dynamics which influence the self-image and the image of the other are closely interrelated.
>
> (Figueroa 1974, quoted in Figueroa 1991: 152)

A newly qualified teacher, Ravinder Bansal, describes his grammar school experiences in Birmingham during the late 1970s and early 1980s when, as a Sikh boy in a predominantly white school, he was subject to an atmosphere of racial intolerance and abuse from fellow pupils. His teachers gave no indication that they perceived any problem within the school. He argues that academic success was achieved at a very high cost:

> I succeeded at the grammar school because the emphasis was on academic achievement and the teachers had high expectations of all pupils, even if they were black. My brother was at a local comprehensive where nothing was expected of him. The price I paid was in terms of self esteem and cultural identity. Through insidious and overpowering means, such as assemblies, subject material and teachers' attitudes, I was made to feel that there was only one way to success: the white, ethnocentric, middle-class way. My brother had none of the benefits of

being in an academic environment while suffering from the same loss of identity.

(Bansal 1990)

Education should permit the development of multiple identities (Osler and Starkey 1996; Richardson 1996b) yet this student's experience of schooling would appear to have undermined his existing identity, while at the same time failing to expand the choices open to white, middle-class students.

Parents

Much less is known about the experiences of black people as parents. An extensive review of research into ethnic minority communities and schooling, including minority parents' views of education and home–school cooperation, concludes that: 'In the literature on home–school liaison minority homes are invisible, are conceptualised as "problems", or are subsumed under . . . the "disadvantaged"' (Tomlinson 1984: 118). It concludes that there is a mismatch between these and those of teachers:

> . . . minority parents have become increasingly anxious that schools did not seem able to equip their children with the required qualifications and skills to compete 'equally' with white children. This anxiety has been particularly acute for West Indian parents . . . [it] has come to dominate home–school relations in West Indian communities . . . the basis of this mismatch of expectations may lie more in the structure and functions of the education system than in any parental failure or teacher obtuseness.
>
> (Tomlinson 1984: 19)

The black voluntary school movement developed in response to growing dissatisfaction among parents of Caribbean origin with schooling in Britain and the particular failure of the education system to meet the needs of black pupils. Such schools have also enabled black teachers and helpers to develop their professional and organisational skills; a study of black voluntary schools noted that: 'One particularly painful lesson is that black teachers do not have privileged access to the souls of black children and must earn their respect by demonstrating genuine commitment and competence' (Chevannes and Reeves 1987: 166).

Many parents from within minority ethnic communities in Britain have expressed the wish that their children grow up bilingual and have been concerned about the attitudes of schools and teachers to their home and community languages. One study reported parents' worries about bullying and racial prejudice, unhelpful teachers, lack of religious and language teaching, and too few ethnic minority teachers (Cross 1978). A number of small scale studies by Ghuman reveal that parents from various Asian communities, although largely satisfied with the children's schooling, have expressed concern that their children's identities and cultures were being ignored by the school; many parents specifically focused on the issue of mother-tongue provision (Ghuman 1980a,b; Ghuman and Gallop 1981). The Swann Report (DES 1985) rejected bilingual education in the languages of various Asian communities, not wishing to endorse any separate provision for ethnic minorities. Yet bilingual schooling in Welsh and English is available and encouraged in Wales.

Rai (1990) emphasised the particular difficulties faced by Asian families with children with special needs. He found that families encounter difficulties with professionals who appear to make decisions without family involvement, including the transfer of children to new schools. Such problems are compounded by the fact that information is not made available in community languages; this would appear to contravene the requirements of the Education Act 1981 which sets out procedures for the assessment of children with perceived special needs. Also many children are being misdiagnosed because they are being assessed inappropriately through the medium of English.

The issues faced by parents of children with special educational needs raise a wider question about consultation processes between schools and parents and the involvement of black parents in decision-making. Some writers (for example Gibson 1987; Brar 1991a) have suggested that much of what passes for public 'consultation' with black and ethnic minority groups is in fact a process of legitimisation of policies which have already been formulated by schools or education officers. Under recent legislation school governors have an increased role in the management of schools. Although the DES highlighted the need for more governors from ethnic minority communities, a survey carried out in the late 1980s found that very few LEAs were monitoring governing bodies and fewer still offered special support or training for their ethnic minority governors (Deshpande and Rashid 1993). Deem (1989) found in her research into school governing bodies that ethnic minority governors 'have a hard struggle and are amongst the quietest in our study' and that some governing bodies expect less of parent governors, noting that 'this is especially marked where there are female and black or Asian parent governors' (Deem 1989: 255).

Recently, 'choice' in education has become a focus of debate, forming an important part of the Conservative education agenda. The political right has drawn attention to the rights and responsibilities of parents in their children's education, and the 1988 ERA has increased public awareness on issues of parental choice and parental rights. Competition between schools has served to place many inner-city schools serving black communities at particular risk, as parents seek to exercise their choice and find places for their children at 'better', more popular suburban schools. The consequences of this 'choice' are inner-city schools with fewer pupils, smaller budgets and less choice for those parents who cannot afford to transport their children to the suburbs. In some areas of the country provision of services to inner-city schools serving black and working-class communities have been neglected: a study into the lack of provision of adequate school places in Tower Hamlets found that the local education authority had failed to plan for increased pupil numbers in the borough, despite available statistics on projected pupil numbers, and that the DES had colluded with the local authority in failing to take action. The report stressed: 'it is unlikely that the DES would have taken no action if the authority had been predominantly white and middle class' (Tomlinson 1992: 445).

Most recently, the demands of Muslim parents for 'separate' schools have attracted wide media coverage. In a study of Muslim mothers' reasons for selecting Islamic or state primary schools for their daughters it was found that most parents with children at a state school perceived themselves to have little choice, being constrained by such factors as the distance they could travel from home. Many of those with daughters attending an Islamic school also saw their choice as something of a compromise, faced as they were with the prospect of paying school fees which some could ill-afford; these parents, concerned with their daughters' academic achievements, recognised the risks in sending their child to a school which lacked the security of state funding and which consequently remained vulnerable to closure (Osler and Hussain 1995).

Black and ethnic minority parents are increasingly more aware of their rights and are demanding action to ensure that their children are not subject to discriminatory practices in education; for example, a parental challenge to the admissions policy of two Watford grammar schools led to a CRE investigation and report which has helped to shape a Department for Education (DfE) circular on admission arrangements (CRE 1992c). Similarly in 1993, Bradford parents challenged the council's schools admissions policy in the High Court, arguing that it discriminated against their children. The council acknowledged that Asian children in the city were less likely to be offered their choice of school than were white children (Young 1993).

Higher education

Research suggests that many black parents are likely to place a higher value on education than many white parents. For example, there is evidence to suggest that in various Asian communities working-class parents appear to aspire to higher education as strongly as those from middle-class backgrounds (Gupta 1977; Kitwood and Borrell 1980; Brennan and McGeevor 1990). Moreover, the high participation rate of Asian women in the labour market has created a greater interest in educating girls than in the past, as Bhachu (1991) demonstrates for Sikhs in Britain. Recent statistics from the Policy Studies Institute indicate that higher proportions of people from Indian and African-Asian communities now stay on in education after 16 years compared to those from white communities. Nevertheless, the proportion of those with no qualifications at all is particularly high among people of Pakistani and Bangladeshi origin (Jones 1993).

In comparison with the substantial research on issues of 'race' in schooling, we know relatively little about the experiences of black and ethnic minority people in higher education, although there is a growing literature on issues of 'race' equality in teacher education and on the experiences of black and ethnic minority student teachers. In a small-scale study of black women university students, all with families from the Caribbean, Tomlinson (1983) sought to establish whether there were any specific factors which accounted for their 'success' and to explore their general experiences of higher education. She found all of the women, regardless of their parents' own levels of education, spoke of the encouragement and practical support they had received at home, and some mentioned the influence of the (Pentecostal) Church. All these women had been educated at predominantly white schools, yet within higher education they highlighted the isolation they had experienced. They noted that although some people from their communities saw them as role models, a number of others, particularly men, were likely to assume they had separated themselves from their communities and were no longer really 'black' in outlook.

The feeling of isolation expressed by the sample of students interviewed by Tomlinson is echoed by Forbes (1990) in a personal account of her experiences as a black student at the Open University. She noted the Eurocentric focus of the curriculum, and her subsequent tactic of hiding her own responses when working alongside students whose backgrounds were very different from her own. She is critical of the 'pub culture' of the summer schools which excludes many black students brought up in a deeply religious tradition, and points out that not only are many white students unaware of black students' experiences and upbringing, but that the Open University made no provision for their needs.

In 1992, in response to a DES consultation exercise on the 'reform of initial teacher training' in which schools would take on greater responsibilities, the CRE expressed a number of concerns about the terms and criteria for that partnership. It was concerned that both the institutions of higher education and the schools should be able to demonstrate a commitment to equality of opportunity, both in terms of their own procedures and as a subject element in their training; it noted that unlawful discrimination and equality of opportunity were seldom being addressed in a systematic way, and that they were not referred to in the proposed list of competencies used to assess students. The detailed proposals from the CRE focused on two main concerns:

> Firstly we wish to argue that specific and systematic steps need to be taken to ensure that people from the ethnic minorities will be recruited for teacher training without unlawful discrimination. We also wish to argue that specific steps need to be taken to encourage people from

ethnic minorities to apply for teacher training in the first place. Secondly, we are concerned that the training delivered equips teachers to undertake their duties without unlawfully racially discriminating, and in a way that meets the demands of schools in a multi-racial, multi-lingual Britain.

(CRE 1992a)

A study commissioned by the Higher Education Information Services Trust (HEIST) found that among British students from black and ethnic minority backgrounds a significant number wished to be counselled by ethnic minority staff but that this was not feasible given the gross underrepresentation of ethnic minority teaching staff in universities (Adia 1996).

In a survey of Asian and white sixth-form students' perceptions of the teaching profession Singh and his colleagues found that both groups shared some general negative attitudes towards teaching as a career; the Asian students also saw racism among pupils and teachers as a significant deterrent to entering the profession (Singh 1988; Singh *et al.* 1988). In a survey of black students in 41 UK initial teacher education institutions, Siraj-Blatchford (1991) found that the vast majority identified racism as a problem they had encountered during their teacher education course, most commonly on teaching practice. Her findings are supported by Adia (1996) who discovered that ethnic minority students from a range of courses were likely to have encountered racism on placements or teaching practice; these students found such placements more stressful and demanding than did their white peers.

Teachers

The Swann Report (DES 1985) devoted a full chapter to teacher education and the employment of ethnic minority teachers, noting the underrepresentation of ethnic minorities in the teaching force and the absence of statistical data. It included information from black and ethnic minority teachers' organisations which suggested that such teachers faced discrimination both in obtaining posts and in subsequent career advancement. The Committee observed a number of ethnic minority teachers who were 'stagnating' in posts which did not match their capabilities or experience (DES 1985: 602).

Arguing that the teaching profession should reflect the ethnic make-up of the wider population, the Swann Report pointed out the potential of black and ethnic minority teachers as a source of cultural expertise and as a reassuring point of contact for ethnic minority parents and children who are unable or unwilling to trust 'authority' to understand their needs. The report stressed that schools had, in black teachers, a potential source of bilingual staff, teachers who might make a particular contribution to schools' pastoral programmes and develop community links. It emphasised the value of ethnic minority teachers as role models to both black and white children. Its call for the introduction of ethnic monitoring as a first step towards enabling equality of opportunity within the profession has since been taken up, although the educational arguments put forward for the recruitment of greater numbers of ethnic minorities into the profession do not appear to have been widely heeded or developed.

A survey undertaken on behalf of the CRE (CRE 1988a) found that not only were ethnic minorities underrepresented in the teaching profession, accounting for only 2 per cent of the teaching force compared with 4.5 per cent of the overall population, but that they tended to be on the lowest pay scales and to be disadvantaged in terms of promotion in relation to their white colleagues. The ethnic minority population in some of the local authorities studied was as high as 33 per cent, so it can be seen that the teaching force was totally unrepresentative of the local population.

The survey provides useful statistical data which confirms the indications of the Swann Report that black teachers do not enjoy the same career progression or support as their white colleagues, with about half believing they have experienced racial discrimination in their employment. The ethnic minority sample was on average older than its white counterpart and had considerably more teachers working in the shortage subjects of science and mathematics, and so might have expected more rather than fewer senior or promoted posts. Yet all the evidence suggests that black and ethnic minority teachers are seen as a cheap commodity by their employers, more likely to be employed at lower pay levels and to be on temporary contracts. Blair (1994) suggests that one of the effects of market ideologies introduced into the education system in the late 1980s is to worsen the already poor employment prospects and conditions of work for black teachers.

While the CRE survey provides some useful statistical data concerning the position of black teachers, it tells us relatively little about the actual experiences of these teachers. This type of evidence is scarce and must largely be drawn from specific enquiries conducted in certain London boroughs; from other reports which were not designed primarily to investigate black teachers' experiences; or from biographical accounts.

An early autobiographical account is that of Beryl Gilroy who came to Britain from Guyana in 1951 and eventually became head of a London infants' school. She observes: 'attitudes to the few blacks then in the country were much the same as they are today but the way people deal with them or react to them has altered' (Gilroy 1976). The experiences of Bangar and McDermott, who entered the profession some 30 years later, having both been educated in Britain, cause them to question both schools' motivations in appointing black teachers and their subsequent expectations:

When we started teaching, we were both aware that our position would necessarily be different from that of white teachers, but we did not imagine that our working lives would be so dominated by issues to do with racism. We soon discovered that black teachers are generally expected to be involved with challenging racism, and throughout our teaching experience we have found ourselves channelled more and more into black issues.

(Bangar and McDermott 1989: 138)

Daniels and Aldred (1986: 25), in advice to black parents on how to overcome institutionalised racism and maintain effective relationships with their children's schools, draw attention to the possibility that 'some black students who have internalised all the negative concepts/stereotypes about "black people" will give black teachers a much harder time than they do their white teachers'. Research with black boys in a London school, confirmed that this is sometimes the case:

. . . we watch him [the black teacher] very closely and see how he behaves towards us and the white boys. If we notice that he is always shouting at us but not at the white boys, we feel that he does not like us and we decide to make life in the class difficult for him.

(Delsol 1984)

Interviews with girls of African Caribbean and Asian descent in three Birmingham schools revealed that these students felt the need for more black teachers, who they believed would better understand their cultural backgrounds and their experiences of racial discrimination. Nevertheless, they also reported that black teachers were sometimes given a more difficult time by both black and white students:

They constantly poked fun at her. Believe it or not, one boy sat at the back of the classroom and started to smoke. I couldn't believe it. Just because a Black teacher was teaching. They made a joke out of her, and hardly did any work. She was good at her job and when she demonstrated an experiment people started to get really interested. But because of who she was people would use any excuse to give her trouble. Black teachers can carry respect but it takes a lot more.

(Osler 1989: 29–30)

The girls in the Birmingham study were also aware that black teachers may be under pressure to compromise in various ways in order to be accepted by their white colleagues; such teachers were regarded by many of the girls as 'acting white'. The young black women in Mac an Ghaill's (1988: 31) study saw their two black women teachers frequently rejected by black students for 'failing to identify with them against the white teachers and not being fully accepted professionally by the latter'. Although the Swann Report stressed that black teachers should not automatically be expected to take on responsibility for the welfare of black pupils, many may find that the circumstances of their employment leave few options open, as this comment reveals:

We are frequently given responsibility for the behaviour and monitoring of Black pupils in 'problem' schools, where attempts are made by the all-white management to exploit our knowledge of our own community to its detriment. For those Black teachers who do push for meaningful and lasting changes, the likelihood is that we will be labelled 'subversive' by our employers and by the white parents, who see us as a threat to the status quo. And those who don't, risk permanent isolation from their own Black community, who regard them as having 'sold out'. Given such a choice Black women have tended to go into the schools prepared to do battle with the system.

(Bryan *et al.* 1985: 87)

Bangar and McDermott observe how they are expected to be experts on black culture, but also note how their very presence in schools as young black professionals who 'fit in' serves to legitimate an inequitable system:

Black teachers are often called upon to fill pastoral and disciplinary roles in situations where they have little control and are usually asked to intervene on behalf of the school rather than in the interests of black pupils or parents. A school can deflect allegations of racism by using its black staff to deal with situations of tension, and even by citing their existence as proof of its commitment to challenging racism.

(Bangar and McDermott 1989: 143)

In his study of the life histories of people of African and African Caribbean descent living in Britain, Henry (1991) includes the stories of seven men and one woman who were teachers. Despite a range of political standpoints, all perceive 'race' to have played a significant role in their careers, and a number express concern about the racism they have observed or encountered in fellow teachers.

The role of senior management would seem to be critical in ensuring that black teachers experience equality of opportunity to progress and develop professionally. The Burnage Report includes accounts of interviews with black teachers who were working at Burnage High School at the time of schoolboy Ahmed Ullah's murder in 1986. The panel concludes: 'the stories and experiences of the black teachers at Burnage are a clear indictment of the effectiveness of anti-racist policies at Burnage High School' (Macdonald *et al.* 1989: 233). Part-time teachers responsible for Indian music and Urdu indicate how the school organisation served to diminish their status and that of their subjects in the eyes of pupils and staff.

Case studies of black teachers of Caribbean origin (Gibbes 1980) also raise questions about the role of senior management, the levels of support offered to black teachers, and the impact of senior management on their careers. Many of the problems and barriers encountered in the career histories recounted to Gibbes occurred before the introduction of the Race Relations

Act 1976, when there was little hope of legal redress. Nevertheless, in the 1970s, when Gibbes was conducting her research, there existed a potential alternative source of support for isolated black teachers through LEA structures.

During the late 1970s and 1980s, many LEAs took steps to implement equal opportunities policies in the recruitment and selection of teachers. Nevertheless, surveys of black and ethnic minority teachers in the London borough of Newham (Newham Asian Teachers' Association 1985; Newham Afro-Caribbean Teachers' Association 1985) found that these teachers were disproportionately represented in lower-scale posts. There was a widespread perception that they were not given the same encouragement as their white counterparts, and were failing in attempts to achieve internal promotion within their schools. One disturbing feature of the surveys was that all Asian teachers and just over half the African Caribbean teachers had heard racist remarks from colleagues. The African Caribbean teachers' survey concludes: 'One of the root causes of inequality might be the assessment of competence of teachers by Heads. There is no set pattern or precise criteria for promotion.'

This conclusion would seem to be supported by the findings of the 1988 CRE survey which found that proportionately nearly twice as many white teachers as ethnic minorities had been invited or encouraged to apply for internal teaching posts by their headteacher. The statistics indicate that headteachers are less likely to recognise the potential of black teachers and when they do identify able black teachers they are apparently unwilling or unable to make use of them in their own schools.

An independent inquiry into the recruitment and promotion of ethnic minority teachers in another London borough found that for the majority there appeared to be a ceiling at what was then Scale 2 (Ealing 1988). The enquiry had been commissioned to establish why a teacher recruitment drive which had explicitly aimed to increase the proportion of black and ethnic minority teachers failed to do so (Brar 1991b). The report found that the all-white recruitment team had relied on word-of-mouth recommendations for the permanent appointment of temporary staff, informal telephone references, and visits to teacher education colleges that were not known to attract black and ethnic minority students.

The Education Reform Act 1988 and the introduction of local financial management has increased the autonomy of schools and significantly changed the nature of their relationship with LEAs. Although LEAs remain the legal employers of teachers working in local authority schools, the power of school governors has been increased and they are likely to be far more influential in the selection and recruitment process; research indicates that governing bodies are unlikely to be representative, being biased in favour of white, middle-class males, who tend not to prioritise issues of equality and social justice (Deem *et al.* 1992). In this context, black and ethnic minority teachers are likely to experience greater isolation and be more vulnerable.

This research would appear to support the concerns expressed by the National Union of Teachers, in a policy document containing recommendations on the recruitment and retention of black and ethnic minority teachers' presented to the 1990 Annual Conference:

> ... the possibilities for discrimination will be even greater if local authority guidance on equal opportunities practice is not heeded. Governors should be made aware that they may be financially liable for Industrial Tribunal cases if they do not take LEA advice and breach the Race Relations Act. The many black teachers who work in support services will also be made more vulnerable under local management of schools, as LEAs seek to reduce centrally held budgets in order to devolve finance to schools.
>
> (National Union of Teachers 1990)

Black people are underrepresented at all levels within the teaching profession, but this underrepresentation is particularly acute in senior management positions and in higher education among teacher educators. An informal survey by the Anti-Racist Teacher Education Network, published in 1988, found that there were just 27 full-time black teacher educators in England, Scotland and Wales, 0.6 per cent (McKellar 1989: 69). McKellar concludes (like Bryan *et al.* 1985, quoted above) that the responsibilities of being a teacher, particularly within a management position, may place black people in a situation in which they are seen to be operating against the interests of their own communities. She suggests this may limit the appeal of teaching as a career in the same way as it affects recruitment into the police force. She argues that the experiences of black teachers, and black women in particular, give them insights into the processes of education which encourage them to challenge inequality:

> It is part of the role of the black teacher to think of the wider concerns of education; the positions of groups in society; the differential rates of achievement of pupils; the ways schools induct pupils into different roles in society. It could be argued that all teachers need to have an overview of the processes of education, but because black women teachers are most likely to be able to understand the issues involved in throwing off oppression then it becomes part of their lot.
>
> (McKellar 1989: 82–83)

Very little is recorded about the experiences of those black people who do manage to achieve senior management positions in education. A study of black women managers at a variety of levels identifies a number of pressures which such women are likely to face, including feelings of isolation, the strain of coping with sex stereotyping, discrimination from colleagues, and pressure from the dominant institutional culture. It explores the specific pressures experienced by black women, who are a small group within a female minority in senior management. They are likely to share many of the same pressures as other women as well as encountering others specific to themselves (Walker 1993).

A number of women in Walker's study identified a democratic and participative style of management as helpful to them as black women managers; they argued that this helped to break down barriers and so decreased feelings of isolation, and was influenced by their experience of oppression, making them particularly sensitive to the effects of their actions on others. They stressed the importance of networking as a means of support and were aware that efforts to achieve cooperative, community-linked and non-hierarchical ways of working were not without difficulties, particularly for black women headteachers who might be experiencing acute isolation. The stresses of implementing change from within an organisation sometimes tempted individuals to adopt more authoritarian or aggressive styles of working.

Summary

Despite demands from black parents that their children's needs be met and their right to education ensured, and calls for racial equality and policy initiatives from within the education service, it is clear that black people do not enjoy equal opportunity with their white peers. Painful personal accounts and a significant amount of research evidence indicate that at all levels black children and adults are forced to challenge racism as part of their everyday experience. The accounts suggest that although pupils may be limited in the range of responses available, adults have developed a multiplicity of responses and a range of strategies to support them in their professional lives.

Four

Researching black teachers' lives

Meanings and interpretations

In researching black teachers' lives and careers, my aim has been to focus on the meanings which the teachers themselves attach to actions, events and choices in their lives and work. I wished to establish why people from black and ethnic minority communities become teachers, what factors encourage them to remain in teaching or to look for alternative opportunities, and what are the subjective experiences both of those teachers who encounter career blocks and of those who achieve senior management positions and 'career success'.

In contrast to much of the research on 'race' and education, the study focuses on black and ethnic minority people who have largely succeeded in education. The areas I set out to investigate were black teachers' own experiences of schooling, the influences and choices which have led them into teaching, work experiences and values and attitudes to work, and the career or work paths they adopt. I consider the meaning of 'career success' for black teachers and identify the personal qualities and environmental factors which make success possible within a context of structural inequality.

Although the intention was to generate hypotheses and theories from the data as it was collected, the study, as originally conceived, was inevitably influenced by my own career experiences, as outlined in the introduction to this book, and by stories told by black colleagues about their experiences. I have sought to exploit this lived experience and use it as part of the context in which the research design was planned and developed. Just as an ethnographer may spend time in a particular institution, developing an understanding of context, so I have sought to use my past experiences in a contextual way.

It might be argued that this is likely to encourage personal bias and influence the outcomes of the research. Interviews, as a method of data collection, have been characterised as particularly prone to bias on the part of the interviewer. The danger is that researchers may not be able to identify their own prejudices, or stand back from familiar settings or accounts (Cohen and Manion 1989). In working to overcome any undue bias, the interviews were conducted in a relatively unstructured way. Although I had a checklist of issues I wished to cover I began by inviting the interviewee to talk about their education and career. The approach used was thus similar to that used by Casey (1993: 24) when she invited women teachers, including African-American women, to respond to her request: 'Tell me the story of your life.' As the narrative developed I asked questions to clarify certain points or to take the story into a new chapter, such as from leaving school to start work or enter higher education. Since I was prompting I asked each interviewee at the end of their narrative if there were other issues they had expected to talk about which we had not covered. In this way I sought to give the subject of the research as much control over the content of the interview as possible.

The purpose of the study is to gain qualitative insights into, and understanding of, the complexities of black teachers' lives and careers rather than to attempt to measure any one objective reality. The research does not set out to establish statistically the overall position of black teachers within the education system but to look in-depth at the experiences of a small sample. Life-history interviews were judged to be the most appropriate and valid method of collecting such data. Such interviews do not measure an 'objective reality' but they are likely to offer insights into the complexities and contradictions of human experience. Since black teachers are living and working in the context of a society and education system which is structured by 'race', gender and class, one aim is to explore the impact of inequality, and particularly the impact of racism, on individuals' lives and careers. In recounting their life histories, teachers are reflecting on their own subjective realities. It was anticipated that this would generate data on a wide range of life experiences: black teachers' experiences are clearly not confined either to racism or to teaching. The research was thus planned to encourage individuals to share the experiences and influences which they judged to be important.

Woods (1986: 34) refers to the process of 'washing your mind clean' when doing qualitative research. Whilst I would argue that this is difficult, if not impossible, to achieve in conceptualising a study, it is what has been attempted in the analysis of the data. In the analysis I have not assumed that each interviewee shares my understandings; I have looked afresh at what each person is saying. However, at the planning stage, and in gaining access to people and agreeing their participation, familiarity and shared experiences have been considerable advantages. All researchers have a personal perspective which, I would argue, necessarily affects their data at all stages.

Given that the few existing studies of black and ethnic minority teachers have suggested that they encounter careers blocks and that they find it difficult to progress to senior positions, I felt it important to study teachers at different stages in their careers and to try to identify changes which might be taking place. Since a longitudinal study was not practicable, I targeted students and teachers at various key points in their decision-making and careers. This approach also has the advantage of providing an opportunity to investigate any differences in experience between those teachers who were educated abroad and migrated to Britain, largely in the 1950s and 1960s, and those who have been educated largely or exclusively in this country. Within the research sample experiences of schooling extend over a period of some 40 years from the 1950s to the early 1990s. They need to be placed within a historical context.

The intention is to allow the participants in the research an opportunity to bring their own perspectives to the analysis. This is particularly important as black and ethnic minority people have often been measured against presupposed white, often middle-class norms in previous educational and other social science research. The aim was to create a context where the teachers and students who are the source of the data might have the opportunity to help shape the research framework by grounding it in their own experience.

The sample

Most of those who participated in the study were living or working in the West Midlands, but there were exceptions. Given the relatively small number of black and ethnic minority people in senior positions, I decided to interview any senior manager who was willing to participate, regardless of geographical location. The geographical spread also helps protect the anonymity of individual participants, particularly senior educators.

The first set of interviewees was made up of experienced teachers, including a number who had achieved senior positions, generally headteachers or local education authority advisers and inspectors. A second set consisted of graduates following PGCE courses and undergraduates following a Bachelor of Education (BEd) course, i.e. people who had chosen to teach and were in the process of becoming teachers. These interviews enabled me to develop an understanding of this process as well as their motivations in entering teaching. I also talked to students who had chosen not to teach. They were interviewed in the final year of an A-level course as they made plans to enter higher education. By including people who had a career other than teaching in mind, I hoped to gain a broader picture of the attitudes of young people from black and ethnic minority communities towards teaching.

The sample was made up exclusively of black people, that is people of African, African Caribbean or Asian descent. No white students or teachers were included as the intention was to consider black perspectives within education. In choosing to consider black people as a group, I am assuming a shared experience of racism, while acknowledging that the forms in which individuals may experience racism are likely to differ, and may vary according to such factors as gender or perceived ethnicity. Nevertheless, the sample includes people from a wide range of social and cultural backgrounds. None of the participants questioned or expressed any difficulty with the notion of a study which focused on a sample made up of black people and all were willing to identify with this descriptor, to a greater or lesser degree. The issue of identities is developed in Parts Two and Three and in Chapter 11.

Where appropriate, I highlight the shared concerns of black teachers with their white colleagues, drawing on the research literature. The notion that a study of black teachers must be set within a comparative framework to guarantee its validity is questionable, and may well be based on a racist premise, as becomes clear when we consider that previous studies of white teachers' lives and careers have not been judged by similar criteria. The concerns expressed by Troyna (1994) that a study which focuses exclusively on black people may, albeit unwittingly, strengthen conceptions of whiteness as 'normal' with black people positioned as 'the other' are, I believe, avoided by using life history and presenting a rounded and complex picture of teachers' realities. Such an approach encourages participants to reflect on the multiple and sometimes contradictory influences which combine to shape their lives. Each individual responded to the request to talk about their education and career in ways that made sense to them. For everyone this involved looking beyond their school or workplace, and included reflections both on personal relationships and on broader political developments.

The sample is not intended to be representative of all black teachers, or all black students, although an effort was made to find both women and men in each category, and for each category to include both African or African Caribbean and Asian participants. In total 48 people were interviewed on an individual basis, 28 women and 20 men. Of these, 26 were experienced teachers and 10 had achieved senior management positions. Additionally, four group interviews were held with a total of 20 students.

Among the experienced teachers all but one were graduates, and the exception was in the process of upgrading her qualifications; seven of them had obtained higher degrees or were registered for them at the time of the interview. All had completed their higher education in Britain. Half of the senior managers also held advanced qualifications. Like the ethnic minority teachers in the 1988 CRE survey, they were thus particularly well qualified.

Whereas many of the teachers in the CRE survey had obtained their postgraduate qualifications in India, the teachers in this sample had obtained their higher degrees in Britain largely through part-time study some years after entering the teaching profession. A survey of ethnic minorities and the graduate labour market found that while members of ethnic minorities tend to place considerable value on education, ethnic minority graduates face particular difficulties in the graduate labour market, generally having to go to more interviews than their white peers. The quality of job is likely to be inferior to that secured by a similarly qualified white graduate and promotion more difficult to obtain (Brennan and McGeevor 1990). It seems quite probable that black and ethnic minority graduates entering teaching may have a perception or anticipation of such difficulties and this may explain why teachers from such backgrounds are generally better qualified than their white peers.

Issues of access

Initially, I approached teachers that I knew and later some of these teachers suggested colleagues in their own schools or from among their friends who might be willing to participate; half the experienced teachers and all the senior managers were recruited in this way. Other participating teachers I met at black teachers' meetings or at meetings between black teachers and parents, and some I made contact with through their participation in in-service courses. In one sense, they might be regarded as atypical, for it is perhaps the most active and high-profile teachers that are likely to be encountered in this way and therefore, one might suppose, the most talented or successful. When teachers who had taken part suggested friends or colleagues they generally named people they believed would be lively or 'interesting to talk to', but on a couple of occasions people were suggested because they were known to have had 'a difficult time', either during their own schooling or during their subsequent careers.

As a teacher educator, I encountered few problems in identifying PGCE students willing to participate in the research nor did I encounter any difficulties when I approached schools and colleges seeking to interview black and ethnic minority A level students. It was more difficult finding BEd students. Although I found one group of BEd students through a college tutor, I encountered obstacles at other institutions, including an administrator who made it very clear when I arrived for a pre-arranged meeting with students that she thought it very strange that I should 'want to meet the ethnics'.

The problems of access which have been described reflect, I believe, the structural position of black people within predominantly white institutions. In institutions of higher education, and notably within teacher education, black and ethnic minority people are significantly underrepresented among the teaching and administrative staff; in some of the colleges and departments I approached they were totally absent. Yet these institutions were all in towns or cities with significant black settlement. Certain groups within the black and ethnic minority communities, notably African Caribbean, Pakistani and 'black other' students are underrepresented in traditional universities, although some of the new universities (former polytechnics) have been successful in attracting more black and ethnic minority British students (Modood and Shiner 1994). While statistics suggest that the numbers of black and ethnic minority British graduates applying for places on teacher education courses may be on the increase (Graduate Teacher Training Registry, 1992), they remain tiny minorities in many institutions. Among five ethnic minority groups, the number of unplaced applicants had risen between 1993 and 1995, although the number of unplaced white applicants fell (Howson 1996).

In such a situation, black and ethnic minority students may not wish to draw attention to themselves, particularly in institutions where staff may be unaware of the different realities of black student life and of the level of overt racism experienced by many students (Siraj-Blatchford 1991; Blair and Maylor 1993). Students may not wish to draw attention to their 'black-ness', since to do so may attract comments or judgements that they have 'a chip on their shoulder'. If I, as a visitor and a member of staff from a nearby university, could encounter lack of cooperation from administrative staff in interviewing such students ('the ethnics'), then it is likely that the students will experience similar unhelpfulness within such an institution. It is per-haps small wonder then, that when students were approached by white staff members to be interviewed by me about their experiences as black students, many were reluctant to come forward, particularly where the attitudes and values of staff may not be have been made explicit to the students.

In schools, sixth-form and further education colleges the situation may be somewhat different. Many of these institutions, particularly those with multi-ethnic student populations, have addressed issues of equity and social justice in a more explicit way. Although the vast majority remain white institutions in terms of their staffing and power structures, black and ethnic minority students may feel less vulnerable or isolated than many of their counterparts in universities, particularly in those institutions where there are substantial numbers of such students or where they are in the majority. In schools, student–teacher relationships are likely to be more established, and sixth-form students will, in such circumstances, know more about the attitudes and values of individual teachers. There may also be an expectation on the part of both teachers and students that students should cooperate to do what is asked of them; the degree to which sixth-form students are genuine 'volunteers' in research is thus open to question. Certainly access was never a problem with this group.

As a response to such ambiguities, when I interviewed groups of black A level students I always renegotiated their participation and was careful to stress the confidentiality of the proceedings and to guarantee anonymity. I also took care to explain that in studying the lives and careers of black teachers I was concerned to understand students' viewpoints. Thus I inter-viewed them about their own schooling and career choices having stated clearly my own value position: I explained that my motivation in the research was a commitment to racial equality and justice. I believe if I had tried to adopt a 'neutral' position in the interviews this would have been counterproductive.

Interviews were arranged to suit the needs and timetables of participants: I offered to visit them at their workplace or place of study, for them to come to my workplace or home, or if more convenient, for me to visit them at home. The majority of students were interviewed at the institutions where they were studying, although about a quarter either came to my home or I to theirs. I visited half the teachers and senior managers at their place of work and most of the others at home. Generally there was a more relaxed atmosphere in people's homes, and refreshments were always offered, generally hot drinks and snacks, although on one occasion a full Trinidadian meal had been prepared. All the participants agreed to be tape recorded. I spent several hours with each of the experienced teachers and we sometimes met on a number of occasions.

Ethical and political issues

When I began collecting narratives I was aware from the very early stages that categorisation of interviews and much of the procedural advice offered by the textbooks did not fit comfortably with what I was doing. Some aspects of interviewing, for example, the number and length of interviews, whether questions are asked according to a standardised format, and how the information is recorded, are generally included in research reports and these aspects of interviewing are seen as 'legitimate'. Other aspects, for example, social/personal characteristics of the interviewer, interviewees' feelings about the interview, and the extension of interviewer–interviewee encounter into more broadly-based social relationships remain 'illegitimate' (Oakley 1981). As Oakley suggests, this has led to a theoretical characterisation of the interview which cannot and does not work in practice.

Interviewees are typically seen simply as a source of data, and it is the interviewer's task to establish a rapport with the interviewee or even, if required, to empathise with his or her concerns. Establishing rapport, as explained in the literature on research methodology, does not really mean establishing a sympathetic or emotional relationship, but 'the acceptance by the interviewee of the interviewer's research goals and the interviewee's active search to help the interviewer in providing the information' (Oakley 1981: 35). It is seen as a skill which will enable the interviewer to obtain the necessary data for the research. To go beyond this, some researchers would suggest, is to enter dangerous territory and to break professional conventions.

Some researchers only advocate a move away from the established procedures towards a sharing of responsibilities between interviewer and interviewee if giving more control to the interviewee will improve the quality of the interview, and thus the data. Questions of power are seen purely as methodological issues; there is no suggestion that the research process might be changed simply to achieve a more equitable or non-exploitative relationship between researcher and researched. Where an interview might otherwise be threatening to an interviewee, interviewers may share and relate their own biographies. They would indicate how, for example, they share experiences, attitudes or tastes with the informants in order for the latter to be more trusting (Powney and Watts 1987: 42–3).

To suggest an interview is democratised merely as a strategy to put an interviewee at ease is, it might be argued, patronising to interviewees who will clearly have their own perceptions, both of the interviewer and the interview process. It is also to ignore the possibility that for ethical reasons, as much as for any desire to obtain the best possible data, the researcher may wish to establish a working relationship with interviewees which is built on a basis of openness rather than passivity and professional distancing, and on values such as equality and reciprocity.

The interviewees in this study, who ranged from sixth-formers through to teachers and senior managers in the education service, were in professional terms a group of people with considerable differences in status. Interviewer–interviewee relationships were likely to differ according to the category of interviewee and their perceptions of their status in relation to my own. I felt it important, nevertheless, to try to work in a non-hierarchical way. I was concerned, first and foremost, to try to engage in the research in a way which is non-exploitative.

All participants were promised confidentiality and anonymity. The significance and implications of this varied according to the category of interviewees. It was clearly of immediate and critical importance to PGCE students who were not only talking about their past educational experiences but also their present courses, their experiences on teaching practice and their relationships with their tutors, pupils and teachers in their practice schools. They were aware of my on-going professional relationships with these tutors and teachers and needed to be confident that not only would their anonymity be guaranteed in any future reports, but that, perhaps more importantly, total confidentiality would be ensured in the immediate future. Information which they gave me might, if shared with tutors, have influenced their assessment.

Some women researchers, for example Scott (1985), have recorded how, in interviews with men, interviewees often try to control the situation. She also found that the more powerful the person's position, the more difficult the interview. I had existing professional relationships with the majority of the senior managers I interviewed, but these were not generally close relationships. Nevertheless, I was always welcomed on a basis of equality, and shown great courtesy. It was also noticeable that interviewees in senior positions also set out to work in a non-hierarchical way. This was not always what I had expected. One senior inspector originally agreed to give me an hour, explaining that he was very busy; this might have been interpreted as a way of him establishing a superior position. Yet when I arrived he set a very different context for the interview: he came to meet me, introduced me to a colleague, made me a drink and, at the end of a long working day, engaged enthusiastically in the interview for some two-and-a-half hours. Although we had not worked together for six or seven years, a good professional relationship was re-established. While this may be explained partially in terms of the personalities involved, I believe that much of the energy which went into interviews stemmed from a belief on the part of the interviewee that the research was worthwhile and important.

The very process of inviting people to tell their life histories, even when the particular focus is of education and work experiences, meant that a familiarity and understanding is established between interviewer and interviewee which goes far beyond the 'rapport' recommended in order to ensure that the interviewee supplies the interviewer with the maximum amount of data in the most efficient way possible. Like Oakley's (1981) interviewees, the students and teachers that I interviewed tended to want to put questions to me. For example, some wanted practical or factual information on careers or courses of study, others asked more personal questions about my own work experiences. On more than one occasion when the interviewee had finished recalling her own life history, I was asked to recount my story, and I found that roles were more or less reversed.

Although I did not start with an assumption that interviewees would be as interested in me as I was in them, I did share aspects of my own biography with those interviewees who asked questions. This generally happened after the participant had recounted their own story, so the question of whether my viewpoints might influence their account did not arise. Sometimes, however, I was asked questions about myself before the individual agreed to participate. On one occasion I rang a young primary teacher. She invited me to her school, and I sensed it was very important that she met me before she agreed to go any further. We met in her lunch break and she wanted to know all about the project, including how I would write it up. She went on to ask me whether I had ever encountered racism at work. It was only when I had answered that I had, and said how I had dealt with it, that she agreed to be interviewed.

Although many of the textbooks advise researchers that it is inappropriate to answer questions (Goode and Hatt 1952; Selltiz *et al.* 1965; Galtung 1967; Brenner 1981; Powney and Watts 1987), not to have done so would have been to ignore the principle of reciprocity. The interviewee may not want or need anything in return, or the interviewer may not be in a position to offer anything to the interviewee apart from openness, but without such a commitment on the part of the researcher the interview process is potentially exploitative. It is also likely that many interviewees would not have been so open if reciprocity had been denied, and in at least one case it is quite likely that I would not have got consent to an interview. In answering questions I do not believe I was allowing 'interviewer bias' to distort the interview, the interviewee would have inevitably made their own judgements about my value position even if I had not been explicit. Interviews are necessarily complex social interactions and it would seem that the critical issue is not whether a particular interview is biased or not, but whether the researcher is aware of their own influence: 'To want to interview without interviewer influence is a contradiction in terms' (Brenner 1981).

Researching success

In Britain, African Caribbean and Asian people have been the subject of much social science research, and black teachers are likely to be aware of this and also aware that black children have been the subjects of much educational research. Although black researchers are now beginning to address issues of 'race' and education, the bulk of research into black people has been done by white researchers, who, whatever their political standpoints, have inevitably addressed issues from their own perspectives.

In asking black teachers to tell their stories, I was asking people to participate in research which would focus in large part on black 'success', rather than 'failure' in education. Although a number of participants welcomed a study which focuses on successful black people, it is not without its difficulties. In the early 1980s, a major study of high achieving African Caribbean, Asian and white pupils was proposed to explore the factors, other than socio-economic factors, which are involved in achievement and under-achievement. After initial consultations the project was abandoned due to serious reservations in some communities about the ways such a study might be used as an excuse for a lack of positive action (DES 1985: 80; Mortimore 1991: 211). There remains an important political issue concerning research about 'successful' black teachers. Careful consideration needs to be given to the ways in which it is reported, and researchers engaged in this type of project need to try to anticipate how it might be interpreted, used or reported by others, possibly to the detriment of black people, either in teaching or in the wider community.

Student teachers, teachers and senior managers all showed a high level of interest and commitment to the research, with many making enquiries about the availability and timing of research reports, and a number stressing the need for dissemination and asking to be kept informed about any future publications. Some gave personal encouragement and expressed delight that I was addressing issues of importance to them. Much of this support came from teachers I was meeting for the first time.

Shared identities

I would argue that my own identity, both personal and professional, had a significant impact on the interviewees. While a number of people felt they would have agreed to be interviewed by a white person, some were quite clear that they would not have consented, and others felt that the quality or tone of the interview would have been quite different. Some women said they would have talked as openly to another woman that they trusted, whether white or black, and others said it was important to them that I was both black and a woman and that they knew me. The response below was fairly typical:

Audrey: You agreed very readily to the interview, do you think you would have said the same things to a white interviewer?

Balbir: I think I would have, but I don't think I would have been so open in the comments that I've made; I don't know whether I would have been so honest, in a lot of the personal comments that I made about some of the staff that I had worked with, about my own life in terms of experiences at college and forming my own identity and so on. Whether those sort of comments would have rolled off the tongue so easily I don't know.

At another level this degree of 'comfort' in the interview and the assumed shared understandings between interviewer and interviewee may pose some difficulties when presenting the results of the research to a wider audience. Some things may be expressed in a more explicit way because the participant is speaking to a black researcher, others are implicit because of the 'shared meanings' which have been assumed:

Audrey: Do you think you would have talked as freely and in the same terms to a white person?

Yasmin: Oh no, oh no! No Audrey, I would have to be explaining it all of the time. There is a lot more behind it, there is a whole package that goes with it and you know the picture and you know what I mean and you know what it is like. This interview would have been 10 times longer! I would find it difficult anyway, without being negative or hostile, to talk to someone white like this. I have got a couple of [white] friends who you could talk to like this and they actually think the same way and they realise that it is quite a racist society, with structures set up to perpetuate that, and they acknowledge that and want to change it. If you were a white interviewer that I didn't know very well, I would find it difficult to say that I find the society racist and I am living proof of it, completely assimilated into the British culture and yet when I am actually faced with something people don't see me as white. It's not British culture, it's white culture isn't it? White culture I have got but I don't look white, and when people look at me what they see is a black woman, worse, worse, an Asian woman.

It was probably equally important to certain interviewees that I had recently worked as a school teacher, and was familiar with the broad working contexts of participants. There were undoubtedly also many professional assumptions made yet having an 'insider' professional position, as when a teacher researches aspects of teaching, is not as commonly regarded as problematic.

Life history and the dangers of intrusion

Life history as a research method may be seen as intrusive if the researcher invites the researched to talk about experiences which are in some sense intimate. For a number of people in this study the research interview was a painful experience, particularly as they recounted stories from their own schooling: for example, incidents where teachers had acted insensitively or taken decisions which had placed them at a long-term educational disadvantage. Sometimes people said they were sharing certain details of their lives for the first time, because they feared these might have been interpreted by friends or colleagues as personal inadequacies. Despite this, interviews were rarely totally sombre and often there was a good deal of laughter. Interviewees were often able to laugh at themselves and to see humour in day-to-day encounters at work.

My research was essentially about people's experiences of schooling and work, but for many people, particularly women, decisions made about careers are often tied to their real or anticipated domestic responsibilities. While just under half of the experienced teachers and senior managers had children, it tended to be women who spoke about their marriages and children, their feelings about them, and the impact they had had on their work. A number of the students that I interviewed, both women and men, were about to get married, and so interwoven with work were many personal details of people's lives. The second interview that I did, that with a recent graduate, made nonsense of the textbook advice that if interviewees ask questions of the interviewer, these should be carefully and firmly sidestepped:

> Another danger that experienced interviewers appreciate is that respondents may become dependent even during a fairly brief interviewing session especially where the topic is one which highlights a major unresolved situation for the interviewee . . . The interviewer may be one of the few well-informed people who has sympathetically listened and apparently understood the difficulties of the interviewee. This same interviewer now has to leave the situation without offering advice or hope for very immediate improvement. Professional interviewers learn quickly about the necessity to maintain distance.
>
> (Powney and Watts 1987: 43)

In this interview, a young Muslim woman graduate told of how she had become involved in an oppressive and violent relationship with a fellow student who had made her a virtual prisoner in their shared home. After several months she had managed to leave him, and with the support of a tutor, resit her examinations. The man then pressed her to marry him and when she refused told her parents about the relationship, which had previously been kept secret. She was now under pressure to marry the man having, in effect, broken her own religious code by living with him. Unemployed and fearful for her reputation and future, she asked me for advice. By interviewing this young woman, I had become involved in her problem, and I believe it would have been irresponsible and unethical to have merely walked away. As Oakley argues:

> A feminist methodology of social science . . . requires . . . that the mythology of 'hygienic' research with its accompanying mystification of the researcher and the researched as objective instruments of data production be replaced by the recognition that personal involvement is more than dangerous bias – it is the condition under which people come to know each other and to admit others into their lives.
>
> (Oakley 1981: 58)

Once an individual has recounted their life history, they have effectively admitted you into their life; a researcher is not merely a researcher but a fellow human being engaging in a relationship with the researched, and as such must act in accordance with personal codes of behaviour as much as with any professional code.

Analysis

The intention was always to continue with interviews until no new ideas seemed to be emerging, what is sometimes referred to as 'theoretical saturation'. One problem with this approach is that the process of data collection can become an end in itself: in my case I found I enjoyed the process of interviewing so much that I was reluctant to stand back from it and judge when the point of saturation had been reached. These concerns echo those of Scott:

> We developed a tendency to press on with the interviewing in the belief that this in itself was the most important part of the research even when we were already 'saturated' with data. We had fallen into the positivist trap even though methodologically we thought we had located ourselves outside that framework.
>
> (Scott 1985: 73)

In the early stages of this project, I feel I was constantly in danger of falling into the same 'positivist trap', first through inexperience and secondly, through a worry that without sufficient numbers, the views of the participating teachers and students would not be accepted.

Clearly there are limitations to the approach I have adopted. Life histories inevitably emphasise the uniqueness of human experience and the open-ended way in which interviews were designed means that analysis is a slow process and it is more difficult to identify common themes. Even when such themes are highlighted in the process of analysis, there are still difficulties in generalising from the accounts of such a group. For example, all the teachers in this sample were working for metropolitan LEAs. It is likely that black teachers employed in shire counties, while sharing some of these experiences, would have very different stories to tell.

One difficulty with research of this nature is that pressures of time cause the process of data collection to be artificially separated from the process of analysis. Ideally the process of analysis should have been taking place along-side the interviewing, but other commitments and delays in transcribing the interviews meant that it was often difficult to reflect on one interview or identify the key themes until after several other interviews had taken place.

In the end, the numbers of interviews in particular categories, such as BEd students were decided by issues of access rather than by notions of reaching theoretical saturation. In the case of the interviews with experienced teachers, I was able to continue data collection until no new ideas were emerging, and among senior managers I increased the size of the planned sample because I felt that these interviews were a particularly rich source.

The processes of analysis are closely linked to the processes of writing. I have identified a number of recurrent themes in students' and teachers' accounts and I develop certain of these themes through discussion of various stages in teachers' lives and careers. A researcher carries considerable power and responsibility in the process of writing up research. I am aware that a number of participants agreed to interviews because they trusted that I would not 'misuse' what they were saying or misrepresent them. Yet, as Liz Stanley and Sue Wise argue, the written product of any research needs to be recognised as a construction and not a representation of the reality it is about, with the writer having considerable power over the researched:

> Within writing, researchers have the last – or rather the penultimate (for readers have the last) – say about what 'the research' meant, found, con-cluded. Writing dispossesses the researched. Although the researched may exert a good deal of influence in the interaction that composes research, when it comes to writing researchers can – and in a sense ultimately must – take responsibility for the research carried out, because it comes to bear their names as textual products of the academic labour process.
> (Stanley and Wise 1993: 218)

Summary

These life-history interviews raise a number of questions about research methodology which suggest that much of the guidance and theoretical categorisation of interviewing are somewhat unrealistic, and have tended to ignore many practical and ethical issues. In interviewing black and ethnic minority people I cannot disregard shared experiences or meanings, or adopt a neutral position. Personal involvement is much more than a problem of unfortunate bias, and personal values are likely to influence research whether or not they are acknowledged. It is more important for the researcher to identify their own value position than to adopt an artificial distance either in the empirical research or in the way it is reported. This permits shared experiences to be acknowledged as an asset. Interviewees become participants rather than respondents or informants in research. Nevertheless, if the researcher is visible in the research process this also places her in a more vulnerable position, open to personal criticism from which other, more 'distant' styles of research or writing may offer protection.

Part two _____

Changing lives

Teachers' narratives: case studies

Introduction

The six cases presented here have been selected to reflect a broad range of experiences from among those teachers not in senior management positions. They give us a taste of each teacher's unique story. As each teacher presents their story they discuss the expectations and influences on them which help shape their identities as teachers and more particularly as black teachers. The aim is to consider questions of professional identity, how these teachers perceive their role as educators, and those of political and community identity, their identity as black people. The chapter considers how the various identities which individuals adopt fit together and identifies some of the tensions and contradictions which may be experienced between professional and socio-political identities.

Case studies

Neelum

Neelum, who at the age of 38 years was one of the most experienced teachers in the sample, had taken the decision to work part-time, as she had young children, and was employed as a Section 11 teacher, based in a primary school. Unusually for a part-timer, she held a middle-management post.

Neelum's decision to enter higher education was closely tied to that of being able legitimately to leave the family home, for she grew up in a small Scottish town where there was no local provision for higher education. Her parents, who are from a farming community in Pakistan, have had very little formal education; her mother never had the opportunity to go to school and her father only attended for a couple of years. They did not discourage her in her ambition to enter university, perhaps because they wanted her to do her best in her Highers, but once these examinations were over they began to make arrangements for her marriage. She immediately said no to the marriage, believing this would ruin her chances of continuing her education, but by the time her father realised the strength of her determination the prospective bridegroom was on his way to her home with an engagement ring. Despite some embarrassment over the proposed marriage, Neelum's parents finally relented. Arrangements were made for her to lodge with cousins while she studied away from home.

Her examination results were not good enough to secure a place on a general arts degree and so instead she accepted one on a BEd course at a college of education. Her main concern was to postpone marriage:

> I actually really didn't mind. I didn't really think of myself as having a career at that point, it was just the thing about going on into higher education and leaving [my home town] and not getting married. I had obviously come to realise by then that if I didn't go on to higher education I would have to get married soon, and I wouldn't have an excuse. This gave me a sort of passage for four years.

It was while she was at college that the idea of becoming a teacher took its hold:

> I think I might have toyed with the idea of doing something else but it seemed just a natural progression. I finished the BEd and had good reports on teaching practice and I enjoyed it and so I just went for jobs.

A teacher surplus meant she was unable to find a post straightaway and so she worked as a resources assistant in a local secondary school for some months before moving to Glasgow to take up an English post in a multi-cultural secondary school. Right from the beginning of her career, Neelum wished to work with black children, and consequently when she left Scotland she applied for a Section 11 post:

> It was a conscious decision. I wanted to work with black children and that is why I had moved to Glasgow and they had offered me that job, and why I took that job. Being used to the Scottish education system and being aware that the English system was different I was relying on vacancies advertised in *The Times Ed* [*Educational Supplement*]. When I got the details through I thought this would be interesting to work on language, which was part of my training anyway, and to work on the language needs of Asian children in particular.

At Neelum's first school in a working-class area of Glasgow, high standards had been set and she was appalled to discover that the same did not apply in the secondary school she moved to in the West Midlands:

> I was really disheartened with the school. I mean, I'd worked in a secondary school in Glasgow with a high proportion of black children,

both Asian, Afro-Caribbean and Chinese children; the majority were black yet there had been really high expectations and high standards. A lot of the children went on to university and it was expected that this would be done. It wasn't a rough area but it was an area of quite high physical deprivation. They were always knocking down these tenements. You walked to school and they were bulldozing this and that and our school was in the middle of it all. But regardless of that environment the kids were really motivated and so were the families. And when I came to this school I was really appalled at the way there was no sort of standard and there was no expectation that they would get O levels or that they would continue to do anything in education. And I stayed at that school for a year as an ESL teacher and I said after that, 'Well if this is what secondary schools are going to be like in [this LEA] I don't want to work in another one.' So I moved to primary where I felt that the children would be more motivated and that the job would be more worthwhile. That is why I changed.

Neelum's concern about the need for high standards and for children to be encouraged and supported in their learning led her to take a new direction in her career and to develop new skills working with younger children. She underlines how teacher expectations can influence children's levels of achievement. Studies from this period (Driver 1977, 1979; Wright 1986) show how some teachers blamed African Caribbean children for low achievement and more recent studies confirm that negative stereotypes are sometimes also held of Asian pupils (for example, Shepherd 1987; Wright 1992; Troyna and Siraj-Blatchford 1993). Teachers' informal assessments of pupils may also be biased and may influence pupils' life chances in subtle or less subtle ways, such as in access to examination classes. Neelum chose to work in the primary sector where she believed children would be less likely to have been influenced by negative assessment and would thus be more highly motivated, where she hoped the general ethos of the school would be more positive, and where she believed she would have a greater personal impact. She remained highly motivated and began to find opportunities for her own professional development despite the feeling that senior colleagues offered little support:

I started taking on extra things then, doing work on bilingual assessment, and setting up assessments that were conducted in Punjabi and English. I started doing bits and pieces of in-service work, mainly with other teachers in the team. I felt that was good experience but I don't think the people in the support service in the LEA really appreciated that as much as I think it ought to have been. They were always setting up hurdles for me to sort of knock down. They weren't very supportive at all although I did do a lot of extra work and put a lot of extra effort into the job.

Neelum decided to study part-time for a Master's degree. At that time, teachers were receiving secondment for further study and so when she was told she could not be released for one afternoon a week she approached her union for support. The union told her her request was reasonable but they could not support her:

> I had to go on a part-time contract; I was nine-tenths for a year and a bit because they just would not release me. I'm sure that was partly to do with being black and partly to do with the fact that the person in charge was a white man. It was really disheartening. I think maybe they might have listened more to a man. And I was young, I'd had only four or five years teaching, and maybe they thought, this young inexperienced black woman, we're not going to give her half a day a week off.

Neelum then moved to the multicultural support service of another West Midlands LEA where she joined a new unit set up to promote multicultural and anti-racist curriculum development. There she had the opportunity to work with a number of other black people. She also sought other opportunities to broaden her professional experience, for example, through a secondment to an in-service team. She describes this period in her career, during the mid-1980s, as an important one for her, both in terms of her further professional development and of her growing political awareness as a black person:

> I began to work with people who also fought discrimination and had their own stories to tell. In [the new LEA] the black teachers were more aware of racism and their experience of it, and in education generally. That was quite good in terms of my own development as a black person. I felt I was able to develop in that way, as well as to develop professionally through that.

The members of the new unit encountered some suspicion from other teachers, particularly during its early days, before its reputation was established. Neelum pointed out that it was sometimes difficult to distinguish between the suspicion and hostility which some teachers felt towards such initiatives and the particular additional resentments they expressed towards black colleagues who were agents of these changes. On one occasion when she drove a new car to school a colleague made it very clear that he felt that positive discrimination was operating in favour of a young black woman in a promoted post. When the LEA first attempted to introduce an ethnic monitoring process for staff, teachers in the same school feared it would be used against them as white people; again the concern was about positive discrimination in favour of black people. Neelum stressed the irony of this, since many black teachers also feared how this information might be used to their disadvantage.

Neelum acknowledged that Section 11 teachers were often given low status but sought to overcome this difficulty by setting herself very high standards and taking a lead role in collaborative work:

> I always make it clear from the outset, I think it is even more important for a black person to do this, that the role I am doing in the classroom is equal to, and probably edging on the superior to, the main classroom teacher. In doing so I can then get the respect of the teacher and of the children. I am definitely not going to be the classroom assistant type of person, it has got to be equal or verging on the more dominant. And that is possibly something which goes right through, you have got to be seen as better than, and then you might be treated as an equal.

This concern to be seen as 'better than' in order to be treated on an equal basis to white colleagues is reflected in many of the teachers' narratives.

Neelum was promoted to a leadership role within the unit, but she had not sought further promotion, or to move back into mainstream teaching, partly because she had managed to negotiate a part-time contract and wished to remain in part-time employment while her children were small. At the time of the interview Neelum was still working in the multicultural support service, developing collaborative styles of teaching and focusing increasingly on language issues. The context of her work had changed with the introduction of the national curriculum and because of changes in emphasis in the ways Section 11 funds might be used.

As someone whose work often meant that she was isolated in schools, Neelum recognised the benefits of networking with other black teachers:

> The Black Caucus for Section 11 teachers, I found that quite useful because in the early days it was quite well attended and there were a lot of debates and things going on that were interesting and volatile at times. It also gave you an insight of what was going on in the city, because everybody is so scattered about and so you might never find out or be able to lend your support. And so it was educative, it was informative and it was also a sort of social meeting place as well, so you would get together for the meeting a little bit before or linger afterwards. And also I think it did have some actual positive results, I think the Authority in a few instances did take notice of what Black Caucus members were saying. And I think that some white people felt they had to be a bit more wary. I think it made people think twice before they did something.

It would appear that the Black Caucus, as a network of black teachers, not only gave individuals personal and professional support but that it also served a broader function, in acting as a pressure group to influence and monitor those LEA policies and practices which affected the lives of black teachers and pupils. The isolation which black teachers may experience within their institutions has led many to seek support through networking.

As Burton and Weiner (1993) point out, networking has long been used by the privileged as a means of professional support, but it can also be adopted by less powerful groups.

Neelum felt that black parents also offered her support in her day-to-day work by their ready appreciation of her presence on the teaching staff of a school. She is able to establish good relationships with them where her cultural background, her linguistic skills and her understanding of their needs are all assets which can be demonstrated:

> For parents to see that a school is actually employing Muslim teachers, when a school actually does it, that must obviously boost them. I may not know the child but immediately there is a rapport there. They come and ask your advice or talk to you about their child, and ask you about yourself and what you are doing there. So immediately there is that point of contact just because of the same colour, the same culture and perhaps the same religion. They don't dilly-dally with the formalities they just start. That's really nice, it really boosts your confidence a lot, and your value, and that value boosting can come quite often more from the parents than from the staff. It gives you your credibility.

Neelum had not set out on leaving school to be a teacher but she had found a career which she enjoyed and in which she was continually setting herself new challenges. Her initial interest in working with black children had encouraged her to develop particular skills and specialisms from the earliest stages of her career. Her experiences as a Section 11 teacher also encouraged her development as a black person, and the two processes, of becoming a competent professional and of developing a particular political awareness, were closely interrelated. Her choice of work meant that she did not experience contradictions or conflicts since her professional goals and her personal beliefs were well integrated; it was a central part of her role to speak out on behalf of the black children and communities with whom she was working. It was parents from these communities, rather than her colleagues in school, who gave her the recognition and support she needed to be effective.

The focus of her job meant that Neelum was as interested in the continuing professional development of her colleagues as she was in children's learning. Networking with other black teachers provided her with support which had been particularly important in her personal and professional development in the early stages in her career; she also recognised the wider political benefits of such networking in seeking to promote the interests of black teachers and children more generally. Neelum did not appear to have made forward plans at the outset of her career, but each 'career move' was designed to broaden her experiences and create new challenges. Although, like many Section 11 teachers, Neelum had been subject to a number of organisational changes, particularly in the late 1980s and early 1990s, she had, after becoming a mother, made career plans and choices which allowed her to integrate her professional life with her parental responsibilities while maintaining her status and level of professional responsibilities.

Wesley

Wesley was aged 35 years and working as a science teacher on a B allowance, with pastoral responsibilities as a deputy head of year. He graduated with a joint honours degree in chemistry and biochemistry and worked for two years as a research chemist before taking up teaching. He entered through a graduate direct entry scheme and obtained his PGCE on a part-time basis. Wesley had been teaching for 10 years in north London, not far from the area where he was born and brought up. Both his parents were from the Caribbean.

Wesley took science A levels without real consideration of the possible career implications; his concern was to keep his education as broad as possible:

> I was advised to go to the sciences because the arts side I could do in my spare time. Like I could continue with my French which I do through correspondence with my penfriends and so on. Even now I've become more linguistically able because I am still very keen on that side, French, German, Spanish, Turkish even.

Teaching was not an option which Wesley considered on graduation. He worked as a quality-control chemist for two years but found it monotonous and was thinking of leaving when he was made redundant. Alternative openings in industry appeared limited but he learnt of a direct entry scheme into teaching:

> I did not really think about teaching; basically I drifted into it. A friend of mine told me about a scheme whereby I could start teaching immediately and then do my teacher certificate within the school system with [an outer London borough] so that's what I did. I came back to London because free accommodation was available and that's how I got set up in teaching.

This non-traditional route into teaching made Wesley rather anxious in the early stages of his career, he felt he lacked the professional training that his colleagues had had access to:

> It was difficult because I was really terrified that I didn't know the system, for instance, writing lesson plans and doing exactly as I should. And whenever the adviser came in I thought perhaps I've missed out on something and I used to show the other teachers who then said, 'Oh no, that's fine, that's how we do it.' When I went to courses then it was confirmed that I wasn't very confident because I felt perhaps I've missed out on something.

Despite this uncertain start Wesley soon found that he felt comfortable in his role as a teacher; not only had he learned the skills of classroom organisation and management but that he also enjoyed many aspects of the job:

> I drifted into it and then I found that I quite enjoyed it. I like the fact that I am able to make my own day. If I feel a bit off then I can change my plans accordingly. And the variety of activities that we can do in the day, I mean some people say, 'Don't you get bored teaching the same thing day in day out, year in year out?' I say no because you're delivering it differently each time. Obviously you look to your lesson plans, entertainment value and so on and you're also delivering it to different characters and personalities and that's quite interesting. Most of them will come out with the same jokes that I've heard for years, but I still find them funny.

Nevertheless, Wesley felt an outsider in the predominantly white, middle-class Catholic environment of his first school:

> It was a very nice place, mainly white, middle class sort of thing. Lots of Irish children, but they were, let's say, from 'good families' because they were recommended by the priests and so on. And we had smatterings of ethnic minorities, at least one black child in the class. And I felt very odd there really in a sense, not basically through my teaching experiences but as a person set in that school with other people, for instance other teachers who were Catholics. I felt inferior and I was always watching my Ps and Qs. It came to a crux when I asked Sister, after I had passed my probationary period, if I could be taken on permanently. I was on contract and it was up to them to decide whether to extend or terminate, and she told me that they had their quota of Protestants. And then I said, 'Well it seems we'll have to part company then,' because I was not going to be second option.

Wesley's next teaching post offered new challenges because the children were less compliant and he had to learn how to motivate them and engage them in learning. However, once he had learned how to manage in this context, he felt much more comfortable, largely because of the make-up of the staff. He observed:

> There was a variety of teachers from ethnic minority groups, Asian, African, West Indian and so on, and you just got on with it. But I noted that there were no ethnic minority teachers in any sort of position. Perhaps they hadn't been around long enough, they were all young. Eventually one of the African teachers became head of humanities, but she had been at that school for about 15 years.

Wesley describes himself as ambitious, but despite being in a shortage subject area, he was unable to achieve promotion in that school. He explained that this was partly related to his perception that teachers were required to serve for a number of years before seeking promotion:

> I feel that the way I entered teaching made me less confident initially in order to go and seek new jobs. For instance, the first five years I didn't actually think of applying for any allowances or positions of responsibility because I felt perhaps that I had not got that experience yet. When I was at school teachers who were in jobs of responsibility were mature people, but now I can see that it's all changing. I've got friends at school now who were probationers one year ago and they are now running a small department. Now me at that time, I would have said, 'No, I couldn't do that,' and just plod on, do the hard graft for years before actually thinking of doing this. So I think I might have held myself back.

Although Wesley does not make the connection explicit, he has also observed that other black teachers are not, in his experience, being promoted, whereas white colleagues have obtained posts of responsibility after only a year in teaching. His initial frustration at not getting promotion led him to make a sideways move and teach overseas:

> I only moved on from [my second school] because I was looking for promotion. I was applying for Scale 2 posts at that time and I had my CV typed up and was applying for anything, willy-nilly. Then I saw this job in Gibraltar, and I thought, in for a penny, in for a pound!

Wesley spent two years teaching abroad and on his return to London found himself having to take a 'supply' contract. It took him several attempts to achieve promotion. He felt unable to say he had faced direct discrimination because he lacked positive 'proof' yet he was aware that other teachers were being promoted over him, even when he had been in an 'acting' post and had proved his capacity to do the job:

> There may have been obstacles but I can't put my finger on them. You go along, you don't get the job and you think well, maybe I wasn't good enough, maybe the other person was better qualified, better experienced. In the teaching world there's no one there but yourself, I feel. Your head wouldn't say, 'You're too good at your job, don't you think it's time that you tried for something?' No one's ever told me I should think of moving on.

The promotion to deputy head of year has boosted his own image as a teacher, and he sees it as recognition by the school management of his skills in working with children. He feels that he has really found his niche in pastoral work:

> I've gained experience in the pastoral field and I feel my career lies there. I just like the social side, being able to talk to children, deal with

their problems, meet parents, the human side of teaching. If you're really concerned about the education of children you want to be there with them, and I think that if I can deal with the more social, personal side of children it will help to promote their learning in some ways, like dealing with bullying and racism and so on.

Growing up black in Britain has made Wesley sensitive to the needs of minorities and to children's experiences of racism. He is particularly interested in the needs of refugee children, a group whose needs he feels are often overlooked:

I've recently had a number of Somali children and Sudanese children coming to the school as well as the Kurdish children from Turkey. I feel if you can make these minorities feel welcome then you're going part of the way to getting them working with you in a more pleasant environment. They relate well to me and they feel they can tell me things about which teachers are racist and so on, and they talk to me like that. Without being unprofessional, we discuss the problems of what they may have done and how the teacher would respond. If you show interest in their particular culture then it helps them to see that you're not racist against them; you are interested in them as people and in their families, you give them time, take the trouble to learn something of their language. When we get a new child who has started school and been round all the other classes where the teachers say, 'Copy this,' and then they come to science I show them things. I talk to them in their language to get them to understand what they have to do in English, then it really pleases them. They come up to me and show me their books and it really pleases me.

It would appear that Wesley's identity as a teacher responsible for pastoral care has clearly been reinforced by his dealings with the range of minorities represented within the school. He has also been able to draw on his own identity and experiences of dealing with racism in working with these children. There do not appear to be any conflicts between his identity as a black person and his general role in pupils' pastoral welfare. As an African Caribbean man working with African Caribbean children there are however a different set of issues which come into play:

I feel annoyed, well intensely annoyed, if I see a black child especially, wasting their time, being rebellious or misbehaving and not getting on with the work. I try to say to myself, 'Well, why is this happening?' Some of them are very able and they get drawn into a group identity stereotype thing. I found this more so in schools where there are a number of black kids. In the first school I taught at the black kids were just part of the class, they were normal, normal spoken, normally behaved, I mean well behaved. They conformed I suppose.

Wesley identifies a strong peer pressure for black children, perhaps more particularly black boys, to adopt a mode of behaviour which challenges authority, and to a certain extent fulfils a stereotype which a number of teachers have of African Caribbean youth (Wright 1986; Mac an Ghaill 1988; Gillborn 1990). He explains this in terms of the racism which these students are encountering at school or in the wider society, but points out that they are also demanding that he, as a black teacher should conform to a particular notion of black identity:

> I think they are obviously meeting – there are external factors. They are either meeting racism where, in a mild form or just simple comments made which affect them, or they have poor images of themselves in their society, their particular group and so on.
>
> I've always had comments, in these schools with a multi-ethnic mix, from black kids in particular saying that I'm trying to be white or trying to be English and I always resent this, and I say, 'Look, you don't know anything about me. I come from England. I am what I am. I'm not trying to be anything, like some people are. I'm not trying to identify with any particular group, I am myself, I am a person.' But their view of this person is of a white middle-class person, well spoken, and he appears not to know or be involved too much with his particular group. And I've had some of them trying to sus me out as it were with language, asking, 'Sir, do you know what this means? Do you know what this food is?'
>
> Well, if I do or I don't what does it matter? I am where I come from. I haven't said to myself, 'I'm going to give up this thing, I am going to act as an English person or whatever.' The black kids here see it as trying to be a white person. These people in the Caribbean, they speak so eloquently in English but with a West Indian accent, it sounds very educated and very good and that distinguishes them as being black. But with me it's different because my accent itself is English and they can't accept that. There's something going round in the community that says, 'no you shouldn't do this, you shouldn't do that, because you're not being black'. Sometimes I feel that the black kids relate to the white teachers more than they relate to me because they think I've sold out or whatever. Once they get to know you and they know that you're not trying to put it on then it does change.

Wesley argues that he has the right to define his own identity and not be tied to a narrow definition of blackness. This is not to suggest that he does not identify himself as black or that he does not feel a responsibility to support these same black students. His description of the ways in which black male students behave amongst themselves and towards him as a black teacher suggests that they have a very narrow view of what is acceptable black masculine behaviour, based on what Wesley believes to be a narrow range of role models. Far from having 'sold out' Wesley is acutely concerned for the future of these black students; he readily acknowledges the impact of racism on their lives. He is concerned that they should not be limited by narrow interpretations of black masculinity:

> They don't seem to have a range of black role models. I know that in all walks of society there are black people present, but they are hidden. The main image that black children get is black dancers, black singers, black rappers, black sportsmen. They see that you can make money quickly in these areas where skill is required.

Wesley has sought to broaden the student's understanding of blackness by introducing a range of perspectives and examples into the science curriculum but he acknowledges that the biggest difficulty is teacher attitudes which he sees reflected teacher behaviour: 'They may not be racist in themselves but the stereotypes are there, and it perpetuates itself because they deal differently with black kids.'

Wesley has applied his own experiences of life as a black person to his understanding of equity issues in school and particularly to ensuring that bilingual and refugee children have proper access to the curriculum. His identity as a teacher is closely tied to his ability to relate to children, but he has experienced some frustration in trying to promote a broader understanding of black identity amongst black children.

As a member of a staff team he has also encountered attitudes which clearly reflect the different experiences of black and white teachers. This is most clearly demonstrated in his colleagues' responses to the question of racism in schools:

> Racism! That doesn't happen here! Some of them are so blinkered they really don't realise that these things go on. It's like, 'Oh he's only mentioned that because he's black.' I get very annoyed when people ask, was I born here. I say to them, 'Well, how often do people ask you were you born here? Doesn't it signal something to you?' I resent answering questions like that. If you say out loud, 'I think that was racist', they think, 'Oh yeah, he's got a chip on his shoulder.' Sometimes you keep quiet because you don't want to be labelled in that way.

He illustrates how some white teachers find it difficult to recognise, let alone accept, the different realities of black teachers. Wesley's determination to avoid being labelled means he is obliged to hide something of himself, his identity and experience.

Wesley clearly finds satisfaction through his work with children and this makes it possible to deal with potential isolation amongst colleagues. He is clearly dedicated to his work and talks about it with obvious enthusiasm and a genuine liking for children. As he puts it: 'I only drifted into teaching, but now I see it's my thing in life.' He demonstrates a high level of commitment to those children who are disadvantaged by the system, or whose needs are not properly recognised in the school, such as refugees; this commitment is informed by his own experiences and understanding of racism. Wesley does not appear to have had the benefit of any careers advice, mentoring or support, nor does he believe such support to be available to teachers generally. Although he is ambitious to progress in his career, no one has advised him of appropriate steps to take or any experiences which would be of particular benefit. He may have disadvantaged himself early on in his career by self-imposed limitations, but given the context in which he is working, in a shortage subject in London, he appears to have encountered considerable barriers.

Wesley has generally worked in schools where he is not isolated as a black teacher, but he has no experience of the black teachers' networks which have been so valuable to Neelum and to other teachers in this study. His case raises important issues about black identities and particularly black masculine identities. He is one of only six male African Caribbean experienced teachers in the research sample. His observations about the expectations which black male students have of African Caribbean men are followed up in Chapter 6 and in Chapter 8 in an analysis of senior managers' perceptions.

Balbir

Balbir had been teaching for nine years in secondary schools and had recently accepted a post as a Section 11 teacher on a B allowance. Her family moved to England from India when she was 4 years old, and settled in Handsworth. Her father was a well-educated man who had graduated in India with a Master's degree and who spoke fluent English but was employed, as were many recently-arrived immigrants in the West Midlands, as a foundry worker. Although he acted as an adviser to others in the local Sikh community on legal and tax matters, he was not well informed about the English education system. Consequently, when Balbir passed her 11 plus examination but was unable to get into the nearest selective school, her father, not wishing her to undertake long journeys across the city, accepted a place at a non-selective Church of England school.

Balbir was happy at secondary school, regularly coming top of her class. She recalls that she was the only Asian girl in her class, with only three other black and ethnic minority children. The remainder of the children in the top band of this multicultural school were white; the third band was made up largely of African Caribbean pupils. At this point in her life, Balbir had not given much thought to her Sikh identity, and it was only at sixth-form level that she began to reflect on the differences in lifestyle between herself and the majority of her school friends:

I am not really from a very strict Sikh family, we do follow the traditions and the culture, but in terms of actual worship we don't. And I was never really aware in school that I was any different from my English or Afro-Caribbean friends, because religion wasn't a very strong force in my life.

It wasn't until the third year of secondary school that one of the teachers actually did a small unit on Sikhism. And I remember reading the book that we were given and it was all about Sikhs on horseback, Sikhs are soldiers, they are a sort of military. It wasn't until then that I started to make connections and think: this has got to do with something I have got at home, and the pictures that are hanging on our wall, they are the same pictures in the book. But I remember thinking, I don't think my father used to ride a horse [*laughs*], because that was the kind of image that was portrayed.

I was the only Sikh in my year, until I went into the sixth form in 1976. That was the year we had the Ugandan Asians coming over, we had ten Ugandan Asians in my school, and they were Sikhs. I remember in the sixth form joining up with a Ugandan Sikh girl and realising we had a lot in common. I think it was that girl's influence on me that made me think, 'I am not white, although I have grown up with white friends, talked like them, and dressed like them.' I was white in every sense really, but I realised, 'hang on, there is something else to me'. I did make a conscious effort to learn more about who I am and what I am, and my family background.

During the sixth form Balbir began to make preparations for a future career, first applying to do a course in journalism. She was the first person within her extended family to consider higher education in England, and although her father did not steer her towards a specific career, he was quite clear about what was inappropriate. Journalism was impossible because it meant studying away from home, and physiotherapy, her second suggestion, was rejected because it would involve close contact with (male) patients. She became dispirited, and it was only the intervention of a careers officer which pointed her towards teaching:

> It seemed to me at that stage that everything that I chose to do he just blocked. It got to the stage where I was thinking, well, why bother? If I'm not going to be able to do what I want then I'm not going to do anything. And I remember those last six months just giving up. I came out with rotten results in the end. And it wasn't until Easter, just before the exams when the careers teachers came round visiting, saying: 'Come on, you haven't put any application forms in, why not?' Because my O level results were good and they were saying, 'You've got to do something.' It was one of the careers teachers, a black woman, when I explained to her the situation, that my parents wouldn't let me move out, that it had to be something fairly close to home and that they had blocked the career choices that I had had, that she said, 'Why don't you consider teaching, you've got several colleges in the area that you could

commute to daily.' She was quite useful in terms of counselling and she was the one who actually directed me towards teaching.

If teaching was a compromise solution for Balbir, so also was the course that she followed at the college of education. She did not get the grades for direct entry to a degree course and was told she could begin a certificate course and resit her A levels during her first year if she wished to transfer. She had applied to study English and history at college, but was told these courses were full and was advised to study religious education:

> They said, 'We are desperately short of black and Asian RE [religious education] teachers and with your kind of background and your kind of culture you would fit in very well.' Looking back, that story about English and history being full, I think, was it true or wasn't it? I went into the college and did RE for three years and hated every minute of it. I had never actually thought about religion, not being a religious person myself, it wasn't a subject I warmed to naturally. But I think I learnt a lot about my own religion; it was actually an education for me, rather than preparation for teaching the subject. I do remember doing teaching practices and feeling, I don't really want to do this. I thought that at the end of three years I would leave college and look for another career option.

Balbir's career options were restricted by careers advice which came too late, by her father and by the college's concern to meet its own goals rather than her particular needs. Once she had completed her course her father wished to see her 'settled'. Like Neelum, she used the opportunity to continue her education as a means of delaying marriage:

> I said to dad, 'I really wanted to do a degree in the first place and a certificate is second best. The subject area is like a second best, and not really what I wanted to do, but maybe with a degree I will stand a better chance of moving into another career at the end of it.'

The honours degree required two further years study but her father was willing to delay her marriage for one year. It was her maternal grandfather, on a visit from India, who persuaded her father to relent, telling him: 'Let the girl do it. What is two years now? She is going to be married for the rest of her life!'

Balbir's first post was as a religious education teacher. She was introduced to her future husband, their engagement was announced and she was married at the end of her probationary year:

> We were engaged in August: he came with his parents to our house and we had a brief talk for about half an hour on our own. Then we didn't see each other again until the actual day of the registry wedding, nearly a whole year later. I was 24 when I got married, which is very

old and very late according to Indian tradition. I was an old maid! I was very lucky to last out that long, because I think as time went by dad mellowed more and more. He was never a strict father in the first place, not a disciplinarian. It was always: 'Do what you like to do, but always remember who and what you are, and never let me down.' And so when it came to marriage it was always negotiable. Satnam, my husband, was actually the third person I saw; the other two rejected me, I didn't reject them!

From her second year, Balbir grew unhappy about teaching religious education (RE) and began looking for opportunities for further professional development. When a vacancy occurred she accepted joint responsibility for the post of head of careers. She had been doing this for some six months when a new headteacher arrived at the school and awarded her a temporary Scale 2 post for this work, but when a new head of careers was appointed, she lost it. She admitted that at this stage she was naive about promotions, she had never seen an LEA vacancy bulletin in the staff room and she did not know about other opportunities within the LEA. Nevertheless, her head of department, who might have supported her career development, failed to offer support:

> She was quite racist in her own way. It was, well, you're a Scale 1 teacher and that's where you are going to stay. Never any encouragement to share any responsibility in the department. Though on the papers I was second in the RE department that was never recognised. In terms of career development, there wasn't any. I often ended up with the rotten classes, I was never actually teaching in the RE room, she would have the classroom and I would be somewhere down the corridor, sometimes three storeys up! Having to cart books up and cart them down again. And generally, not been encouraged in any way.

Nevertheless, in her fourth year, when an opportunity arose Balbir sought to change the balance of her work:

> I came back from maternity leave to find there had been somebody on long-term supply covering my timetable, who was a displaced head of department. She was quite an experienced RE teacher. She actually wanted to carry on, but was being directed towards this vacant history post. I said, 'Look, she wants to carry on doing the RE and I want to do history, so what's to stop us sharing the timetables and doing half each?' But the head of RE was quite autocratic and she just wouldn't have it. And it did get nasty from January through to about Easter. And I wanted to bring the union in and the head said, '*No, we can sort this out internally.*'
>
> My father got taken seriously ill, he'd had a heart attack. I had problems at home, not getting on with my in-laws, I had pressures from the other home side with my dad in hospital, and then pressures from

work. It was like everything was coming to a crescendo, and then dad died in June. I took two or three weeks off, sick leave, and I came back off sick leave with a resignation note and no job to go to.

Despite this apparent setback, Balbir found promotion and began working as a member of a GRIST (Grant Related In-Service Training) team covering for teachers engaged in in-service training. The move suited her and confirmed her worth as a teacher, but it also highlighted her dissatisfactions with her first school where she had applied internally three times for promotion. She explained it in terms of a senior staff attitude which recognised the value of black teachers, but did not consider them as suitable material for promoted posts:

> Each time it was, 'I'm sorry you haven't got experience,' or, 'We can't have you this time round,' always an excuse. I always felt it was something deeper than that, being blocked every time. I felt it was something to do with the lack of confidence, among senior management, in terms of employing blacks or Asians in heads of department or heads of year posts, even though you had the kind of qualifications they wanted in terms of background and experience of minority children.

Unlike Wesley, who assumed he would have to 'serve time', Balbir determined that as soon as she had completed her probationary year she would actively seek opportunities for development and thereby enhance her career prospects. While Wesley assumed that lack of support and encouragement was the norm and that teachers as a profession show no sense of collegial responsibility for junior staff, Balbir explained her head of department's attitude in terms of racial stereotyping: an assumption that a young Asian woman would remain in a junior position.

As a member of the GRIST team, Balbir broadened her experience through teaching in a variety of schools and felt considerable benefits from seeing other teachers' approaches. After four terms she felt she had gained as much through this experience as through any course or training. However, the project was folding up and she was advised to apply for alternative posts. Although she had been promoted to a Scale 2, during this period teachers' salary structure was revised, with the first two scales merging, and she lost this small advance in status.

Her next post was as a head of religious education, but she was offered no additional salary for this responsibility, although the previous head of RE held a B allowance. After nearly six years of teaching, Balbir was finally a head of department, but her achievement was clouded by the fact that she received no acknowledgement in terms of pay. However, like Wesley, Balbir found that when she was given the responsibility and status of a new post, she felt she was able to develop as a teacher. It was at this point in her career she came closest to accepting the identity of a teacher, and felt most comfortable in her role. Balbir also echoes Wesley in her view that the freedom to plan her own work and develop her own ideas is, for her, one of the most attractive aspects of teaching:

> I thought at least the experience will do me good. So I went back to RE, but this time, because it was me being my own boss, it was a lot better. You really had the flexibility and freedom to do what you wanted, but it was hard work as well, coming from quite a relaxed flexible time-table. I had two GCSE groups which were new to me and I had to learn all that work, but it was tremendous experience and a real boost to my career. Here I was in charge of my own department. Everything that I'd been stopped from doing, I'd actually try it out now.

In this respect both Balbir and Wesley are very similar to the primary school teachers in Nias' (1989) study, over half of whom stressed that autonomy in the classroom, 'feeling in control' was a major source of job satisfaction.

Nevertheless, this period was not without problems, particularly in terms of relationships with a small group of well-established staff. Balbir was the only full-time black teacher in a school where black and ethnic minority pupils, mostly Asians, formed over 95 per cent of the pupil population:

> Apart from the languages teachers, who used to come in and out, I was the only one. I think maybe the colour of my skin fooled a lot of them, because a lot of them weren't sure. And you would hear conversations, not really aware of whom or what I was. I think it slowly dawned on them, and I did notice that conversation would turn to whispers some-times, and that was quite obvious. And I think throughout my career I have become more acutely aware of things like that, whereas maybe growing up in a school as a student you are not aware.

Not only did Balbir now feel more at ease in her role as a teacher, she had also begun to reflect on her Sikh identity and her experiences as a black woman, and consider the implications of these in developing the curric-ulum. Unlike many of her colleagues, she saw decisions about curriculum and school management as political, recognising that language policy, for example, would affect children's access to the curriculum, their access to employment opportunities and their parents' access to the school:

> Politically I was quite strong in my views, in terms of multicultural education. I think that in those early stages I probably upset the kind of people that I didn't want to upset, and maybe that had repercussions on the applications that I made internally. In simple things like saying: 'I think letters should be sent home in mother tongues, rather than in English all the time,' and then to be told by senior teachers, 'We think parents should learn to speak English,' and feeling very annoyed. I commented in the staff room that I didn't think that was right, and that

I thought that was racist. But then walls have ears and information gets passed back. But I was feeling, 'Well this is who I am, and this is what I am all about, multicultural education is what should be on board and I am going to stand up for it.'

Balbir's identity as a Sikh woman, 'this is who I am', led her to espouse a multicultural curriculum. She has become critical of those aspects of her own schooling, such as streaming, the invisibility of her home culture, and the school's failure to communicate effectively with her family, which she had not questioned at the time but now perceives to have been damaging. She sees each of these features perpetuated in the education of her pupils. A strong sense of injustice leads her to speak out, possibly to her own disadvantage in career terms. As Balbir finally accepts the identity of teacher and reshapes it according to her values, conflicts emerge over equality issues.

Some of Balbir's colleagues are overtly hostile to a multicultural curriculum. From their perspective, Balbir is stepping beyond her designated role when she suggests changes in the school's approach. Whereas Neelum is experienced and skilled in advisory work, Balbir is not; her approach attracts the animosity of her colleagues.

After three years as head of RE Balbir achieved promotion outside the school as a Section 11 resources advisory teacher. A reorganisation of Section 11 posts led to the immediate disappearance of her new job, and so she began working as a curriculum development teacher. Although disappointed with the way her career had developed, Balbir still showed considerable interest in broad educational issues and in the needs of black and ethnic minority pupils and parents. She had also started researching parent–school relationships for an MPhil degree. I first met her at an Asian teachers' meeting where Madan Sarup spoke on strategies for challenging racism. She played an active part in the ensuing debate.

Like Neelum, Balbir entered teacher training not really believing she would become a teacher. It was only as a head of department that she felt fulfilled in her work and that she finally began to accept the professional identity of a teacher. Her strong sense of social justice led her to advocate multicultural education and challenge what she perceived to be racist attitudes among colleagues. Her own identity as a Sikh and as a black person in a predominantly white profession was reinforced by barriers encountered in seeking career advancement. Her behaviour often contradicted colleagues' stereotypes of an Asian woman, and this led to situations where there was a conflict of interests between her political identity and her career aspirations: she chose to speak out and found herself frustrated in career terms. At the time of her interview Balbir was considering leaving teaching: her political commitment to the black communities found expression in her work, but this satisfaction was largely outweighed by frustrations in career advancement.

Janet

Janet was born in the Caribbean and came to England as a young adult without any formal qualifications. Her ambition was to be a teacher. While her children were small she took part-time work to pay for a correspondence course and began by taking O levels. She tried A levels, but then found an alternative route into higher education through the Open University. Success in this led her to a BEd honours degree, and so by the age of 30 years she was training to teach. As the result of experiences at college, she felt very alienated from the formal education system and so after graduation she began working first as a Christian education worker and then in environmental education.

Although Janet enjoyed this work, she felt that she was not making the best use of her qualifications and skills and so took a temporary teaching post in a primary school; this led to a permanent position. Janet was on a B allowance with a responsibility as a curriculum leader and had been teaching for six years. She had completed a further Open University course in educational management and at the age of 41 years was looking for a deputy headship.

Janet's motivating goal was to become a teacher and to achieve in England what she knew other black people had achieved back in the Caribbean:

> The people who taught me were quite young. These people could have been only about four years older than me. I was thinking, 'Jesus, I would like to be like them;' I really wanted to be like them. I came here and because I had seen those people in the West Indies, I wanted to be like them in England. [I thought] 'I am going to be a black teacher in England.'

This theme of role models from the Caribbean runs throughout Janet's account of how she became a teacher, as does her desire to fulfil her mother's high expectations and find a worthwhile career:

> My mother brought us up on her own and she always wanted us to be something, and she always said I was the bright one. It was high family expectations. My mother had the will but she didn't have the know-how. I wanted to go for something that I thought had status. When you are in the West Indies to be a teacher is one of the high-status jobs. And I think to be a school teacher, as far as a West Indian family was concerned, that would have been a brilliant target to make, and I wanted to make it.

Janet's account was one in which her experiences as a black person, and as an adult migrant to Britain, led her to see things quite differently from most of the people around her. When describing her career it was always very clearly from the perspective of a black teacher rather than simply as a teacher; for example, she never generalised from her own experiences to talk about teachers in general. Although this may have been due, in part, to the fact that she understood the research to be concerned with her experiences as a black person, her account is quite distinctive in this way.

Janet believes her first headteacher used her presence on the staff to benefit her own career:

> She thought that she was helping me and I later found out I was helping her because she had plans for her own promotion and she wanted to show the city that she had an understanding of what we call multicultural education issues. To have worked with a black teacher gave her this perspective.

Janet went on to explain that the head was not simply seeking to gain credibility by appointing a black member of staff in an LEA which stated it wished to recruit black teachers. Janet felt her headteacher set out to systematically exploit the situation to demonstrate her knowledge and understanding of black people and thus prepare herself for her next job. This understanding of black people did not, however, appear to extend to supporting Janet, whom she clearly found competent, in her efforts to gain promotion. Janet applied for a promoted post in another school and the headteacher of that school came to see her teach. This head then wrote to Janet explaining that her own headteacher was unable to recommend her for the job.

Janet remained in this school until the appointment of a new head brought her first promotion: an A allowance for equal opportunities and coordination of staff development. She enjoyed these responsibilities but experienced further difficulties with the new head:

> He also had a problem. He said things like, 'I have never worked with a black teacher before,' as though I was a monkey. I was like a kind of curioso. It wasn't the kind of celebration of 'Janet is going to bring different positive experiences;' it was like, 'God, you are different!' It was like he was going to lose his virginity; it was a new experience. I found that offensive and I had to deal with that and I knew that it was going to be very difficult for me to develop under somebody like that.

Despite these difficulties Janet enjoys her work and recognises that she gets a strong sense of purpose and achievement from children's achievements:

> I have got a kind of attitude in me where I like to be needed, where I love to be important. I want to be an important human being in the lives of the children so that when they grow up I can hear people saying things like, 'Oh, I was naughty but my teacher, boy, she wanted us to read and she got us reading.' I want to be a useful human being really.

Clearly Janet identifies with her job and sees herself very much as a teacher. Her difficulty lies in a conflict between her perceptions of her responsibilities towards children and the ethos and direction of the school. She feels this particularly in her school's approaches to the education of black children:

> My current post was like jumping from the frying pan into the fire. It is a school with 90 per cent black children, including Asian. All of the staff are white; not one black member of teaching staff. One black member of the non-teaching staff and about 10 Afro-Caribbean children. Each one of those children has had problems in the school. I was very conscious of this issue to do with black learners. And the head, his expectations of those children are that they wouldn't succeed. And so he rubbed them up the wrong way and the children responded.

Janet has learned that open challenges are ineffective, and so she has tried to find a personal compromise:

> I had to develop professionally. What is described as being professional is to see all that is happening and to shut up your mouth. I am ambitious and I want to move on. And so on the one hand I am ambitious and I am appreciated, but on the other I am a black female person who is articulate and able.

So it is as a black woman concerned about the welfare of black children that Janet experiences conflicts within her role. To achieve a position of power in a school and have some future influence over children's education, she feels she has to remain silent about perceived injustices. Her compromise is to offer individual support to children: she supports children sent out of her colleagues' classes by asking them about their ambitions and hopes for the future. The greatest difficulty is when she is asked to support the school in dealing with parents of black children who are in trouble:

> When there is trouble about black kids, I am called in and told, 'Well, as a senior manager, give your point of view.' Everybody knows I am reluctant to give it. It is obvious that the odds are stacked against the black child. To bring a black person in to make a comment would only legitimise the already made-up decision. In other words, I am saying the judgement is the black child is wrong, the black child has failed, the black child was naughty, the black child was bullying. And they only bring in me in front of the parents. In other words, 'If your own black people are saying your black child is naughty, well madam, what do you expect me to do?' I will not participate. I think that is downright injustice.

Like Neelum and Balbir, Janet has gained support in her personal and professional development by joining a wider network of black people:

> I belong to an organisation called NAME, National Anti-Racist Movement in Education. And that organisation really does take on board the issues that affect my life. Those people were instrumental in making me

aware of what goes on in school in terms of 'race' and colour and strategies with which to counteract those. They were really good about supporting me when I had negative experiences at school. They were teaching me how to support other teachers not to be negative towards black children and how to use their professionalism to meet the needs of all children. In NAME I was fortunate enough to be able to get black people from different parts of the country coming together in one group.

Burton and Weiner (1993) identify some of the benefits of networking, which include support and solidarity, overcoming pressure and isolation, and the sharing of expertise and advice. Janet confirms how her membership of a national network of black educators has enabled her to benefit from others' expertise, demonstrating how the network has filled a critical gap in her own professional development. Not only was this national network of value to Janet, she also gained support and encouragement from more senior black educators in her own LEA, in practical terms and by example:

In the LEA there was one black teacher who was always interested in my career, even when I started; she was then a senior teacher. She was always making sure that I made the right career moves and there to offer advice. Someone who I could call over situations at work, in terms of my legality, in terms of being astute and wise, in terms of acting as professional as I could be. I could call on her as the one black female adviser we had in the city.

This type of support and networking between black women has a long history. Angela Davis (1982: 129) recounts the history of the Black Club Movement, led by black professional women in the United States from the late 1890s, noting that black women of middle-class and working-class backgrounds established a greater sense of solidarity than their white counterparts through a 'shared consciousness of the need to challenge racism'. Janet also has been encouraged by the appointment of a number black men as headteachers in her LEA: 'the fact that they were there, that was support for me'. Networking of this kind has been critical to Janet because within school she has found it very difficult to get access to training and support: 'I have had to ask and badger, and persuade, and be persistent to get the professional development that I believed was mine by rights.'

Janet believes herself to be a competent professional who, nevertheless, needs constantly to work hard to achieve recognition as a black teacher. Her words echo those of Neelum, Wesley and Balbir when she stresses the constant need for black teachers to set themselves high standards, be seen to be working hard, and to recognise that they are inevitably high profile because of who they are:

I see myself as equal to my white colleagues and I will stand with them and succeed with them. In so many ways as a black teacher, and as a forward-looking black teacher, I think I do twice as much. I compete so that people won't see me as a deficient practitioner. I aim for excellence, and I try not to take chances, because I think my mistakes are taken up very sharply, they are pointed out. And I cannot afford to be human, someone who people could relax with, I can't! I think that is the racism, because other people could get away with things, other people are preferred.

Janet's narrative reflects her strong determination to achieve the goals she has set for herself. Unlike most of the women in this study, and many of the men, she has planned out where she wants to go in her career and is constantly aware of the next career step. She sees this as critical to her success in teaching, as a black woman and as a mature entrant. The conflicts in Janet's working life stem largely from the contradictions she experiences as a black woman concerned for the welfare of black children, in a context in which these children are treated unjustly. Janet's sense of her own worth is particularly striking. She is not afraid to highlight her strengths and to publicise them in a way which is perhaps unusual among women brought up in England, whether black or white. She sees her non-British upbringing as a distinct advantage in giving her the confidence to succeed.

Denise

Denise was in her second year of teaching in a primary school. Aged 27, she had left school at 16 years with few examination passes, but with a determination to become a teacher. She studied part-time for A levels and financed herself by working as a sports coach. After six attempts she gained mathematics O level, an entry requirement for teacher training, and was accepted on a BEd course.

Born in the West Midlands to parents who had migrated from the Caribbean, Denise has wanted to be a teacher since she herself was at primary school. She remembers one of her own teachers who inspired her:

There was one teacher who I really admired and I think seeing her made me really want to become a teacher. I remember doing an assignment about her once, because she was the greatest influence on my life of becoming a teacher. Mrs Moore was her name. I remember at seven always wanting to be a teacher.

Denise also wanted to teach netball, and might have trained as a secondary teacher had a physical education option been available at college. Looking back, she has some regrets but recognises that she would not wish to teach sports forever. She describes herself as a reserved and quiet person who would not have been noticed at school, apart from her skills in sports. Although she was encouraged in this area, no one seemed to give her any advice about careers, and she feels that no one took her wish to become a teacher at all seriously. Her parents had not had much education and were unable to offer any advice:

> I was left to my own devices really and that was very difficult because nobody had gone as far as this before and I was the first one. And they just didn't know how to support me. I just wanted better for myself than my parents had. At first it was a distant dream that I didn't think I would ever fulfil. But now I am here I am thinking it wasn't that difficult after all.

Denise's school, although multi-ethnic in its make-up, had relatively few African Caribbean children. She expressed a concern about black children's education, reporting that many teachers, both black and white, experienced black children as relatively difficult to manage. She felt upset by this, but unable to explain the problem fully. Nevertheless, like Wesley, she felt the problem was largely one of teacher expectations to which children respond: 'I think they have got an expectation, they have been built up to being naughty children. Everywhere you go they underachieve and they just live up to whatever stereotype.' Research in infant, junior and middle schools (Wright 1992; Connolly 1995) supports Denise's perception, suggesting that relationships between white teachers and young African Caribbean children are characterised by conflict, suspicion and heightened control.

Denise had struggled hard to gain a place in teacher training, and had shown tremendous determination in gaining the formal mathematics qualifications she needed for entry. Now that her primary ambition was realised, she clearly found her job challenging and was eager to talk about her work. After some 18 months in teaching she was looking forward in her career and had ambitions to gain a senior position, although she was not clear where she wanted to go. Her ambition was still fired by a need to prove herself, this time as a good teacher. She also linked professional achievements to an expectation of future motherhood, and a need to give any children of her own a good start in life:

> If you had asked me when I had just started, when I had finished college, I would have said, just to be in the classroom, and just teach, teach, teach; that is all I ever wanted to do. Now I am in the classroom and I am teaching, teaching, teaching, I wouldn't mind just going up to prove to myself that I am capable of doing it and to prove to others as well. Because I don't have to be at the bottom of the pile. I am thinking that if I eventually have children I would like my children to have a smooth journey and not the rough ride I had. So thinking ahead really, perhaps too far ahead.

It was not just as a teacher that Denise wished to prove herself; she felt this pressure particularly as a black teacher:

> Nothing has been asked or expressed of me, but I feel because I am black that I have to prove myself, I don't know why, I just feel it. And

I have got an added sort of burning, because I am new as well, I feel I have got to prove that because I have just come out of college. I have got to be seen doing all of the right things.

Denise had attended a black teachers' meeting but had not felt the need, at this stage in her career, to actively network with other black people in education. In any case she had some black teacher friends who were fellow church members. She felt the need to have black role models in teaching and to know that other people had 'made it' and felt she was particularly fortunate in having a black deputy head (Angela) within her school, with whom she had formed a close working relationship. Nevertheless, she was wary about being seen with the deputy, for fear of criticism from other teachers:

It is nice to go somewhere and see another black teacher there, that in itself is sheer encouragement and support. I really don't know, just to see other black teachers is good. But then again, if you cling too much to black teachers they might think, 'Gosh, she is another one with a chip on her shoulder.' I feel really conscious talking to Angela at times; they might think that there is a riot going on here. That is how I feel they perceive us.

It has made a difference because she has been my voice as well. If she hadn't been here I think I would still have been very timid and very quiet and not be able to do anything. And she is not just another black teacher; she has achieved. She has got ability and that is encouragement for me. I think to myself, I can do it, because someone else has done it and she is black as well.

While Denise is still working hard to establish herself as a teacher and learn a full range of professional skills, it is clear that she already identifies herself as a teacher and is beginning to plan a career in teaching. Her identity is also very much as a black teacher, and this is linked to the struggle she feels she has endured as a black person getting into teaching. Her identity as a black teacher is strengthened and supported by working closely with a black deputy head who not only gives her the practical everyday support that she needs, but her presence also prevents feelings of isolation and is a source of strength. This black deputy headteacher is clearly seen as a powerful role model propelling her forward in her career.

Amarjit

Amarjit was 26 years and working on a long-term supply contract at a large grant maintained secondary school. He had wanted to be a teacher from the time he himself left school and had studied chemistry at university followed by a PGCE. He completed his probationary year in a predominantly white school in a small town in the north of England and then worked for a year at a school in Handsworth, Birmingham, where he had grown up. He was in his third year of teaching and in his third teaching post.

Amarjit's family had migrated from India and, like Balbir, his father had worked as a foundry worker, his mother had worked in a laundry. During his own secondary schooling, Amarjit had encountered racism in the form of racist taunts from other students, but felt that he had not allowed this to hinder him in his progress or in his more general enjoyment of school life. He recognised that the curriculum had been rather narrow and anglocentric, and that the school had made no attempt to communicate with his parents other than in English, but his family had resolved this by sending his brother and sister-in-law to parents' evenings. Amarjit appreciated the fact that his boys' grammar school had given him, a working-class child, access to higher education and a choice of possible careers. He held his own teachers in particularly high regard and identified with them:

> I always wanted to be a teacher when I left grammar school. I had such a great experience of being at that school and I thought, 'I could do this.' And the teachers were very confident and very relaxed, and I sort of associated myself, my nature and character, with a job such as that.

Although Amarjit wished to play down any significance that pupils or colleagues might attach to him as an Asian teacher or as a black teacher, he wished to be seen to be succeeding as an Asian:

> I think if I do my job as well as I think I can do it, then I think I will be serving other Asians or other non-white people as much as I think I would like to, in a sense that people could see that an Asian person or a non-white person could do the job very comfortably, and they are very enthusiastic and know the topic. There is no sort of language problem, or stereotypical situation: why can't a black teacher just be like any other teacher?

There were, however, two issues he felt black teachers need to address which reflect differences in experience from their white colleagues:

> I think you can have challenges to authority, people testing you out perhaps even more so because you are black. Once you show your competence I think the other thing is about racist comments, what you do when there are various taunts. I think that is a personal strategy which has got to measure with the school and school rules and school policy. But at the end of the day I think you have got to do it in a calm manner and not go over the top just because you are black, but at the same time not ignoring it because you are.

He also acknowledged that it was particularly important for him to promote equal opportunities and to see all students, and particularly Asian girls, achieving:

I do promote equal opportunities for everybody, that is obviously a very nice thing to say about yourself, but I do. I like to see girls doing very well, but especially Asian girls. At [my last school] I was quite proud of the fact that a lot of the Asian girls were getting the best results. But again here I find I want all the students to do well. I mean I demand discipline, I demand. And it is as strong as that.

He was scornful of what he saw as tokenistic attempts to introduce multicultural education, particularly when it was left to black people or designed largely for black students:

I find it [multicultural/anti-racist education] a valuable thing to do but I mean most of the Section 11 people that I have met are black. Why only black people should do it or be in charge of it? Because it suddenly loses its significance in a predominantly white society. I do acknowledge that it is very, very important. But again it's only significant in a school where the majority of the pupils are black, so again it loses significance and weight if it is not done in all schools.

He had been asked to translate at a parents evening and felt unhappy about this:

I really didn't want to get involved for a number of reasons. I just didn't think that I ought to be the one. I thought the school ought to have some facility, and for it to be done properly and not just take advantage of the person who is doing it. And also I want some acknowledgement of the fact that I was doing it and not just expected to be doing it. I felt really uncomfortable and I didn't do it.

Amarjit believed he did not make a distinction between black and white teachers and hoped that others, including those in authority, would respond in the same way. Although he clearly identified himself as an Asian person, with a particular set of experiences, he did not wish to overplay those experiences and certainly did not wish to be identified as an Asian teacher. Over the three years he had been teaching he had been less and less inclined to adopt the identity of a teacher, not because of any conflicts with his Asian background, but because of the general status of teachers and the realities of teaching as he had experienced them:

I think the way people view teachers, the respect that I certainly have for teachers, I found that it is not mirrored by other people, and I am not just talking about the students, but society in general. They are not held in very high esteem. I think the way school operates is a very strange thing to me. And it's changed over the years, I mean from when I was taught eight or ten years ago, to the way teachers teach now. And I am sure it's not for the better.

Consequently Amarjit no longer saw his long-term future in teaching:

> I would like to do a few other things. I mean I would like to have my own business, and I think the more I have been abroad; I can see the import–export idea keeps flashing in front of my eyes. For the time being I think it's OK [on a supply contract], but I can visualise a situation when I am going to come back from my holiday and not want to do it any more.

Amarjit's lack of commitment to teaching as a long-term career had not come about through any obvious difficulties or through lack of 'success'. Instead, it was the changing nature of teaching and the gap between current realities and those of his own teachers a decade or so earlier which had led him to consider alternatives. Although it appeared he would not stay long in teaching, it would seem that he had learned many of the skills which would enable him to develop as a teacher if he so chose. He did not wish to be seen or judged as a black teacher or an Asian teacher, yet he had given some thought to the ways in which both racism and his own experiences as a non-white person might affect his experiences of teaching.

Six

Teacher identities

Black identities and teacher identities

This chapter sets the six case studies presented in Chapter 5 within the wider sample of 16 experienced teachers. Teachers' professional identities and their socio-political identities are explored and potential tensions identified. Through analysis of the teachers' narratives, common themes are identified and some of the organisational and management implications considered.

The students and teachers in this study were invited to participate as black people, and none of them questioned or challenged this at the outset. It was generally acknowledged by each of the participants, despite their varied histories, languages and cultures, as a term which might be applied to them as people of African Caribbean or Asian descent, and as a shorthand way of acknowledging some shared experiences within the socio-political context of Britain today. Nevertheless, the understandings which individuals attached to it, and the degree to which they accepted the term as a way of identifying or describing themselves varied considerably, and were elaborated as each recounted their story. Only one individual, a woman of mixed Nigerian/Scottish descent who had grown up in a foster home, expressed discomfort with the term 'black', arguing that she had encountered racially prejudiced behaviour from among both black and white people.

One theme running through each teacher's narrative is the individual's professional development, and part of this is their changing understanding, at various points in their career, of what it means to them to be a teacher or educator. A parallel theme running through each account is the development of another identity, what Neelum (Chapter 5) describes as 'my development as a black person'. Amongst the more experienced teachers, this second element comes forward most strongly, although it tends to be taken either as something which is 'given' or as something which is developed in childhood among those born and educated in the Caribbean.

Among those educated abroad, part of the sense of self as a black person is confidence and expectation of success, which individuals explain in terms of their family upbringing and own schooling; this sense of self is not permanently undermined by any experience of discriminatory treatment of black people in Britain. Nevertheless, some individuals describe the initial shock of encountering racial prejudice on arrival in Britain and the temporary damage this does to self-confidence. This study, focusing on teachers' lives and careers, necessarily concerns itself with those who have overcome many of the damaging effects of experiencing racist treatment.

Beverley, a Section 11 teacher, who like Janet (Chapter 5) came to Britain as a young woman from the Caribbean, described how when she was working in a promoted post, as a head of year, she came to realise that colleagues were giving her a particularly difficult time. She raised this with her headteacher, telling him: 'I think these people are giving me a hard time because I am black and I am a woman.' He simply replied: 'Oh my dear, I knew that all along.' Beverley goes on to criticise those 'nice people', like her former headteacher, who 'do a lot of damage'. It would seem to be the inaction of senior managers, who observe differential attitudes and behaviour of their staff towards black colleagues and towards black children, which has such a significant impact on black teachers, and leads them to challenge injustice, often from relatively junior positions and at some personal cost. As Beverley expresses it: 'I have a passion for seeing justice done for black children. And that drives me on, and I do give a lot more of myself than a lot of white people I have worked with.'

The inequitable treatment of black children by many schools has led Beverley to become involved with black parents' groups, helping them to organise and to be better informed about their children's schooling. She acknowledges that this is not something expected of her as a teacher, but it is something which as a black teacher she feels compelled to do, for the sake of justice.

While Neelum emphasised the immediate rapport she was able to establish with black parents which she felt gave her 'credibility' with her colleagues, not all teachers reported similar experiences. As we have seen, Janet, working in a school where there were a minority of African Caribbean children who were generally regarded as difficult, felt she had sometimes been placed in a difficult position when asked to defend to parents what she perceived to be unjust disciplinary measures. Salma, a young primary school teacher, recalled how she encountered initial difficulties establishing her credibility both with colleagues and with parents. She felt she had little in common with her 'official' mentor and sought the support of her (black) headteacher:

> I wanted to do something for these kids on their level, as in multicultural/ anti-racist and anti-sexist education. I said to the head, 'Oh God this place is like 1870, when are you going to pull them all up?' and he

would laugh at me. It was a time when I knew he was listening but he was trying to get me to loosen up a bit and away from a notion of this is the only way of doing it.

The mums didn't trust me. My Punjabi wasn't very good and I still wore the black trousers and I always wore a black scarf around my neck, but they didn't trust me. They didn't think I could be a good teacher if I was like them. I have had to actually *learn* it, so how could I teach it as well as someone that *was* it, that is, a white person? It took me a long time to understand why I didn't get on with the Asian mums. And Asian dads would never look at me, they just couldn't face me at all: a young enthusiastic, confident Asian female who had the signs of some traditional elements, and yet wouldn't speak their language! It was only after I got married and my husband determined that my Punjabi improved and I became more confident in myself. But it is great because now I get to the mums and I speak to them in their own language. I feel confident speaking to the mums, but not so much the children, especially if there are white people around. I feel good now, I feel they have started to accept me and started to respect me. And I think they are wanting it now for their own kids, their girls especially.

Salma's account reveals some of the complexity of teacher–parent relationships and how they may be closely tied to an individual's sense of her own identity. It was only when Salma had managed to unlearn the self-consciousness she had acquired at school concerning her own culture and background that she became more assured. She was then able not only to win the trust of parents but also to begin to challenge the sexist attitudes she encountered both in school and in the local community towards women, and particularly Asian women; her challenge was more effective because she had become a role model for the children. Others, like Amarjit (Chapter 5) and Surinder, a young mathematics teacher, felt that colleagues did not really appreciate their bilingual skills. Surinder had to explain that she could not take on the role of a professional interpreter or guarantee an accurate translation. She felt strongly that a school should be willing to acknowledge teachers' linguistic skills with payment where appropriate, or pay for a professional service.

A number of black teachers in the sample find that they are better positioned to challenge narrow attitudes or injustices from outside the confines of the school, often in Section 11 posts. A number reflected on the liberating experience of advisory work which allows them to develop their skills as educators away from the day-to-day pressures of those (white) colleagues who seek to restrict their creativity, talents and professional development opportunities. Other teachers see the dangers of marginalisation in Section 11 work and dismiss it as a career option. This issue is explored with reference to the careers of senior educators in Chapter 8.

Knowledge of black success in the country of his upbringing helped give Eric, an economics and politics teacher, the same determination to succeed as it did Janet. He spent some of his secondary schooling in Trinidad and some in London and was acutely aware of differences in teacher expectations:

> In London I found that things were very relaxed and do as you like. I was totally shocked. It seemed fine at the time but, of course at the time I didn't have the vision to see the dangers of that. I would say that comprehensive school contained 95 to 99 per cent working-class kids, and black kids weren't expected to do well. You would do pieces of work and you would be marked down. Plus the fact that most teachers never took any time in their lesson preparation. It was just a matter of going into the class and throwing an out-dated text book and saying, 'Well, copy from the book.' And from what I understand that isn't really teaching as such.

Eric's case supports research carried out at about this time in a multi-ethnic school in the West Midlands (Driver 1979) which suggests that negative teacher expectations are likely to be conveyed to students and to adversely affect their performance. Although Eric was disadvantaged by his London schooling, he did not let this deter him from his ambitions. He believes his schooling in Trinidad helped confirm that he was capable of success, even at the point when he left school in London with only two O levels. He also found he was an outsider, with little in common with the black boys he encountered in London:

> When I came back from Trinidad in December 1977 there was a distinctive black British culture here, which at the time was pro-Rastafari. I think the unwritten code amongst black youngsters at the time was not to do well in school. I think it was a sort of resistance to a perception of racism in wider society. The only people I actually identified with were people who actually had some experience of the West Indies, and African peoples. But the black British, no experience of the Caribbean and so on, I sort of played a game with them. Basically I was taken from a very comfortable environment in which I was quite happy, and thrown into a very hostile alien culture.

Eric goes on to express similar concern to Wesley (Chapter 5) about the limiting forms of black male identity which he has encountered, both as a pupil in London and as a teacher. His concern is such that he hopes he will be able to leave Britain so that his own children will be educated in an environment where they will be presented with wider choices as black people. At least one of the teachers had sent her own children 'back home' to Guyana to experience a year or so of schooling there, in the hope this would foster the strong sense of identity she herself had acquired growing up there. Caribbean states estimate that several thousand people have made the move from Britain in the 1990s. Although a large number of these are retired people 'returning home', a growing proportion are parents, not all of whom were born in the Caribbean, who are dissatisfied with the opportunities available to their children within the British school system and concerned about such issues as the gross overrepresentation of African Caribbean children among those excluded from school. The Organisation of Returnees and Associates of Jamaica has been set up to advise those considering the move (*The Times Educational Supplement*, 1 November 1996).

Men and women in the study sometimes expressed different priorities in working for justice and equality in school. Eric had attended a black teachers' meeting but had felt uncomfortable with the women there; he did not share what he described as their 'predominantly feminist' agenda. Salma described how when she shared understandings of racism with her black male headteacher she had sought to 'educate' him on gender equality. Another teacher, Bhupinder, found from the beginning of her career that she had more in common with two young white female colleagues than with other Asian teachers in her school, whose 'conservative' attitudes led her to believe there could be little, if any, shared understanding between them. Moreover, she argued that the assumption that an 'Asian' teacher will necessarily be able to get closer to her pupils than a white colleague is first, to assume that they will have similar upbringings and, secondly, to assume that similar experiences are necessarily more important than individual attitudes:

At my first school, a girls' school, I made friends with two women who still remain incredibly close friends . . . They're sort of my age and feminists, very strong viewpoints, very student-orientated and anti-establishment and what have you. But the majority of the staff were racist, sexist, bigoted in their views, tremendously destructive of students' self-perception.

The whole make-up of the school was appalling: there was a rigid banding system with mainly white middle-class girls in the top bands, mainly Asian and black students in the middle band and all Asian students in the bottom band. The bottom band was just a dumping ground for students with 'language problems', students with conceptual problems, students who clearly needed language support but were highly intelligent. There were two other Asian teachers. One was a 'safe' Asian in terms of the other people because she was married and she wasn't threatening. She had been a student at the school and came back and was a teacher, and taught home economics; very safe. The other was a chemistry teacher who wore a sari and was very traditional. I didn't find either of those teachers particularly keen to cause a revolution.

I know teachers defined me very much as a new 'Asian teacher'. In my report at the end my teaching practice [at the same school] I was described as, this is a quote, 'the best Asian teacher I've ever seen'. I took issue with this, but my teacher at university said I should take it as a compliment! I think the [Asian] students thought I could understand them better but I don't actually agree with that philosophy. I think you can be white, you can be middle class, you can come from a background where both of your parents are in the National Front, but depending on your individual views you can still be just as close and you can understand just as much. Because my own background is very, very different from those students who have had an orthodox religious background.

The labelling of Bhupinder as 'an Asian teacher' so that her performance is judged not by a general standard, but against the perceived attributes of other Asian teachers, is a serious cause for concern. Ghuman (1995), in his study of Asian teachers in British schools, found that older 'first-generation' Asians who were educated abroad were often judged to be more 'authoritarian' in teaching style than their white peers. He concludes that such perceptions were partially justified; such teachers had been schooled under a different system and their teacher-training and experience in India or Pakistan left them with very different initial expectations of children in the British school system from those of their white colleagues. However, he expresses the concern that younger Asian teachers are still being categorised in a similar way by certain of their white senior colleagues; these same senior colleagues are likely to have considerable influence over their career development and promotion prospects:

> Most second-generation Asian teachers are apprehensive that they are still being labelled as authoritarian by their white colleagues despite their full education in British educational institutions and resulting acculturation into British norms and value systems.
>
> (Ghuman 1995: 99)

Being labelled by others as an 'Asian teacher' or as a 'black teacher', with a stereotyped set of assumptions is potentially very damaging. For individuals, like Bhupinder, who contrast strongly with the stereotype, it may be difficult or impossible to function effectively in such a setting and at the same time be true to themselves. Her feminism, for example, may in such circumstances be magnified and thus more threatening to her colleagues than that of her white friends. However, Bhupinder acknowledges that a recognition of Asian cultures and languages in her primary schooling was very important to her. What is important to her as an adult is that she should define her own identity.

For some teachers in this study, particularly those who like Balbir (Chapter 5) were educated in predominantly white schools, black identity is linked with a reassertion of a cultural identity which her own teachers 'overlooked'. Yet others, similarly educated, explain their black identity more or less exclusively in political terms, as part of the process of accepting the role of a teacher and dealing with the contradictions and conflicts as they respond to racism within schools, and racist attitudes amongst colleagues, which they begin to see impinging on their careers or the opportunities and chances of black pupils in their care. Neelum and Wesley and a number of others fall into this category. They all seem to have avoided the disadvantage of negative group labelling at school either by having secured a place at a selective school or by growing up in isolation from other black families. In some respects their experiences may be compared with that of Ravinder Bansal, who as a newly qualified teacher recalled his experiences at a Birmingham grammar school during the late 1970s and early 1980s, arguing that he succeeded because in a selective school the teachers had high expectations of all children, but that this was at the cost of his self-esteem and cultural identity. He concludes:

> Education has given me a voice: it has given me dignity and a critical awareness ... At the same time, it has disrupted and made life more painful because it stops me from acting without thinking.
>
> I can't go into the City and earn pockets of money – what use would that be? I can't cut myself off from what I see around me and say it has nothing to do with me when I see the conditions that children live in. I come from a family and background where people shared what little they had. I am fortunate, and at the same time unfortunate, to have experience of different classes, people and places. Education has allowed me to transcend social class and helped me to give something back.
>
> (Bansal 1990)

The majority of the participants in this research study show themselves to be acutely aware of the needs of black children and of other disadvantaged children in their schools and share Ravinder Bansal's desire to 'give something back'.

Other teachers are conscious of the ways in which black children have been negatively stereotyped or are the subjects of low teacher expectations from first-hand experience. They have consciously had to challenge racist attitudes among teachers and fellow students from a relatively young age, growing up in multicultural city schools. Trevor, a head of mathematics, described his own schooling which appears to have been conducted in an atmosphere of violence. At primary school he was singled out for violent treatment by his teacher and he entered secondary school with a reputation as a troublemaker:

> I found it very difficult in those early years [at primary school]. On many occasions my parents were called in. I liked maths, I was doing quite well, but I felt I was held back and that I wasn't given the opportunity to succeed. Possibly the teachers felt that my attitude was wrong, hence I was denied the opportunity. Something I remember was that lots of boys who [subsequently] went on to grammar schools would

come to me for assistance with their work. But it was sort of covered up and the boys got the credit. I was told that because my English wasn't very good there was no way I could read the questions on the higher books. Also the teachers' attitudes towards myself and some of the other black kids wasn't desirable. I remember on one occasion coming in late from the playground and I was asked to explain my lateness, and for some reason I was laughing and being silly at that age, and I was repeatedly slapped in the face by the teacher. I didn't tell my parents anything about it. My parents, at that time, were more or less in favour of the system; they had put their faith in the system. My report when I left said that before long this person would end up in trouble with the police. That was actually written on my [primary school] report.

Trevor's account is an indictment of his teachers and a frightening reminder of the power which teachers can wield, for good or bad, over the lives of young children. Trevor was only able to salvage something of his schooling in the middle years of secondary school when a shared interest in chess caused a particular teacher to take an interest in him and support him in achieving. Personal experiences of this nature gave Trevor and others interviewed for this study an acute sensitivity to their power as teachers and to the power of teacher attitudes generally in relation to the achievement of black pupils.

Among the younger teachers who had been teaching for less than three years, there was more emphasis on establishing their credibility with colleagues and pupils, and less emphasis on their personal identities. Amarjit and Denise (Chapter 5) both sought to play down their experiences as either Asian or black people, not wanting to be seen as having 'a chip on their shoulder', and this extended in Denise's case to not wanting to be seen with the black deputy head who was in many ways acting as her mentor. This raises questions about the climate of this small primary school where a young black teacher felt she was open to criticism from colleagues if she were seen together with a black senior colleague. It is perhaps useful to set this within a context where some teachers still express concern about black children who group together. There is rarely a similar concern expressed about white children congregating together. Denise's case is in contrast to that of Salma, who benefited considerably from the support of her black headteacher. This, however, was in a school where there was a more explicit commitment to racial equality, where members of the local community were actively involved in the classrooms and in other school initiatives and where there were other black members of the teaching staff.

The decision to become a teacher may be made consciously after considerable thought and deliberation or more casually, as a result of chance or circumstance, as when an individual states, 'I just drifted into it'. However, once the decision has been taken, in whatever circumstances, there follows a long process of adaptation and acceptance of a professional identity, the process both of *becoming a teacher*, learning certain professional skills and norms of behaviour, and that of *feeling like a teacher*, of adopting a particular identity. In this respect the teachers in this study are similar to the white primary school teachers in Nias' (1989) study who tended not to define themselves as teachers during the early part of their careers. She found that those who remained as teachers often took up to four years to identify themselves as such.

The way in which an individual enters teaching does not seem to have any direct relationship to their level of commitment once they are established in their profession. Neelum's BEd course was for her a means into higher education, it was her enjoyable teaching practices which encouraged her to see herself as a teacher. Similarly, Wesley found himself working as a teacher as the result of redundancy at a time when he had no obvious alternative options. Yet both of them had worked hard to develop a range of skills and develop within their profession. Their commitment to their work was no less than that of Janet, Denise or other teachers in the study who had set out from childhood to become teachers and had had to struggle to realise their ambition.

Denise's story, and her struggle to become a teacher is very similar to that of Hazel, a mathematics teacher in her late twenties, who had been channelled away from teaching and into those types of occupation, nursing and social work, seen as 'natural' choices because they matched the caring and serving roles expected of black women. In Denise's case, poor examination results and lack of career counselling served as barriers, as did her difficulty in obtaining mathematics O level, an entry requirement for teacher training. By contrast, Hazel found mathematics easy and achieved success in this subject, yet the barrier of teacher and career adviser stereotyping was a formidable one.

Hazel describes vividly how she was forced to challenge negative teacher stereotyping more or less on a daily basis, and of how her family were her only source of support. Her own school experiences have lead her to make a special commitment to the education of black people, not just in the sixth-form college where she is employed, but as a voluntary teacher at a black Saturday school:

> If the black teachers don't do the children a service then we are going to regret it. It is a sort of long-term thing; I would always feel guilty that I didn't help them when they needed help. It is a process of regeneration, otherwise we will be perpetuating the cycle of black failures, children failing and failing. I think they need to be caught at a young age.

Commitment to their work is something which runs through each account. This commitment is sometimes closely related to an individual's need to prove themselves. As Denise acknowledges, this is something which may apply to any teacher, but there appears to be an additional pressure on black teachers to prove their equal worth. This pressure is expressed as a need to work harder and always perform at one's best. It is felt as acutely by Amarjit, who has no intention of remaining a teacher, as it is by Janet who is seeking promotion and further advancement. It is not just a need to convince others that a black teacher is as capable as any other, but it is also expressed as a responsibility to other black people, a question of not letting others down or conforming to a stereotype of inadequacy.

All the teachers in this study were invited to consider their possible futures, and one feature that came across in a number of accounts was a sense of geographical mobility; a number were considering the possibility of moving abroad, either for a short period, to take up a fixed-term contract, as Wesley had already done, or as a permanent move. At the time of writing, I am not in touch with all the interviewees, but know of teachers who have moved to the United States, the Caribbean, Australia and South Africa, and at least one who has worked abroad since the research interview and subsequently returned home. Other possible destinations discussed included other African countries and Canada. Individuals' motivations for travelling varied considerably, but included: a desire to find more attractive working conditions; to work in a black community or alongside other black colleagues; to be of service to children living in disadvantaged conditions; and a desire to bring up their own children in a more positive environment, in a culture which acknowledged black achievement and where racism was not part of their everyday school experience.

Common themes

Relationships with black students

Each teacher expresses a special commitment or concern for black pupils, and this often extends to any pupil who may be disadvantaged in the education system by other factors, such as those of gender or class. Regardless of their attitude towards particular equality initiatives in schools, each teacher stressed issues of equity and justice in their own practice. All six of the individual case-study teachers, for example, are concerned about the achievement of their pupils and of black pupils in particular, and this issue comes across more strongly than questions of curriculum content, being seen as closely related to teacher attitudes and expectations. In this respect they are representative of the wider sample.

Black teachers may find that in order to support black children achieve in school, they not only have to confront teacher attitudes which have racist outcomes but also students' understandings of blackness and particularly black masculinity, enabling them to see that it does not have to be interpreted in a limiting way. Willis (1977) has explained how social class styles or identities become translated into school resistance for working class boys and Mac an Ghaill (1988) found similar responses among African

Caribbean boys. A number of teachers in this study perceived some African Caribbean boys to be acting in a 'self-defeating' way in school. Their particular understanding of black identity was one which challenged those black male teachers who were, in their eyes, 'acting white' through their association with the school. The teachers in this study did not express similar difficulties in relationships with African Caribbean girls. Fuller (1980), in her study of black girls, notes how they challenged negative labelling by focusing on school achievement and the gaining of qualifications and Mirza's (1992) research confirms this response. Many of the female teachers and student teachers in this study had approached their own schooling in this way. It is possible that both black and white teachers have experienced fewer difficulties or conflicts with African Caribbean girls whose approach to school appears more utilitarian and whose understandings of black female identity may be broader and more positive.

Isolation

Black teachers in this study frequently described the problems of being isolated in school. Whether they are silent on issues of inequality or whether they speak out and risk being labelled, they remain equally vulnerable. A central issue is that of black identity, and the need to have one's professional and personal experiences valued and taken into consideration. Another is a deep concern about the attitudes of many white colleagues towards black people and the impact which this has on their treatment of black children. Closely related to the issues which black teachers must face concerning their own identity in schools are the understandings which black children have of blackness; this can sometimes lead to children believing that teachers are 'acting white' when in fact they are simply being themselves and expressing their own tastes and interests. Such challenges to black teachers by black pupils may be stressful, particularly when the teacher concerned has a strong black political identity and is fully aware of the impact of racism on children's lives.

Promotion

This sense of isolation, and lack of direct support from colleagues, is more acutely felt at times when an individual is seeking promotion or further professional development. Balbir, Janet and Wesley all provide examples of how they struggle to overcome this type of problem. Neelum, as a member of a Section 11 team appears to have avoided this difficulty, although the question arises of whether she would have experienced similar difficulties if she had not had the support of a black teachers' network to which she belonged. It is interesting to note the case of Yasmin, who worked for many years as a science teacher and who actually left teaching at one point because of the lack of career opportunities. Unable to secure a permanent post on her return, she accepted a temporary contract teaching science in a school where there was a science vacancy. No-one offered her the post, but she was offered a job as a language support teacher in the same school although she lacked appropriate qualifications, skills or experience: 'It brought it home to me that they saw only a black woman, not a science teacher. So I thought I would go out there and use the system. It was at that point I applied for a job in a multicultural support service in another authority'. Yasmin quickly secured promotion in this way but reflects that the test will come when she seeks to return to 'mainstream' teaching where she predicts the majority of schools will not value her skills and experience in Section 11 work.

Networking

The majority of teachers in the study valued the support they gained through networking with other black colleagues, and also generally felt happier in school environments where there were other black adults, either teachers or parents, with whom they had regular contact. Some younger teachers were concerned as to how networking with other black colleagues might be perceived by white colleagues. Nevertheless, those who had had the opportunity to work in predominantly black or exclusively black teams during the mid-1980s, when a number of anti-racist initiatives were established, emphasised how this had been a particularly beneficial experience which had given them confidence and often encouraged them to seek promotion.

Senior management support

Although this study has concerned itself with the experiences and perceptions of black teachers rather than the perceptions that (white) headteachers and senior managers have of black teachers, there are some implications for the ways in which school management teams seek to support black teachers' careers and recognise the ways in which their experiences of the school may differ from those of white colleagues. Within schools, staff development programmes need to be planned so that they are genuinely inclusive of the needs of all. As well as reviewing formal programmes, attention needs to be given to the processes of internal promotion and to the professional development experiences offered, for example, when a teacher is in an 'acting' post.

Mentoring

A number of teachers named an individual teacher who had supported them at school, and some identified a senior black educator, either a headteacher, deputy or an adviser who they were able to turn to for advice, particularly during the early years of their career or when they were planning a career move. Those who have a senior member of staff in their schools to whom they can turn are exceptional, but with some foresight and planning it should be possible, particularly within urban LEAs with sizeable black populations, to support links between senior black educators and new teachers. Models for such schemes already exist: for example, the Birmingham-based Imani Venture, an organisation set up by black people to offer work experience and mentoring by professionals to young black people, especially graduates starting out on their careers (*Birmingham Voice*, 15 February 1995), and the black male mentor scheme, also operating in Birmingham with the endorsement of the LEA, to offer support, encouragement and a 'sense of direction' to African Caribbean boys (*The Times Educational Supplement*, 10 February 1995). The issue of mentoring is a complex one and although in some cases it may be desirable that a teacher finds a mentor from the same ethnic background, this may not always be necessary or even desirable (Osler and Starkey 1996).

Bilingualism

While the majority of teachers interviewed for this study had bilingual skills which they saw as an asset, they were not convinced that schools necessarily acknowledged or valued these skills in their everyday work with children and their families. Many were concerned that schools should not assume such skills or exploit them by demanding that they took on extra responsibilities without remuneration. Some colleagues did not seem to appreciate the level of technical competence required to act as an effective translator or interpreter. I explore a number of these issues in greater detail elsewhere (Osler 1994c).

Gender and identity

It would appear from the sample that black women teachers are networking more effectively and more consciously than the men. The sample is biased in favour of women because these were the teachers it was possible to locate. Black people generally are underrepresented within the profession, but there are strong indications that black men in particular are not entering teaching. This in turn is likely to have an impact on students' perceptions. There is a particular concern about the differing experiences of black boys and girls at school, particularly the narrow interpretations which black male students are giving to black identity and black masculinity. A number of black educators have identified a crisis in the schooling of African Caribbean boys.

Summary

This chapter has explored the particular experiences of black people in teaching and considered the differing ways both professional and socio-political identities are established. It has highlighted some of the factors which support and hinder black teachers in their working lives. Although many of the teachers in the sample have encountered career barriers, they remain highly committed to their work and feel a strong sense of achievement.

The foundations of success: senior educators look back

Introduction

Theoretical and historical analyses of racism may provide us with a framework within which we can explain the underrepresentation of people from black and ethnic minorities within teaching, but existing theories of racism do not adequately address the experiences of those black people who do reach senior positions. This chapter draws on the narratives of ten senior managers to consider how their own schooling, either in Britain or overseas, and the impact of migration have helped shape their thinking and actions. The senior managers reflect on their various routes into teaching by examining their experiences of higher education and their subsequent career paths.

Six managers were headteachers in primary, special or secondary schools and a seventh was a secondary school deputy head. The remaining three all held senior positions in the inspection and advisory services of local education authorities. There were six women and four men in the sample. Seven of the ten had migrated to Britain from India, Africa or the Caribbean as children or young adults. They range in age from those in their mid-thirties to those in their fifties; they were thus people who commenced their careers in Britain during the 1960s and 1970s.

Adler *et al.* (1993), in their study of women in educational management, remind us that we should be careful to avoid presenting women managers as a homogeneous group. It is equally important in a study of black senior managers that we guard against sweeping generalisations, since they are likely to have both common and varying experiences. These are likely to be influenced by such factors as self-identity, gender, family and social class background, age, religion, nationality, culture and perceived ethnicity. The experiences of the ten individuals presented here do need, therefore, to be recognised first and foremost as individual experiences; they cannot be seen as representative of all senior black educators in Britain. Nevertheless, they do have some common threads running through them and all of the participants recount episodes which mirror those of a number of others. I will therefore develop some of the themes which emerged from the last chapter in the analysis of black teachers' careers.

The career progression realised by these senior educators is particularly noteworthy within an education system which has disadvantaged black and ethnic minority students and in which there is plentiful evidence of structural racism. Moreover, their own narratives reflect their sense of achievement taking on the challenges of leadership. These are men and women who in their own terms have achieved considerable success. For these reasons I have adopted a traditional concept of 'career success' as a starting point in this analysis, whilst acknowledging that concepts of career and of what makes a successful teacher are often male-orientated and may operate to exclude or disadvantage female educators (Evetts 1988; de Lyon and Migniuolo 1989; Adler *et al.* 1993). My intention is to explore potential contradictions in defining career success for black educators, and to examine some of the costs of success, both personal and professional, for individuals.

Overcoming barriers

Schooling

Given the evidence available which demonstrates how the British education system has disadvantaged certain groups of black and ethnic minority children over the past 30 years (for example, Coard 1971; Eggleston *et al.* 1986; Troyna and Williams 1986; Tomlinson 1987; Gillborn 1990; Klein 1993) we might expect that those of the senior managers who attended school in Britain to have encountered some barriers at this early stage. Four of the senior managers (two men and two women) underwent all of their primary and secondary schooling in Britain, with a fifth arriving in Britain towards the end of her primary schooling and the sixth during the early years of secondary school.

In the 1950s and early 1960s when they started school, the patterns of migration to Britain from the Caribbean and from the Indian sub-continent meant that, although there was a growing black population in Britain, many families were divided, with some school-age children remaining in the parents' home country. Although the black population was concentrated in particular urban areas, there were few schools with significant proportions of black children. It is not surprising therefore that most of the British-schooled senior educators attended largely or exclusively white schools. Those who had the experience of being the first black children to attend their schools recall the curiosity of both teachers and children, stereotypical learning materials and name-calling by other children. This account relates to the 1950s:

I was brought up on a big white council estate in Manchester. I started [school] at four, and I remember most of the time we were treated in a special way, patted on the head and that kind of thing. We were [treated like] dolls really but we were actually encouraged to work hard at home and at school. We were brought up to believe that you just got good results, full stop. That's how it was in those days, well in our family anyway. And I think that because we were so 'special' the teachers wanted us to do well. We were a curiosity to them and certainly to some of the children. I don't remember anything terrible happening in the early infant school days except for some of the books; I remember not liking the *Black Sambo* books. I didn't like playtimes, mostly because of things like name-calling and stupid things like that, finding friends at that early stage was quite difficult. I was so glad when I was made a prefect in junior school, where you didn't have to go outside.

[Starting secondary school] was another hurdle. By the sixth form I was probably more aware of things going on. I did English A level and the teacher was very embarrassed about reading parts of *Othello* and he got quite nervous about it. He asked to see my mother and said: 'I don't think your daughter should be taking part in this because it's embarrassing for her.' I remember a lot of rigmarole over that and that made me think about him in a different light, because we hadn't read any other books which made him nervous before.

(Pauline, primary school head)

The following account reveals a similar situation a decade later:

My parents moved out to Lichfield when I was about six years old. There weren't any black families in Lichfield and I remember the first day, walking to my new primary school. I remember seeing all these children hanging on the fence staring. And I remember thinking, 'Why are they staring at me like that?' And it suddenly dawned on me that they were all white faces and I wasn't. And I think that's the first time that I was made aware of my colour because in Birmingham there were other black children in the school. And of course my mother was in a sari, so probably none of them had ever seen a sari before. So it really hit home that I was different.

(Geeta, secondary school deputy head)

A senior inspector describes how he began his primary education at a village church school in the Midlands. The family moved to London when he was about 10 years old. He explains how living in a white village community had an impact on his developing perceptions of racial prejudice and racism, and the ways he responded to both white children and black children:

When I started school we were the only black family in the village and so the only black family in the school. And then coming to London was the first time I encountered black children *en masse*, and I had difficulty understanding how to relate and how to interpret the behaviour of the black children. I found that I could easily manage the white children, no problem, and I mean manage. I had to manage them. The first questions I remember being asked when I came to the infant school was: 'Your skin is brown, does it rub off? What colour is your blood? Do you wear grass skirts? Do you live in a mud hut? Don't you speak posh! You learnt to speak English very quickly!' And that was all much of a culture at that time. And the questions weren't necessarily being meant to be nasty, half the time they didn't know. Genuine curiosity, but it was just so ignorant, and at times I felt, do they really mean it? We didn't discuss it at home. We didn't start to discuss those things at home until 20 years later, at least, if not longer.

In London, what was going on with the black kids was their interpretation of the behaviour of white pupils and teachers. They would quickly analyse the situation as being: 'This has happened to me because I am black.' Whereas for me it might be true but it hadn't been my experience. I managed those situations where if somebody had been unjust I would find some way of dealing with them, as I had learnt to manage people before.

(Ken, schools' inspector)

Rather than assume an overarching explanation of racism as a cause of all injustice, he explains his childhood strategy of learning to manage each situation and person, as events developed. This required a range of management strategies which enabled him to cope and which he believes stood him in good stead as he grew older and learnt to recognise patterns of behaviour. Many other teachers and senior managers reported that they did not discuss such incidents with their parents. Some felt their parents would have been incredulous or disillusioned, and such discussions appear only to have taken place between brothers and sisters, or with other black children. No one felt they were consciously protecting their parents, though this may have been the case.

Parental support was echoed throughout all the senior managers' accounts of their schooling, but was stressed particularly by those who were educated here as being a critical factor which enabled them to achieve:

Both my parents were, and still are, very supportive and very ambitious and always believed that the next generation should be better than the previous generation. I always remember my father saying to me that his mother said to him that she used to be a maid and she worked cane fields. He quoted her, saying, 'I expect you to do better than I did,' and that was the encouragement. Just as his mother was proud of him, so he is obviously proud of me. He is an ordained minister and he has been now for over 30 years. When he came here he was studying theology mainly through correspondence. He worked in a factory, but he felt that the calling to the church was the strongest.

(Clifton, primary school head)

Migration

The process of migration was in many ways a disruptive one, but for those at school it was eased by parents, family and sometimes by the local black community. This headteacher recalls arriving in Britain in her early teens:

I suppose I've often said that had my parents known more about the education system here they might have pushed me to go to the local grammar school, but they weren't aware of it, so I had to make do with where I was. Obviously I'm not talking secondary moderns or comprehensive schools down, but the fact is that in 1967 if you went to a secondary modern girls' school nobody expected you to pass exams. I didn't do the three sciences because in a secondary modern girls' school you did biology, biology, biology. But I think, retrospectively, that I had got that sort of inner strength and courage and knowledge about my own potential.

Many did not have what I had: I had a mum and a dad who did not have children outside of that relationship, so we didn't have to contend with a new stepfather or a new mum. And certainly there was the church, that was a very secure community. The other young people I am thinking of, they came and joined a new mum or a new dad and there were conflicts there. And I am thinking of two people in particular, their parents expected them to go out to work and earn money, whereas my parents didn't expect that.

(Lesley, secondary head)

A schools' adviser recalls her experience of starting school in Britain at the age of 9 years:

We came to Manchester and that was my [first] experience of white teachers at that time. There were no black teachers of course and the whole transition was fairly traumatic. We weren't seen as being educated, and we were. We had achieved quite high primary standards. We were the only black children and the first in our school, and we did create a bit of a drama. We didn't realise until we started to work through the school that all of the images and all of the textbooks and all of the songs had very negative and disparaging images of black people. This is the early fifties so you can understand. We were shocked and surprised, and there was a fair amount of hurt, but I think having a supportive family, and having a great deal of confidence in our own identity, we weren't intimidated but we were distressed by it.

(Yvonne, schools' adviser)

The disruption, shock, hurt and distress described by these women occurred in a context where they knew something different: 'having a great deal of confidence in our own identity' came from early years spent in schools where there appear to have been good parent–teacher relationships, high pupil expectations and strong role models. Black-led churches in Britain also provided some of the senior educators and their parents with an effective support system.

Seven of the senior managers had all or part of their schooling overseas, in either the Caribbean, India or Kenya; in all but one case each individual chose to stress how important these early years were in terms of a sense of self-identity or self-confidence which gave them either the expectation of success or the determination to succeed in their chosen career:

> I think there was always an expectation on the part of my family. I had family who had gone to secondary school and some of them had done very well indeed. When I was back in Jamaica I was going to be a doctor, no two ways about it. We all knew that, potentially, we could do well.
>
> (Lesley)

> I loved learning and nothing was ever a problem, particularly things like mathematics, science, geography or history. But in history I used to be a pain because I used to challenge all of the time as to why we were learning about the British. We used to take part in these debating championships. I was always winning those championships, it was really great fun. And the topics were always political because India was very young. I was born in free India and therefore everybody was always talking politics . . . I wouldn't have liked to have been a student here . . . I think in India of all the wonderful things that were given to me that were denied to my children in a very big way.
>
> (Balwant, female)

> A model that I had that was influencing me all of the way was my headteacher in Jamaica, he is dead now. But even the way I teach, the way I do things, I think I can feel that teacher in me. I suppose I had the advantage of not being born in this country. I knew that there were black lawyers and black politicians and teachers, and that is what I was used to. When I came to this country and found these people were missing from key places in society I wasn't fooled by that.
>
> (Frank, secondary head)

One senior educator who came to Britain at the age of 4 years, and had only six months of nursery education overseas, chose 'symbolically' to begin the narrative of his schooling back in the Caribbean, believing that this episode had some lasting impact:

> At the very beginning I very much wanted to talk about the Caribbean because I still subscribe to a view that the majority of the black people

who seem to be successful one way or the other, are the people who have had significant education experiences outside of the country. And so I reflect on myself and I am just wondering how critical those early years of education may have been for me, in order for me to form a view of what school could be. I had a view of school where all the teachers and all the pupils were black, well, not all, as the Caribbean is multiracial, as you know. The first Father Christmas I saw was black.

(Ken)

The process of transition was not necessarily any easier for those who arrived in Britain having completed their secondary education or higher education and who were hoping to study for professional qualifications or take up work as teachers. One of the primary headteachers had been schooled in Kenya and had gone into higher education in India, where he had studied first for his degree and then for a postgraduate teaching qualification:

I worked in industry, in the factory as a machine operator. And I worked nights as well as a machine operator. I remember walking, in London, the Great West Road and every factory I went to the person at the gates said: 'There are no vacancies here'. I was asking for a job and in the end it was through someone I knew, he had come over and he worked in this factory. I didn't spend long in factory work but I spent a total of four years in industry.

(Kuldip, primary school head)

This man's story of his arrival and search for work has much in common with the 'first generation' Asian teachers that Ghuman (1995) interviewed. Of the 25 teachers in his study who migrated to Britain expecting to find employment, the majority were first employed as bus conductors or factory workers. Some found their qualifications were not recognised in Britain. A secondary headteacher who arrived in Britain from Jamaica around the age of 19 years, had similar problems but did not let this deter him 'because I was determined that I was going to be a teacher and not only a teacher but a headteacher' (Frank).

Factors supporting career success

Among the senior educators three broad factors seem to support their success in rising to senior positions within the education service. The first is the early development of particular skills and attitudes in managing racism which support them later in life in seeking and fulfilling leadership roles. The second is a desire for further study and advanced qualifications. This would often seem to be rooted in family cultures, but many senior educators recognise early in their careers that they are likely to be disadvantaged in the labour market as black people; higher qualifications are sought partly in an attempt to outweigh anticipated discrimination in employment. The third factor supporting success is a vision of education which develops out of an experience of disadvantage and discrimination. All the senior educators, particularly those schooled in Britain, have a desire to transform education so that it serves future generations better than it has the black and ethnic minority communities to date, and so that it meets the needs of all.

All the senior managers in this study have undertaken some form of higher education in Britain, with seven of the ten holding a British first degree and an eighth a Certificate of Education from a British college. Five held higher degrees at the time of the interview, with a sixth studying for a PhD. Those in the most senior positions generally held the highest qualifications. A survey of ethnic minority school teachers (CRE 1988a) found that they were generally better qualified than their white counterparts, with 23 per cent of the ethnic minority school teachers holding Master's degrees compared with only 2 per cent of the white teachers in the sample. It would certainly appear that the teachers and senior teachers in this study held, as a group, higher qualifications than one might expect to find across the profession as a whole. This not only reflects a strong commitment to study but also a widely held belief, expressed explicitly by all the senior managers that black teachers have to work harder and be seen to be working harder and achieving more in order to be treated on an equal basis with their white colleagues.

Nevertheless, for many, particularly those attending small colleges of education with few if any other black students, entering higher education proved something of an ordeal. One man recalled how his college ruled that he had not achieved high enough standards to be transferred on to the BEd degree course, yet at the same time he had successfully competed for an international scholarship to study in the United States. Difficulties encountered by senior educators during their higher education were not restricted to academic matters, but covered many aspects of student life, including accommodation and the attitudes of other students. Two British born students who were both primary heads encountered extreme difficulties when they sought to find lodgings while at college in the 1960s and early 1970s. They discovered that the owners of many privately rented rooms operated a 'colour bar' and that colleges were unwilling to make alternative arrangements or offer residential places. In one case the student was forced to seek a transfer from a London college to one within commuting distance of his parents' Midlands home. In the other case this experience encouraged the woman concerned to become involved in the struggle for civil rights within the local community. In yet another instance a school refuses to accept a black student teacher. The individual concerned, a mature student who had worked as a civil servant and in industry, responds by further developing her self-reliance:

> Being the lone black person I spent a great part of my life not expecting to have any dialogue or any peer group support from other black

people but I suppose you think, 'This is the way it is, I am not going to worry about it,' because there was a feeling that there is not an awful lot you can do about it. Interestingly enough, my first teaching practice nearly didn't happen. I was told the school I was going to, but the tutor probably didn't attribute blackness to my name. [I met] a rather horrified headteacher, who when I turned up promptly rang up the college saying that the parents or the pupils would be alarmed at me being there. She suggested that I should be placed elsewhere. It did make me realise that I was going to be in a situation where I would have to develop survival skills and, being a determined person and having had a career in which I was successful, I persevered.

(Yvonne)

A woman who studied history at a traditional university in the early 1970s recalls how she was the only black student on her course. The narrow and prejudiced attitudes of fellow students educated in exclusively white environments convinced her that she would be happier and better employed as a teacher in an area with substantial numbers of black people:

I remember having lots of arguments with friends about ethnic minority groups and being engaged to try and challenge people's very stereotypical visions. And they were, I couldn't believe how stereotypical they were, we were all painted in the same way! And I remember getting very engrossed in conversation and getting very upset and storming out and it almost breaking friendships. And it was then at the end of university I decided I didn't really like the South and that actually there weren't enough black people there for me and I wanted to come back to the Midlands. Because I felt that if I was going to be a teacher and a black teacher then it would be far more valuable for me to work in the Midlands.

(Geeta)

One headteacher argued that it was sheer determination which enabled her to survive and achieve. She outlined the strategies she adopted on teaching practice:

I was the only African Caribbean student in my year. As I was the only one, the only black person, and going [on teaching practice] to places like a coal mining district in the nether reaches of the country, I set out to succeed. I had good teaching practices but I think it must have been because I was a fierce young person. Going into the classroom I was determined that you were going to listen to what I wanted you to do. And I can remember only on one practice I had problems with one group of youngsters who were just bad anyway. I can remember the first morning this child decided he was going to faint and he made himself, or at least he tried to make himself, faint. So I just picked him up and said: 'You are getting on with this lesson.' So it wasn't that

difficult, but that doesn't mean I wasn't aware that the kids were saying
'Blackie' and that sort of stuff. But I got on with it, because it really was
a sort of do or die.

(Lesley)

Securing a first teaching post

Apart from one woman who came as an experienced teacher to Britain and
whose husband had undertaken the process of arranging for her overseas
qualifications to be considered by the authorities before her arrival, all the
senior educators had experience of discriminatory treatment or attitudes
which they had already had to overcome before their first appointment. As
we have seen, many had already developed attitudes or approaches, such as
determination, hard work, and careful selection of geographical area, which
may have offered some protection against certain barriers of discrimination.
None encountered difficulties in securing a first appointment during the
1960s and 1970s, when there was full employment and teacher shortages
in some areas.

One woman, herself schooled at a girls' school in India, chose a selective
girls' school for her first teaching appointment as she felt that was what she
was used to, but for others there was a strong desire to work with children
from 'their' communities. A schools' inspector describes his 'quasi-religious'
notion of teaching as a vocation:

> I made a conscious decision to return to an inner-city area to teach, and
> on that basis I returned to London and promptly looked for and found
> a teaching post close to the area where I had grown up, an inner-city
> area. I judged that the kind of experience I had to offer really needed
> to be in a situation where there were more children from ethnic minor-
> ity background, particularly of Caribbean background. Because by then
> it was really apparent to me, the different challenges that had to be
> addressed in terms of racism, in terms of discrimination, in terms of
> understanding the cultural background, in terms of empathy, and also
> in terms of the sense of allegiance and solidarity to what I identified as
> *my* community.

(Ken)

A decision to live and work in the inner city in the early 1970s did not
necessarily mean that settling into work and accommodation was an easy
process:

> I was involved with a black self-help group in Handsworth. I had no
> choice in my own mind, I was going to stay in Birmingham and I
> wanted to work in Handsworth. So I said to [the interviewers selecting
> for] the pool: 'I don't want a job unless you can give me one in
> Handsworth.' And they gave me one. When I got the place I still couldn't

find anywhere to live. We were trying all over the place, flats saying 'No blacks' or 'No room'. I would take my mother with me and do this experiment [her mother was white] and she would go on her own and they would say 'Yes, yes'. And of course the Act [Race Relations Act 1968] wasn't protective. So I took this horrible place with my sister, horrible because it wasn't self-contained, but it was Handsworth and it was only supposed to be for a year.

(Pauline)

The young man who had arrived in Britain with postgraduate teaching qualifications to find he could only get factory work had no further difficulties securing a post once he held a British qualification. He accepted a post in a predominantly white school, but found he had to work hard to gain the respect of local parents and children:

To start off with I was called: 'Paki bastard', and some of the parents used to tell their youngsters, 'I saw your teacher on a camel today,' the children told me that. But children challenge their parents, and when I left there I was 'Mr Ruprai' rather than a 'Paki bastard'.

(Kuldip)

Career planning

The concept of 'career' is often interpreted to mean progression up a hierarchical pyramid and has been seen as problematic since most people will not reach the top of the pyramid. It has been argued that men and women often have different understandings of career; many women who do rise to senior positions do not follow parallel career paths to their male colleagues (Adler *et al.* 1993) and may face different and frustrating experiences (Ozga 1993). It is possible that black senior educators, both female and male, might have some similar experiences to white women teachers. Evetts (1989) adopted a life-history approach to study how external structural factors and internal labour market processes are worked out in individual circumstances in the lives of female, married headteachers. She concluded that the characteristics for promotion success are likely to vary according to whether there is a plentiful supply of teachers or a teacher shortage. The ways in which individual senior black educators perceive their careers may enable us to identify how individuals manage the particular structural barriers they are likely to encounter.

One headteacher explained her seniority in terms of her 'professional attitude' and strong career orientation, together with her desire to achieve some freedom as a woman. This account echoes that of the narratives of all the senior managers and many of the experienced teachers that black and ethnic minorities need to make twice the effort of their white counterparts in teaching:

Because I was aware of women's oppression, I always wanted to be a career woman. My father treated me as a son because I was the eldest and maybe he made a mistake, but that is it. I don't think intentionally I planned to be where I am at present. Nothing was going to stop me, neither my husband nor my family, as far as professional concerns go. I always say to Asians that you must commit yourself twice as much as other people if you want to be successful.

(Anju, special school head)

Throughout their accounts, all six female senior educators make reference to personal and family commitments and to the demands these place upon them. A number of the women describe choices they have had to make between work and other commitments. One highlights how she was so involved in her career she never considered having children, something which she now regrets, another describes how she does not find time to visit her parents as much as she would like and a third discusses whether her commitment to her work was a contributory factor in her marriage break-down. Both single and married women integrate aspects of their lives beyond work into their narratives in a way which the men do not. The four male senior educators rarely mention their families, children or friends in their accounts, accept in passing; for example, those who are married list their wives among the people who have given them support.

Only one of the sample, a male secondary headteacher, had apparently planned his career right from the beginning, although it is clear that once in post, the two male primary heads quite quickly set their sights on head-ship. One of the primary heads explains that it was the headteacher in his first school who first encouraged him:

He was exactly ten years older than me and he had got this headship by the time ten years was up. And he just said to me that if you put your shoulder to the wheel and believe that, you can also do it. Even then I thought to myself the same laws apply, but if you put within the equation the 'race' factor, I will probably reach there a couple of years after, you have got to allow for racism and whatever. So I got there after 14 years, which is not too bad.

(Clifton)

Nevertheless, this head was exceptional in the sample in having direct encouragement from a headteacher. He explained his achievement in terms of his own determination and he also felt that those people who had really inspired him to achieve were black people whose life stories he had read:

Even though I had the encouragement I also had the beliefs there in the first place, because I was determined I would reach there. The encouragement certainly helped but I wouldn't say it was the motiva-tional force. The engine did it, the encouragement was the added fuel. Other people helped, my father, very strong, very positive and very determined, and I would say my wife. Also the lives of people like Marcus Garvey, Martin Luther King, Malcolm X. All those people have been very important, feeling their determination, feeding off their determination.

(Clifton)

None of the women seemed to have a clear vision of their careers when they set out, although a strong motivational force among the women was to be 'successful' at what they were doing, and many developed this vision as their careers progressed. The other man in the sample pointed out that although his original vision of his career was that of a traditional move through from assistant teacher to head of department and into a senior management position in school, this pattern proved to be unrealistic. He stressed very strongly that where he was now was not necessarily where he had wanted to go:

Career development? I didn't have any long term plans of that kind at all. What I did have was the recollection of some advice one of my English teachers gave to me. One of the things he said to me was, 'Never be afraid of responsibility.' I said, 'Yes, I will remember that.' And I did remember it though I didn't quite understand it at the time.

(Ken)

Summary

We have seen a variety of approaches to 'career' among the ten senior managers, although some common factors emerge: most have an expectation of success, and all are very determined to do their work to the best of their ability, sometimes seeing teaching as a vocation and often seeing their work as an expression of allegiance to the black communities. Individuals, although experiencing some setbacks to their education at various stages or in the process of migration, have built upon these early experiences and developed a high degree of determination and self-reliance.

Eight

Managing success

Introduction

This chapter examines the career paths the senior educators have followed, seeking to identify elements that have enabled them to achieve promotion and 'career success'. It considers patterns and constraints in the choices and decisions they have made, and examines individual motivations in taking on managerial responsibilities. The ways in which individuals have interpreted their roles and the priorities they have adopted are also explored, particularly their commitment to racial justice and the development of political identities. Consideration is given to relationships with students, staff and the communities with whom they work.

We have seen that black teachers are often employed in inner-city areas, in schools where there are substantial numbers of black and ethnic minority children, but that they are not necessarily considered for promotion to senior posts. While black teachers may be seen as classroom teachers and role models, some have experienced barriers in achieving leadership positions. Others fear they are in danger of being used by senior management to support patterns of control imposed on black pupils. Yet others find they are stereotyped into particular roles linked to their perceived ethnicity, such as English as a second language teacher, roles which may bear little relation to their qualifications or experience; they become, in the eyes of their employers, 'professional ethnics' (Blair and Maylor 1993). In examining the senior educator's career development, I consider whether such attitudes or assumptions have also been part of their experience, and if so, how they have dealt with them.

Routes to promotion

The pastoral route

One role perceived as particularly appropriate for black teachers is (black) pupils' pastoral care. One of the senior educators achieved his early promotion through the pastoral route. He believes the school made a radical decision in selecting him for the post of head of year, as a young black man who did not share the dominant 'machismo and control ethos' of the all boys school:

> The pupils tested me out in a different way as a black person . . . By the time I was a year head I was already well established in the school, I had already established a mythology of how I operate and how I behave. I think [with] the white pupils, a key concern was that I could wield power fairly. So I felt it was very important to be seen to be dealing with issues even-handedly. Whereas with the black pupils there was a question of being able to deal with the power and not lose my blackness.
>
> (Ken)

Ken's narrative reflects similar concerns to those of the experienced teachers in Chapters 5 and 6; he sought to develop an alternative model of head of year based on justice and fairness rather than control and was conscious of potential tensions in his relationship with both black and white pupils. He is also sensitive to pupils' perceptions of black male identity and mindful to retain his own political and cultural identity – his blackness. He defined his role as head of year and was aware of the pitfalls; acceptance of the role does not imply acceptance of the dominant model of pupil management in the school. He also enjoyed the support of senior management.

The special needs route

One headteacher, Anju, already had considerable experience as an assistant inspector of schools in India before migrating to Britain as a young adult in 1963. She began again from scratch, recognising that as an Asian woman she might encounter additional barriers, but determined to prove herself in her chosen career. After a number of years teaching she studied full time for a certificate in special educational needs and subsequently took work in this field. She later took a Master's degree in special education and eventually secured a deputy headship and then a headship. Her career is characterised by her considerable determination and by efforts to secure additional qualifications.

The traditional route

The one headteacher who achieved promotion exclusively within 'mainstream' education was exceptional among the senior educators:

> I didn't consciously avoid Section 11 [posts], I just never had cause to even consider them. Looking back on it now, I am very glad I never did take on [a Section 11 post], because it is an area which I think has

additionally stifled black teachers, and stagnated them in the profession
because you become stereotyped into these positions.

(Frank)

Others recognised the potential problems of such a career move but took
Section 11 posts when unable to secure promotion in schools:

> I was aware that I was taking a gamble, because I felt at the time that
> I had been teaching at my first school for eight years and it was time
> to move on. I applied for a few deputy headship posts and was unsuc-
> cessful. But I had the ambitions. I chose the [Section 11] curriculum
> post because I felt the scope was broader. I wanted to have the experi-
> ence of a whole-school perspective, a whole-school view of things, to
> be involved in curriculum management, organisation, development. I
> did it for a purpose, it was a means to an end: I wanted to become a
> deputy and I saw this as a road to it.

(Clifton)

A schools' adviser argued that promotion would have been impossible for
her within a school context, largely because she was speaking out for racial
justice:

> I became an advisory teacher because I was being crushed, absolutely
> crushed [in school]. Once almost dismissed, then every job I applied for
> it got blocked. I don't set out to create trouble, but if they are wanting
> to withdraw black children out of their classes and label them remedial,
> then neither do we have the time or patience to say: 'Let's try it out for
> six months.'

(Balwant)

The 'race' equality route

It would seem that the traditional route to promotion within schools was
difficult, if not impossible, for some yet they were able to benefit by the
move into advisory work, gaining new skills and confidence. Eight of the
ten senior educators achieved promotion through 'non-traditional' routes,
that is by taking posts which were not school-based. On the whole these
posts were Section 11 funded. One worked teaching English as an additional
language (EAL) and seven worked as advisory teachers during the mid-
1980s, at a time when some LEAs developed creative projects to promote
the achievement of black pupils. A number of LEAs also developed initiatives to promote multicultural education in predominantly white schools
through the application of educational support grants (ESGs). These projects
often enabled teachers to engage in curriculum management and adopt
leadership positions in ways that were not possible for their school-based
colleagues; the projects thus provided a springboard for their careers. Black
teachers have been disproportionately represented in Section 11 posts and

a number benefited, as did many of their white colleagues, from the professional development opportunities which certain projects offered.

None of the senior managers who adopted such a route was employed, first and foremost, as an advisory teacher of an academic subject. Although LEA advisory services were expanding and employing subject specific advisory teachers during the mid- and late 1980s to meet the demands of inservice education and training, in every case the individual was employed in a post directly connected to the goal of racial equality.

Lesley, who worked for two years leading a team of advisory teachers, referred to this period as 'the best years of my life'. She outlined the ways in which she felt this experience gave individuals the chance to realise their potential and prepare themselves for more senior positions:

> It gave us the opportunity to explore a lot of ways of working that we probably would not have had, had we been in a school. I think also that the opportunity to work across a range of schools in a sort of advisory, supportive capacity means that you have actually got to be quite alert and you can't allow yourself not to know the answers, or at least know where to go and find the answers when you are asked those questions . . . You had opportunities which they [school-based colleagues] couldn't grasp. The education and 'race' area was probably one of the most difficult areas to work in at any given time, because from the start you were going to have to battle against people who felt it wasn't important.
>
> (Lesley)

Advisory teachers working in the field of 'race' and education not only have to be prepared to take on the intellectual challenge of justifying their work and their goals in education, the work invariably also involves engaging with the emotional reactions that people (both black and white) have to 'race' issues. Managing such reactions may enable individuals to understand the processes of change and is arguably a strong preparation for the challenges of senior posts in education, including those of inspector and headteacher. Ken referred to how he had to learn to 'manage' the white pupils he encountered when he was in primary school, children who held ignorant and sometimes prejudiced attitudes. It is possible that such childhood encounters, learning how to respond in a non-aggressive but positive way, were part of the process of preparation for senior management. A number of senior educators believed they began to acquire the skills of managing people in childhood.

Developing political identities

For a number of black managers, who had previously been isolated at work, the opportunity to work as a member of an all black Section 11 team proved to be a special one. There was still the need for the team to 'prove' their competence as black professionals, but this was no longer an individual struggle:

> It was the first time that I had worked in an environment where all of my colleagues, my immediate colleagues, were black. It was the most invigorating and exhilarating phase of my professional development. It was the contingency of the values, the aspirations, the energy, the enthusiasm and the commitment. And also having the affirmation of blackness, seeing people around you who were highly competent, not just competent but highly competent and highly effective, in all the various ways. It was an incredible spur for you not to let the side down. There was good leadership . . . we really were very privileged.
>
> (Ken)

This 'affirmation of blackness' that Ken highlights was also echoed by other senior educators as a particular feature of their advisory teacher posts. They confirm the experiences of other teachers, notably that of Neelum, who characterises her personal and professional development in terms of her development 'as a black person' (see case study, Chapter 5). Geeta (see Chapter 7) explains how she benefited from working closely with black women colleagues:

> It was a developing politicisation. I came into contact with black teachers in a very close working relationship. It was good to work with these people because we had really good discussions about being black women. You felt some sort of sisterly bond growing up, because you shared such a lot of common experiences. And it was actually the first time that I began to share those experiences and find out that other people had similar experiences.
>
> (Geeta)

Other senior educators confirmed that such work not only enabled them to consolidate and develop their professional skills and develop a political consciousness but also that the experience of working in a team with other black people had a personal and emotional impact:

> It was quite an emotional experience and I mean strongly emotional, because to actually meet other people who had been in similar situations on their own, as black professionals in education, but also to be able to talk about the dimensions of 'race' and education, that too was quite emotional. Quite a bonding took place then, and it is something which has never been repeated in all of my career to the same extent again . . . It took me back to what it might have been like if I was in the Caribbean.
>
> (Yvonne)

It would seem that the opportunities for professional development which the post of advisory teacher offered these senior educators is for all of them a key to their future success. Away from the restrictions which schools imposed, they were free to exploit their talents and skills to the full. For some, the experience of working in this more open environment convinced them that they could never be fully effective at school level; for others, it encouraged them to return to school as headteachers or deputy headteachers. The experience of working closely alongside other black people was also a great liberating experience; 'an affirmation of blackness' not only contributed to a continuing process of politicisation but also gave individuals an enduring source of strength.

Managing as a political activity

Schools are political institutions and managing them is a political activity (Ball 1987). Moreover, the management of education, as these interviews suggest, cannot be separated from the politics of the wider society. The senior educators were generally very aware of the political dimension of their work; in fact, it was this aspect of their work which acted as a strong motivational force. There is some indication from particular individuals, like Frank and Anju (see Chapter 7) that personal ambition was a primary motivating force propelling individuals forward. Nevertheless, the majority of senior educators in this study are also strongly motivated by a sense of justice which is closely related to their understanding of the political situation of black people in a racially structured society. Lesley worked as a senior inspector but returned to school as a headteacher because she believes it is here that she can be most effective:

> As an inspector I knew that I could not sustain long-term relationships with any pupil or teacher or colleague for that matter, because we were working in teams that changed according to the inspection that you were doing. I do believe that a headteacher with a vision of what education can do, and with staff who are supportive of that vision, can actually change pupils' lives.
>
> (Lesley)

Balwant believes there have been tensions between her political goal of achieving greater justice in education, particularly for black children, and personal career progression:

> There are friends who will say: 'I can bring about changes but I do it quietly.' I am afraid I will say: 'Bullshit to that, because there are times when you just have to face everything directly.' You do have to speak the truth about this control phenomenon. If you don't you are selling your soul, and if you like that is the price I have paid, although I am known nationally I could never get promotion. I think this [Local

Education] Authority employed me after knowing my views and they had seen some of the writings.

(Balwant)

While Balwant chooses to speak out on the issues she believes in, Kuldip, as a primary headteacher, does not feel as free to speak his mind on issues relating to racism as when he was an assistant teacher. He feels his isolation as an Asian head among white colleagues has effectively incorporated him and restricted any initiatives he might make beyond the school:

When you are not a head, you are not in this, you can say things, but once you are in it becomes very difficult to say things, because of your colleagues [fellow headteachers], you might offend them. It is very frustrating at times.

(Kuldip)

Yvonne feels that in the changing political context of education she is not best placed as an LEA inspector to bring about the fundamental changes in schools which are needed if racial equality and justice are to be achieved; this responsibility, she argues, now lies most firmly with headteachers and governors. The power of the LEA had been eroded to such an extent that her own influence has to be indirect. Change is best achieved through the local community:

As the LEA erodes, how are you going to actually effect change? And I think the answer is, encourage more black people to put themselves forward on governing bodies. Address meetings and encourage them to be involved. Advise parents on what questions to ask. I'm a resource, anyone in the community knows that they can ask advice. I do a lot of career counselling for black women in particular, through networking. It is a case of trying to work under the system as well as on the system. I think as isolated black people that's the only thing we can do. I would rather be in school as a headteacher. That is where you have influence and power.

(Yvonne)

The two female advisers, Yvonne and Balwant, have to some extent subverted their role and channelled quite a lot of their energies into supporting young black teachers, particularly young black women.

In making an explicit commitment to racial justice, those working as advisers or inspectors may be placed in an ambivalent position. There is a danger that they may be seen first and foremost as black advisers, rather than people with a range of professional and managerial skills; in other words, even at a senior level, they continue to be 'professional ethnics'. Career opportunities may also be tied to the development of a particular political consciousness, to the experiences of being black:

I joined an inspectorial team and I was the only black person on that team, [with] particular responsibilities for equal opportunities . . . They call it accelerated promotion but none of it is in the area in which I would say I am academically qualified. So it is like a continuation of the pastoral phenomenon; it is multicultural by virtue of my racial experience and cultural experience more than my formal study. My credibility is built on my capacity to articulate and analyse who I am.

(Ken)

Ken has attempted to transform the situation from one in which he is seen as a black inspector, responsible for 'race' issues, into one in which he able to set his own agenda for change. This is a satisfactory strategy while he has control, is free to apply for other positions and avoids being labelled. Nevertheless, such a strategy requires constant vigilance if an individual is to leave themselves free to manoeuvre and not be viewed as someone whose only expertise is in matters of 'race'.

Although the headteachers and inspectors in this study adopted a range of techniques and approaches to their work, the one overall aim is the promotion of racial justice, particularly to effect changes in children's lives. They recognise management as a largely political activity, and seek to direct their power to promote particular goals.

A transforming vision

One message that comes through from senior educators' narratives is the responsibility they attach to the power they hold – a responsibility to the black communities. While they are realistic about the limitations of their roles, they retain much of the idealism of their younger and less experienced black colleagues, and express a sense of solidarity with them. An overriding aim is to transform education.

I accepted that the system was not created for me I just happened to be here. If the system is going to do anything for me I have got to make it do it. I have got to go in there and change it from within. I have argued with the more radical of my friends because they don't want any part of the system; they want to drop out of the system in many ways, but they want to attack it from the outside. To me that is confusion, if you are going to attack it, it means you must bother about it enough to want to change it. So it would make more sense to use those energies positively and constructively, and by that I mean getting into the system and getting into some positions of power wherever possible, and then changing it from there.

(Clifton)

One way in which these senior educators effect change is through working closely with the black communities. Nevertheless, relationships between senior black educators and the black communities are likely to be as complex as those between black teachers and their black students: if those in a position of power are to be fully accepted they must demonstrate that they have not lost their 'blackness'.

> What is happening to us as a people? What have we absorbed? What sort of values have we got? We don't even appreciate ourselves. When I stand up to this window now and look out sometimes I see a lot of black children passing this school and going to white-run schools. They won't come here because there is a black headteacher here, and they have got a lot of black kids here. And yet these very same black people, at meetings you hear them say: 'What we want is more black teachers.' But at the end of the day, inwardly, they don't believe that blacks can produce the quality they are clamouring for.
>
> My position is an extremely difficult one. There is a demand that the black community expect of you, you have got to be absolutely perfect; you have got to be able to solve all their problems, you have got to be there to answer all their prayers. At the same time, the white communities out there are watching you make one error and they will shoot you down and they will get you. So I am in a no-win situation; I have got to be better than better.
>
> (Frank)

Frank highlights two contradictory tendencies he has observed within the black communities. First, the internalisation of racist ideology and a reluctance to accept that a black-run school can be as good as a white-run institution, and secondly, the expectation that a single black person in a position of power or authority can somehow miraculously transform the condition of all those black people who seek their help. African-American feminist Pauli Murray (1987) argues that: 'A system of oppression draws much of its strength from the acquiescence of its victims, who have accepted the dominant image of themselves and are paralysed by a sense of helplessness.' Other headteachers and senior managers are not in absolute agreement concerning the internalisation of racist ideology; they are prepared to engage in dialogue with others in the black communities to ensure that people do not become participants in their own oppression.

As a headteacher, Lesley also feels the pressure of tremendously high community expectations, but also recognises this pressure as partially self-generated; it stems from her desire for change and belief in the power of education as a transforming agency:

> Teaching I consider to be a real mission, education does matter. And it matters for young black and white kids in inner-city Manchester, inner-city Birmingham, inner-city London. And I can remember in my first school there were kids who were absolutely spaced out because they had never seen a black teacher before and they certainly didn't have a black teacher who, as one kid said, 'Talked with a Parker Pen voice,' but who could also go into Creole and level with kids. When I went into

the classroom, the first thing I said was: 'I am not here to play, I am here to work and you are here to learn, so if you are going to play you can stand outside. Your parents are working hard in shit houses for you to be here, they are working anti-social hours and you are not going to mess about.' Now that sort of understanding of the potential of education I think has stayed with me and I think that is the most important thing. I understand what parents want, I understand that education is potentially liberating and useful.

(Lesley)

A vision of the transforming power of education, so vividly expressed by this headteacher, is perhaps both the motivating force and the key to career success for each of the senior educators. Although the details of the vision may differ from person to person, all share a commitment to greater justice and equality, to high standards of achievement and to a close working relationship with parents and local communities.

For some, there is also a need to demonstrate professional competence. Anju explains how she had to demonstrate to parents that she was a fully qualified professional, capable of taking responsibility for the education of their children. In this respect, she has had to challenge notions of white superiority among certain parents in the Asian communities which are similar to those Frank has encountered in the African Caribbean communities. Her story also has some parallels with that of Salma, a young primary school teacher in this study, who had to persuade parents that an Asian woman could be a good teacher.

In the beginning, some of the parents, especially your own parents, Asian parents, as they are not used to seeing somebody [Asian] in authority, they wonder. They do wonder if it is the right person to go to. You want to prove to them that you are not there *just* to speak their language. Yes, you are one of them but you have got the qualifications and ability to be a head of school. Fortunately that situation has improved. The parents are [now] much more fluent, they have built up confidence. So the relationship with parents has developed. In inspection, that came out as a model of good practice at the school. I have acquired their respect.

(Anju)

The relationship between black headteachers and the black communities is one based on reciprocity. While headteachers acknowledge a special responsibility to the communities they serve, one head also highlights how the same black community, and particularly the black-run church in which she was brought up, have enabled her to develop both her sense of self-worth and the skills which she now deploys as a headteacher:

I mustn't underestimate the support from the local church community. [It] . . . replaced the extended family and the local community back

home, through things that went on after church . . . They had very high
expectations of me and of many other young people I grew up with.

(Lesley)

The costs of success

A number of senior educators, particularly the women, feel that the personal costs of success have been high, in terms of family and personal
relationships. While this might be true of any senior manager, such costs
may be particularly acute among black senior educators who feel the need
to work harder than their white colleagues in order to be accepted and who
also feel under pressure to 'prove' themselves at all stages in their careers
and especially in senior positions.

Primary headteacher Beryl Gilroy (1976), in her autobiographical account
Black Teacher, makes it clear that she was not free from racism, even when
she achieved a relatively senior position. All the senior educators believed
they had experienced some form of personal or institutionalised racism
while in junior posts but it was upon achieving headship that the most
shocking stories of racism emerged. Given the relatively low numbers of
black people in senior positions in schools, it is perhaps not surprising that
black headteachers might be 'high profile' within their local communities,
attracting media attention. Nevertheless, one expressed concern about the
way in which some of her actions had been 'leaked' to the press by a
member of her staff team and wondered whether a white head would have
been treated in quite the same way.

Two primary headteachers told what can only be described as horror
stories about events following their appointments. Difficulties began for the
first with an anonymous and intimidating phone call the evening after he
was appointed. By the time he took up the headship the teachers at the
school had destroyed most of the school records, removed plugs from electrical appliances and colluded with the secretary and caretaker to have keys
cut to give them independent access to the building and head's office. The
second headteacher faced a hostile campaign by her teaching staff which
included a racist note on her desk, official complaints to teachers' unions
and an assembly on the theme *Ten Little Niggers.* The media became involved
and she was subject to public attack in local and national newspapers but
was unable to secure support from either her LEA or her union. She took
her case to court claiming serious defamation of character and eventually
accepted an out-of-court settlement. She believes the case permanently
damaged her career; when she made enquiries about the headship of a
larger school she was told by an LEA adviser that she should not apply:

She said: 'Management potential, have you got proven management
potential?' And I said: 'I have been a headteacher for nine years!' And

she said: 'Oh well, there is no smoke without fire, don't forget what happened to you when you were in the newspapers.'

(Pauline)

Just as ethnographic research suggests that there is a high degree of conflict between many white teachers and their black pupils, irrespective of those teachers' stated commitment to equality (Gillborn 1990; Wright 1992; Connolly 1995), so it would seem that black managers may experience greater resistance from their white colleagues, even from those who are 'liberal or "anti-racist"':

> There are large numbers of white people, even white people who are anti-racist or liberal, who find it difficult to be managed by a black person. A lot of the time they don't even realise that is happening ... there is a kind of ambivalence whilst you are dealing with them. There are umpteen ways where you as a manager can be undermined, so it is recognising the different guises and forms undermining can take. One of the most common ones is where decisions are not necessarily challenged but not implemented fully or properly. To what extent do you as a manager divert energy in order to get a full compliance? I do have a personal commitment to collaborative and more participative ways of working. As a manager there is a tension between that and time, and the ability to reach a decision, especially in this context of volatile change. If you allow time for consultation and things run slowly then you can't decide: black man can't decide, can't manage, too slow and incompetent, so you are going to lose either way.

(Ken)

The senior managers' narratives more commonly reflected the kind of non-compliance which Ken expressed than the overt hostility experienced by the two primary heads on taking up their positions. Whereas it is relatively easy to monitor and report on overt racist actions, it is much more difficult to find ways of assessing or challenging indirect actions, such as non-compliance or non-cooperation.

Both Ken and Clifton noted the dangers of being stereotyped as an aggressive black male. Throughout Clifton's narrative he emphasised the positive, and his sense of satisfaction in his work. As he finished he was anxious to stress that he had rather underplayed the racism he had encountered: 'I know that I have missed out aspects of my life where racism has played a major part, but if I was to begin to itemise I would never finish.' Both sought to speculate on how their experiences as senior managers differed from those of black women:

> I can't honestly say that I comprehend what it must be like for women managers. So when there are responses to my line manager, I find myself rehearsing in my mind: 'Are they taking this stance because she

is a woman? Is it because she is black? Is it because she is a black woman? Are there layers of this?' Because at times I am quite taken aback at things that are said and the manner in which they are said . . . it is interesting how men respond to a woman being directive, and it is almost as if they feel there is a right not to accept it.

(Ken)

Clifton argued that black men in senior management face very different barriers from black women because they were more likely to be feared by white men in positions of influence. He suggested that black women in senior positions were often considered as a lesser threat by white men. Nevertheless, he felt that many white female senior managers might not so readily accept black women in positions of authority since to do so would require a changing of priorities and agenda. The root difficulty, as stressed in many narratives, is that of accepting black people as professionals, with a particular expertise and authority:

What you find very often is that there is almost this *surprise* on their part that you can do something; that you are educationally-minded, that you can teach, and that you do know your business about education, how to monitor and evaluate progress, how to measure attainment, how to assess good quality.

(Clifton)

Managing self and others

Walker (1993), in her study of black women in educational management, highlights the stress and isolation which these women experience; the senior educators' narratives suggest that this stress and isolation is likely to be more acute in senior positions and may be encountered by men as well as women. The women in this study explained that they needed to be in touch with other black women managers who understood both their professional responsibilities and their particular personal experiences as black women. They had arrived at a point in their careers where the well-developed networks of black colleagues which they had built up over the years no longer served them in the same way as parallel networks might continue to serve white female colleagues; many found themselves alone, without any other black women in a similar post within their LEA.

It gets lonelier the further you get nearer the top. I don't have the same networking as I used to. It's important I think to know black people in similar positions. I still keep in contact with black women friends on a very regular basis, and we can still talk about those issues, but as part of a senior team, there isn't the same network. It is not the same talking about those issues to your white colleagues, certainly not. And to some extent it is not part of their agenda, your personal experience, that is not part of their agenda. And that is not to paint an unsympathetic view of those senior white colleagues.

(Geeta)

Many of the feelings encountered earlier in their careers were re-occurring in a senior position: isolation, invisibility, the responsibility of being the first or only black woman in post, being the outsider. Such feelings and experiences increased the burden of responsibilities on the individual. Yet these women did not wish to speak on behalf of the whole black community, or all black women or even all black teachers.

Sometimes I feel I have an enormous weight on my shoulders because: 'Gosh, you are a black person who has made it to senior management. Right, forge ahead!' As if this is the only one banner you have got to carry. I mean, one of my responsibilities is equal opportunities, but by God, that is not my only responsibility. I find that an enormous burden sometimes that people are saying: 'Senior position in the school, we can really get things done.'

(Geeta)

Different styles of school management are required if this isolation and the unreasonable burden of 'black representative voice' is to be avoided. It is only where more democratic forms of management are developed, with an emphasis on cooperation and negotiation, rather than confrontation that black teachers generally will have an opportunity to make an input, and reduce this pressure on the few black heads and deputies that exist. High expectations from within black communities are matched by those of black colleagues who, while expressing pride and support for the black colleague who has 'made it', are also hoping for real change.

There are, however, situations encountered by black women in senior management which will be familiar to many white female educators:

How many times do we still go and find ourselves invisible? I went to the launch of TVEI [Technical and Vocational Education Initiative] a year or so ago and one of the first things he [the speaker] said was: 'We emphasise the importance of equal opportunities and not just in terms of gender. I am looking round and I notice there aren't any black teachers.' And I thought: 'Hold on a moment! I am sitting on the bloody front row, what is he on about?' . . . I am always struck when I go to meetings and they are all men in grey suits, there is never a black face, or rarely a black face, unless it is someone from multicultural support, not very many women, and often the women are there next to their male heads. My heart always sinks . . . I feel an outsider. There I am in a senior position and I still feel isolated.

(Geeta)

Geeta's expression of isolation was echoed by all the senior educators, but
most strongly by the women in the sample. In response to this situation,
some had set up networks; these had not developed gradually through a
'natural' process but had been carefully planned. The impetus to organise in
this way was also a result of reading the works of black feminist writers,
including African-American novelists:

> I found that I had one or two situations where I had to challenge
> attitudes . . . So wanting to network with a women's group came as
> a result of that. And of course there was quite a lot of feminist liter-
> ature coming out at the time, and black women writers had come
> into the fore . . . it made me see how important it [networking] was,
> because of course black women's experiences were not white women's
> experiences.
>
> (Yvonne)

Local networks were useful but did not meet all the professional needs of
those women in very senior positions; black women headteachers had had
to look nationally to find others in their position. They felt they experienced
greater isolation than their black male colleagues:

> It is easier for black men to get into the club than it is for black women
> to get into the club. We don't go to the cricket and we don't drink, it
> is that sort of thing. I know that there are interests that they share that
> we, the black women, don't necessarily share. I know two black male
> heads who actually go and play chess and go to cricket with white
> colleagues . . . The black women heads that I know, our relationships
> are very different, much more supportive, much more questioning the
> educational objective of any work we are doing, as opposed to socialising
> . . . We ask: 'What have you done in terms of policies here? Can I have
> a copy?'
>
> (Lesley)

Unlike black men, who had some access to existing (male) networks, black
women found they had to consciously develop their own special support
systems with clear professional goals.

'Race' and gender would appear to have acted together to exclude black
women in senior management positions from the support networks which
sustain many of their white and male colleagues. It is not entirely clear why
black women should find it more difficult to join existing (white) female
networks, than black male colleagues who have become part of existing
men's networks. It may be because women tend to network on a different
basis, meeting, for example, for a meal rather than through a sports club;
such networks might therefore be, albeit unintentionally, more private and
exclusive. Another reason why heads such as Lesley do not find themselves
part of an established network of local headteachers is their 'untraditional'
routes to headship. Many of her white female colleagues will have begun

to develop their networks when they were heads of department or deputy heads together, but 'non-traditional' career paths may have excluded many black senior managers from such networks.

The senior educators recognised that a more cooperative style of management might empower others similarly positioned and include those voices which would otherwise not be heard. Nevertheless, because black people were often not recognised as professionals or as people who might appropriately hold leadership positions, it was sometimes more difficult to achieve their goals using their preferred styles. There is some evidence to suggest that the senior black educators were sometimes placed in confrontational situations not of their own making, and that they were sometimes at the centre of conflicts which had no easy solution.

Futures

Given the considerable challenges facing black managers it seems important to establish whether they feel that the rewards of the job compensate for some of the difficulties and whether they are optimistic about the future, either at a personal level or in terms of achieving their wider goals of justice and equality.

Two of the older headteachers were looking forward to their retirement, but even at that stage one had deep concerns about the rights of black people in Britain and her own future security:

> On the whole I am pessimistic for the future of black people in Britain. ... People like me, I still worry, will they give me my pension? But young people what can they get out of Britain? No jobs, differences of opinion in families, no role models, marriages breaking down between educated people every now and then, and they are still putting things under the carpets. And the white person is saying: 'Go to hell, it is your problem, I don't want to know ...' There was a time when I wanted to go into the advisory field, develop a wider horizon so that I could help our people more. I don't want to do anything else, I am tired. The challenges, the conflicts, the battering, it has killed me.
>
> (Anju)

For younger headteachers, recent changes in education meant there was no obvious career structure; advisory or inspectorial posts no longer offered an attractive alternative.

> All those options that I considered feasible five years ago are no longer there. I must admit that to some degree it has worried me. But it has forced me to look at my situation in a different way. I can see myself now for the next few years perhaps remaining as head of this school,

but being a head of a different sort. I can also see myself having fingers
in different pies in education, perhaps lecturing more.

(Clifton)

I will never be a head for seventy years, do you know what I mean?
[*Laughing*] I will probably go off and work with children but in a very
different way. I think it's important though for me to keep my links
between myself and the communities. It may be the way to do it is to
actually get back into working through the community and empower-
ing parents and the young people to raise questions, to make demands
and to make the schools and institutions work for the communities.

(Lesley)

Both these headteachers saw themselves working more closely in partnership with local communities, and acting on community priorities to transform schools. This was not expressed as a vague dream or hope but in the
belief that participation in community and decision-making would empower
both students and their parents.

One senior inspector had experienced so much change that he found it
difficult to anticipate the future. He stressed the continuing vulnerability of
senior black colleagues:

'We lost a lot of black staff in the restructuring exercise, at least four
staff went, and took premature retirement or voluntary severance
because they were facing potential redundancy . . . even at this tier black
people are much more vulnerable.'

(Ken)

He was emphatic that if he had his time again he would not go into teaching, because he is so angry at what has happened:

It is very difficult to convey the sense of betrayal I feel . . . This is not
to say that I am averse to change; I am averse to the direction of the
change. I actually believe that there is much about what has happened
in education which is dangerous and, I think, potentially destructive, if
not counterproductive. There are some things which I think are excel-
lent like the shift towards more precision in planning, and the elevation
of teacher assessments as part of the professional bread and butter. But
I think those could have been achieved in other ways . . . I think propelling the management of schooling into the market ethos and the
competition between institutions is not likely to generate the kind of
improvement in standards that has been talked about. And I find that
very difficult to take.

(Ken)

He suggested he might have better served the cause of racial justice and the
black communities by using existing legislation to bring about change:

I think perhaps I could have achieved more by being a lawyer, applying myself to education law, and taking test cases earlier under the race discrimination and sex discrimination laws. If you talk about the disproportionate number of children who were sent to schools for the educationally subnormal, where were the court cases? And that would have been the response in the [United] States.

(Ken)

Summary

The majority of senior educators have followed untraditional, possibly 'high-risk' career routes, but many believe the alternative would have been stagnation or being crushed within the confines of particular schools. The benefits of non-traditional routes were that they provided management and leadership opportunities which many school-based teachers do not encounter at the same stage in their careers. The challenge for those who wished to return to schools was in finding individual heads or governing bodies who valued this breadth of experience.

All the senior educators were conscious of structural racism in Britain and all, in different ways, have sought to challenge racism in the education service and in society more broadly. All share a belief in the potential liberating power of education. Despite changes in education which leave a number feeling disillusioned, most manage to retain some hope for the future. One inspector expressed it in terms of the ebb and flow of ideas and progress, and believed strongly that the tide would turn yet again.

Part three _____

Daring to teach

To teach or not to teach?: sixth-form students' viewpoints

Introduction

Given the underrepresentation of black and ethnic minorities within teaching it seems important to explore the attitudes of young people from these communities to teaching, attitudes which are likely to be influenced by their own experiences of schooling and their perceptions of their own teachers. When young black and ethnic minority people decide not to pursue teaching, is this because teaching is perceived as unattractive in itself, or is it because they are aware of a range of other more interesting options?

This chapter is based on data collected from a series of interviews with three groups of students, who were following A-level courses in a school sixth form, a sixth-form college and a further education college. All hoped to follow a traditional route into higher education. Each group included young people from a range of cultural backgrounds, including students from African, African Caribbean and Asian families. All the groups were mixed, with a total of six female and 11 male participants. Two were recent migrants to Britain, the rest had completed all of their schooling in this country. Most were from working-class backgrounds, with parents employed in factories, as care assistants or unemployed. A small minority had parents with professional backgrounds, one of these a lecturer in further education. The intention was to explore their experiences of schooling, their attitudes to higher education and their perceptions of their futures, in particular their ideas about work and careers.

Own schooling

Most students attended schools where the majority of the pupils were from black and ethnic minority communities. All had been successful at school, gaining a substantial number of GCSEs at higher grades. Although many felt a sense of achievement and said they had many happy memories of school, particularly primary school, most were also critical of their schooling, high-lighting the low expectations of teachers and lack of access to examination classes.

> The people who were doing high level maths were all boys and were actually in the centre of the room. Whereas I was sitting in the corner with a group of girls who were doing intermediate. I did the higher level work, but I found I didn't get the attention. I would have to go to the teacher rather than the teacher come to me.
>
> (Nurida)

For those students who felt that their teachers were underestimating their potential, there seemed no alternative than to work hard and insist that they were given help. Few of their parents were in a financial position to opt for extra paid tuition, although one family took this route. Some, unfamiliar with the British education system, may not have been aware that their children might have been missing out in any way. It was not simply a question of parents failing to comprehend what was happening at school. A number of students clearly felt that teachers were quite ignorant about their home backgrounds and that this placed barriers between their teachers and parents, particularly at primary school. The students believed that their feelings about teachers' levels of awareness were shared quite widely in the community; one group referred to the appointment of a white teacher to a primary school home liaison post. This appointment and local parents' anger attracted national media attention:

> There was a lot of controversy when a teacher from my old primary school was given a post including culture and some interpretation. The Asian community was disgusted because she was white and she couldn't speak the languages and therefore an Asian or black should have got the job.
>
> (Nazir)

Although a number of students felt that at A level some attempt was made to examine the Eurocentric nature of the curriculum in subjects like history, they were very critical that there was little attempt to do this for younger pupils. They argued that this was as damaging to white children as to them-selves and that white children would have fewer opportunities to learn about different cultures or perspectives at home and less incentive to under-take independent research:

> We didn't learn anything about Asian or African history; it was all white history. The only thing that we did do was slavery, which encour-ages people to take pity on the slaves and believe there was nothing they could do. We did civil rights and Martin Luther King, but even that was taken from a white perspective. I think that causes the white

students to have particular opinions of how they see other students. It forces a lot of stereotypes.

(Satnam)

Two students who both attended predominantly white schools, felt they had been singled out as bright black children and given considerable encouragement, largely because they challenged the prevailing teacher stereotypes. Despite these generally positive experiences of school, they were both critical of what one described as the 'gaps' in her education:

> I feel a bit angry about history in particular because I think it is so unfair just to teach about white Britain, or white America. Just think what I could have learnt. They should try and do something for the children, not just for black children but for white children. White children go through school and they are never taught anything different, they always think that whites are supreme.

(Naomi)

An isolated successful African Caribbean student, who received praise and favourable treatment from teachers, explained how he was consequently subject to racist taunts throughout his schooling:

> I was popular with the teachers, but then again I was unpopular with all the kids. I felt pretty left out because I was like the teacher's pet. It was the usual racist names like 'Golly' and all that about the 'jam jar', and that went on through infant school, to the beginning of secondary school. If it got really bad I would tell the teacher and they would have a word with the parents and then they would say I was making too much fuss. I think you have got to grin and bear it. Kids are still going to do it regardless of what the parents say. When black children are clever, it is seen as a novelty; when white children are clever, it is seen as normal.

(Tom)

This type of bullying and racial harassment was not confined to school. An Asian student who moved home a number of times recalled how, when living on largely white housing estates in Luton, his family had been subject to racist harassment from neighbours. Each time the problem was compounded as he encountered similar harassment at a new school. These experiences allowed him to develop prejudiced views about other communities which were eventually challenged when he went to a Catholic secondary school. The school's emphasis on equality had a positive impact on pupil culture:

> They always brought equal opportunities in, it was sort of imprinted on you. You were taught about it really well and I was glad I went to that school. It really was a melting pot school, there were loads of people there, blacks, whites, Vietnamese, the lot. I learnt a lot about other

people's cultures and I am really glad about that. We had a lot of visits from priests and many of them were black, and it changed your views.

(Arun)

Overall, the accounts of these students, who had all survived the negative experiences they recounted, confirm many of the research findings on the educational experiences of black and ethnic minority pupils, suggesting that racial harassment can be a regular occurrence for some (Gillborn 1990; Wright 1992; Connolly 1995) and that despite the positive stereotypes of South Asian pupils held by a number of teachers (Mac an Ghaill 1988, 1989; Gillborn 1990) they may be inappropriately placed in classes or excluded from certain activities (Wright 1992; Troyna and Siraj-Blatchford 1993). These students' accounts suggest that these findings apply not only to low achievers but also to a number of high achievers. They also indicate that the students themselves are very much aware of the disadvantages and low teacher expectations they face and that they are ready to challenge such injustices.

Career influences and future plans

One particular issue about which students were critical was the level of careers guidance offered to them at the time of GCSE option choices. Schools which made connections between GCSE options and future career and higher education opportunities were praised, but a number of the students, particularly those who believed their teachers had low expectations of them, reported that little advice was available. This is a potentially critical time for many pupils when allocation to certain sets and selection of particular subjects can mean that certain examinations or career paths are closed.

All but one of the students interviewed were certain they wished to enter higher education, with those at the further education college having looked most closely at possible degree courses. About one-third of the students had a firm career goal or ambition, a similar proportion had more tentative ideas and the remaining third were as yet undecided. Architecture, dentistry, engineering, industrial design, law, marketing, performing arts, the police and social services were among the options they were considering. There was no clear differentiation by gender, with girls considering dentistry, the performing arts, the police force, law, social services or 'something scientific', as possible career avenues.

Students felt that the formal careers guidance they had received at school or college had made little positive impact, although it was clear that this varied considerably between institutions, from a brief interview with a careers officer to a regular timetabled slot. They saw careers advice aimed more or less exclusively at those who did not wish to enter higher education. Most students who had formulated a clear idea of their future plans seemed to have taken the initiative, sought information from libraries and other sources and made their own appointments with careers advisers. One student, who hoped to study to become a solicitor, and then hopefully a barrister, reported that teachers in his school appeared to have limited expectations of their pupils:

> At school there wasn't really much, there was careers advice, it was just once a year. It was just the basic jobs, like building and construction, quite a few science jobs, but no one really pushed you into careers like management. It was just a case of finding out the information for yourself. I've found out by going to careers conventions, to the careers office myself, finding teachers, asking friends and parents.
>
> (Tom)

Most students emphasised the important role that their parents and other family members were playing in helping them make decisions about their futures, but although a few stressed the practical advice and contacts that families provided, most students talked about the general encouragement that they received:

> My mum has been a great help, she hasn't pressured me or anything, she just says, 'Go the way you feel.' Mum works in a surgery, she is a practice manager, so that's why I'm interested in medicine-related careers a bit more.
>
> (Arun)

Each group of students discussed whether parents were likely to have different expectations of their daughters than of their sons. While a number of students acknowledged that their parents shared some commonly held notions that certain careers were more appropriate for one sex than the other, none of the girls felt their parents' attitudes would prevent them from following the career of their choice:

> In some ways my dad has ideas about what is suitable for a girl. If I said to him, 'I want to do engineering,' he would be a bit reluctant. At the end of the day, it is my decision. I am sure I would put up a good fight and say that I want to do it. And in the end I am sure he would come through.
>
> (Nurida)

> All my parents are concerned about is me getting a good education, getting somewhere in life.
>
> (Fiaz)

Some of the boys, however, did not think that it would be that simple and noted how many Asian parents had a vested interest in the education of boys who they expected to support them in their old age, whereas girls would marry into another family. They reflected on the experiences of their sisters and female cousins, which clearly varied from family to family.

My father hasn't really pushed my sister into education much. He would have liked her to do A levels; she is at O level standard. He encouraged her into getting a job and she is doing quite well now, but I don't think he would have pushed her into higher education as much as he is pushing me.

(Nazir)

There is a thing about tradition in our family. Asian girls [are expected to] stay at home, because if they go away to university or poly[technic] they will start mixing with boys. I think that is the distinction between letting boys go and letting girls go. They are more careful . . . I think now this is breaking down but it's still quite common.

(Abdul)

While teachers have sometimes held low expectations of Asian girls, assuming that their futures will be restricted by early marriage and domestic responsibilities (Shepherd 1987; Wright 1992) and these stereotypes have perhaps been most persistent in relation to Muslim girls, research among parents presents a mixed and possibly changing picture. Interviews with young Muslim women found that around one-third of their parents were opposed to their entering higher education (Brah and Shaw 1993) yet interviews with Muslim mothers (Osler and Hussain 1995) found that they showed a high commitment to their daughters' education, expecting their daughters to gain qualifications and take up opportunities which they themselves had not had.

A number of students were conscious of their parents' often difficult experiences of migration, and wished to achieve something in terms of education and a career partly for their parents' sake:

They have come to Britain and they wanted to be successful, and they want their children to do better than they have. My dad had his own business and he works as an engineer now. All my dad's qualifications in Kenya mean nothing here and he said: 'I don't want the same thing to happen to my kids. I want them to do better.' It is very important to them.

(Meena)

Meena's comments echo those of the teachers in this study who remain conscious of their parents' struggles and their ambition for their children 'to do better'. Meena wanted to become a solicitor but was one of a few who was ready to consider teaching as an alternative if she did not achieve her first choice of career. A number of students agreed that it is far easier for many Asian students whose parents were unfamiliar with the British education system to gain their parents' support for traditional courses and careers than for new types of career which are less understood.

My father is rather old-fashioned. He says, 'What is business studies? It is nothing really, what you want to do is accounting.' He keeps on giving me these statistics about accountants: 'If you were to become a chartered accountant you get to earn this amount of money.' He doesn't know what business studies is really; he wants me to do more traditional subjects.

(Makhan)

My sister is a freelance designer; if you want to do something different they all kind of attack you at the same time and so you are put in a difficult position. I think it depends on the individual and what sort of family you have got. My family are great because whatever I want they will back me up.

(Meena)

The students discussed whether they felt any particular responsibility towards their own communities, or towards society in general, and whether this might have any impact on their career choice. It was clear that for a number of the sixth-formers this was an important issue which encouraged them to consider particular careers:

That is one of the reasons why I was interested in architecture, I would have liked to go back home [to Zimbabwe] and maybe help with building. I can't say I really need to give something back because I haven't been living in that country for over 10 years; I just think it is something I feel I have to do.

(Godfrey)

When I think I would like to help the community, I don't want to particularly help the Asians only. I don't want to distinguish one group; I feel that is wrong. I feel that would be racist of me and having double standards.

(Makhan)

I think it is important for myself to work with black people. I feel I would understand the black people better and it's as simple as that. I know where they are coming from; it's the same culture. A lot of black people and Asian people are not represented.

(Naomi)

Students held differing views on whether money was a critical factor in selecting a future career:

I think money is really important, because society influences in that way, we live in a really materialist world anyway. For example, when I was at nursery school you had to behave yourself and if you did something good the teacher gave you sweets, you get rewards for it. And that is like that all the way through the education system; if you behave yourself you are rewarded.

(Meena)

Money isn't important to me because my first choice is the creative arts and you get peanuts for doing that. One minute you could be in a job and getting paid loads and the next you are unemployed. I am doing it because it is something I enjoy.

(Laura)

One student felt he had an obligation to his family to secure a well-paid job, so that he could offer practical support to his parents:

Status and pay are really important to me because my parents work in factories you see. All my relatives are basically the same, they are working class really, and I feel I should do better for my parents because they work really hard.

(Deepak)

Career choice, identities and citizenship

Each group of sixth-form students was asked to think about their futures in broad terms and a number discussed whether they saw their futures in Britain or in other parts of the world. In the school group, this developed into a debate about black identities and black experience, which may be important issues in making decisions about futures and careers:

I think there is a common black identity and I think that one of the reasons why sometimes the Afro-Caribbean community and Asian community seem to be split is because, I might be wrong and this might sound racist, but white people try to make that sort of distinction in their minds because in their eyes you are either this or that. For me, really there is not that much difference. I think I have been fortunate because I have experienced the white culture, I have also experienced black African culture, the Caribbean and Asian cultures. So I can look at it and compare all of them. A lot of the things that I see and a lot of the things that I hear my [Asian] friends talking about – about their parents, about their background back home – is the same for me.

(Godfrey)

Other students, particularly boys, wished to emphasise their religious identity as Muslims:

There are similarities between people's behaviour and attitudes, but when it comes to religion the two may diverge. I think being a Muslim, Asian, being Pakistani, helps to make me as a person. At the time of the cricket a lot of people were asking, 'Why are you supporting Pakistan when you were born in England?' I think that is wrong. Everyone has their own identity, everyone has their own feeling. Both my parents come from Pakistan, and that influence is reflected in me. It makes you as a person.

(Abdul)

Others saw identity as something which is hybrid; for them, identity is not either/or but both/and. Nevertheless, although identity is something which should be self-defined, racist attitudes could act to limit personal choice:

I see myself as an Asian, but I think people expect contradictory things of you. There are times when you do go for the British side of things, but it's just a fact that you are both an Asian and born in Britain. I would be happy with the term 'British Asian,' but a lot of people find that off-putting. And a lot of people disagree with it and think that if you are Asian you are not British at all.

(Fiaz)

I was born here and I have the right to be a British citizen, even though I am Asian. I don't think that should have any bearing on you what-soever, but it does come into it in a lot of things like jobs. I know a lot of people who are Asian and born here in Britain, have gone to inter-views, and on their CV it says 'Nationality – British', and yet they are asked their country of origin.

(Nurida)

That's why I say you can't have it both ways, not because you don't deserve those rights that everybody else has, but that because you will never get them, because of the colour of your skin. You should but you won't. You are not really a British citizen because you don't have exactly the same rights as a white British citizen.

(Yousuf)

Yousuf's reluctance to accept a hybrid or multiple identity is based on his experiences of racism and social exclusion. His viewpoints echo those of other students from various parts of Europe from ethnic and linguistic minorities who feel unable to identify with their legal, national citizenship (Osler and Starkey 1996) largely because they are not able to enjoy their citizenship rights on the basis of equality. The two girls, Nurida and Fiaz, recognise them-selves as having multiple identities; the relative emphasis of a particular identity appears to depend very much on context. The choice is not com-pletely open; the perceptions of others can restrict an individual's choice. These students' range of perceptions concerning identity and nationality correspond closely to those of the young black Londoners in Alexander's (1996) study. They suggest an urgent need to address issues of citizenship and identities in schools, and encourage a much broader, inclusive under-standing of national citizenship, particularly with students from majority communities.

The majority of students saw their futures in Britain, despite the fact that many held an emotional attachment to their parents' or grandparents' countries of origin:

> I would like to go to Jamaica and to Italy to find the roots of my family. But I was brought up here and I don't know any other culture so I think it's likely that I'll stay here.
>
> (Laura)

> Definitely in England is where my future lies; my education has been here and my upbringing. Most of my family are based here and so that is where my future is. I think you have got to be in touch with traditional beliefs and everything. You shouldn't forget those traditional values, even if you don't believe in them.
>
> (Meena)

Some students, like the teachers in this study, felt that their experiences or their families' experiences of migration gave them broader horizons, or that they would be willing to travel to secure interesting jobs:

> I might stay here but I would consider Europe if I go into something where there are international opportunities.
>
> (Fiaz)

> I think living all over the world is in my blood; I can't stay in one place for long. I don't mind if my future is back in Bangladesh, but I would prefer it to be Germany.
>
> (Ahmed)

> I think I will take a radical view that I am going to use this country as this country has used other countries. I am going to take what I can, but I may go off to Pakistan at the end of the day.
>
> (Abdul)

Selecting the right university

While black and ethnic minority British students have long been under-represented in traditional universities, it was only in 1989–90 that for the first time higher education admissions statistics offered an analysis by ethnic group, revealing that South Asians formed a higher proportion of admissions than they do of the relevant age group and that African Caribbeans form about the same proportion of admissions as of the population (Jones 1993). Statistics published by the DfE record that in 1992 10.5 per cent of first-year undergraduate students enrolling in English higher education institutions were from black and ethnic minorities; the figure for 1991 enrolments was 11.7 per cent (DfE 1994). Yet ethnic minorities form only some 8 per cent of the population in the age group from which most higher education students are drawn.

Nevertheless, while these figures indicate a higher participation rate in higher education among black and ethnic minority communities than white, they do not reveal whether black and ethnic minority students are gaining access to the highly selective high status courses or institutions. Black and ethnic minority students remain better represented at former polytechnics and other higher education institutions where in 1992 they formed 11 per cent of first-year undergraduate student enrolments, than at the traditional universities, when in the same year they made up just 8.5 per cent of first-year undergraduate students. The statistics also reveal that among Chinese and African Caribbean students, men and women are entering university in approximately equal numbers but that in all other communities, including white, female students are outnumbered by males. This differential is most striking amongst Bangladeshi students where men outnumber women by 2:1.

The A level students in this study differed in their attitudes to different types of institution: some felt that black and ethnic minority students were more likely to be comfortable in a university where such students were better represented among the student population, and where the locality also reflected a range of minority communities, whereas others argued that for them an important aspect of higher education was mixing with a range of people from beyond their own communities.

> Many universities are very white institutions so I have deliberately chosen to try and stay as close to home as I can, because of that.
>
> (Godfrey)

> I would like to go away. Somewhere that has got a good balance of all races. I suppose I would find it a little daunting if there were a minority of Asians, but I think that would give me more confidence in proving myself. In this day and age, you have to get along with people in any situation.
>
> (Fiaz)

> I talked to my law tutor about it and she recommended some good courses at poly[technic]s and universities. Then I decided it would be more interesting going to poly[technic] than to university. I know it sounds racist, but I have always just felt that universities tend to be white middle class; I never really felt I would be comfortable there.
>
> (Tom)

In deciding to study away from home students were not only aware of the need to select an institution and locality where they would feel 'comfortable', they also considered threats to their physical security, posed by a high level of racist violence in society (Gordon 1986; CRE 1987; Amin and Richardson 1994).

I think it would make me feel much more secure if there are other Asians and people like me. Racist attacks worry me, I have got a fear of it. It is something that you hope never happens to you, so you try to block it out.

(Deepak)

That sixth-formers should be particularly conscious of this issue is perhaps not surprising: in December 1994 the National Union of Students launched a 24-hour hotline to tackle growing harassment and intimidation of students by far-Right groups in response to a growing number of racial attacks on school children and college students in or near school and college premises (Klein 1995).

The St George's Medical School case (CRE 1988b) revealed that a respected institution of higher education had been systematically discriminating against ethnic minority and female students in its admission procedures. While all the sixth-formers were conscious of particular difficulties that might be encountered by ethnic minority students planning to enter higher education and some chose their university taking such factors into account, others were determined that neither the fear nor reality of institutionalised racism would allow cause them to restrict their options:

I am just going for the best education I can get. But I have heard tales of people trying to get into Oxford and Cambridge, they have been stopped because of their colour. But I wouldn't think twice about applying. If I am going to get there, I will get there. I am not going to let them get me down.

(Arun)

Perceptions of teachers and teaching as a career

Despite students' criticisms of their own schooling and in particular the low expectations and lack of awareness among teachers of their students' family cultures, most believed they had been well taught and many were sympathetic to the difficulties that they observed teachers to face. However, it was teachers' own comments about the status of teaching, and their explicit criticisms of the conditions under which they worked which discouraged many sixth-formers from considering teaching as a career:

I think we are put off from when we start school because all the teachers say, 'Teaching is rubbish. I wouldn't become a teacher because it is boring.' That is why I think people are reluctant to take it up. If the teachers are saying it is rubbish, and they have gone through the whole system, then there is not much hope for you.

(Abdul)

This type of reaction on the part of teachers, and an expression of their low morale was confirmed by a teacher who noted my tape recorder and asked,

'Are you going to interview somebody?' When I explained I was going to talk to sixth-formers about their attitudes to teaching, he responded: 'Well, I can tell you what I think about it. I wouldn't do it again.' This expression of low morale which is often reported as commonplace in the teaching profession, was not something which was widely echoed amongst the black teachers in this study. By contrast, they retained considerable enthusiasm and even idealism about their work, while acknowledging the difficult conditions. Negative attitudes towards work expressed by (white) teachers might nevertheless have a disproportionate effect on potential black recruits into teaching. Given the underrepresentation of black people within teaching, black and ethnic minority students are generally less likely than white students to have teachers among their own families and communities. They are consequently less likely to encounter someone beyond their school who might encourage them to see the positive aspects of teaching as a career.

Reservations about teaching focused on questions of pupil discipline, low status, teacher stress, workload, low pay and the feelings of individuals that they lacked the particular qualities that teaching requires:

> It's just that I haven't got the patience to teach. Discipline and things like that would bother me.
>
> (Nurida)

> Being educated in a school like this, teachers get a lot of stick from the students. I wouldn't go and teach, no way, that is the last thing I would do. I don't want a job which is as stressful as teaching.
>
> (Makhan)

Some students felt that teachers were not necessarily badly paid, and others argued that although they might get high levels of personal satisfaction from their work, it was their low status in society that caused them to discourage their students from teaching:

> When you push that idea [of taking up teaching] to them they say, 'Don't do it, do something else, do something worthwhile.' I think they are saying that because the pay is not so good, but I think they are getting satisfaction doing the job.
>
> (Yousuf)

One student felt the biggest barrier to becoming a teacher was that it might prevent her from being true to her black identity and culture:

> The 'race' issue comes into it because if I was to teach secondary or junior school, I would want to teach them something about black history. Why teach British history and not include anything about black people? Black teachers may have to sell themselves short, maybe they will have to agree with certain things that the textbooks are saying. And they will have knowledge that they won't be able to put across.
>
> (Naomi)

Concerns such as these are likely to be felt by students from ethnic minority communities while schools continue to present a narrow, anglocentric curriculum. They may contribute to the relatively low take-up of teacher education places amongst black and ethnic minority students. A prescriptive, content-laden National Curriculum, which provides teachers with few opportunities for school-based curriculum development, will only exacerbate such concerns.

Some students felt that they were not in a position to make an objective assessment of teaching as a future career while they were still at school themselves and argued that once they had graduated they might feel quite differently. It is perhaps unsurprising that students were able to identify some of the more difficult aspects of teaching and to make assessments about its appropriateness in ways they were unable to do for other careers about which they had little first-hand experience. On the positive side, teachers were respected by their parents and communities:

> My mum sees it as a success, a number of my uncles are teachers in Pakistan. That is the reason why she jokingly forbids it. Everybody in Pakistan is a teacher and she wants us to be something different.
>
> (Abdul)

> My mum used to do childminding and I used to help her. I got to know the children very well and their parents thought I had a good relationship with them. A lot of them said to me that they thought I would make a good primary teacher, as did my mum.
>
> (Nurida)

Only two of the boys admitted any interest in teaching, but a number of the girls saw it as a possible career path, although not their first choice. These young women recalled the positive experiences of their own schooling and a fondness and respect for some of their own teachers:

> It would be an option for me if things didn't work out for the legal profession. From a very young age when you are in nursery you look up to your teachers and you respect them. And you think, 'I wouldn't mind doing that.' Teaching appeals to me in the sense that I have had a good time [as a pupil] and I wouldn't mind going through it on the other side.
>
> (Meena)

> I have considered teaching as one of my last options. If I go to university I would like to do a degree first and then do a teaching qualification, but I wouldn't go to teacher training college. I would keep my options open.
>
> (Laura)

This is not to suggest that all the girls were in agreement about teaching. Sonia, who had been schooled largely in Jamaica felt that her teachers had been too harsh, and had no desire to be like them. Naomi spoke passionately about the damage that teachers caused to children, both black and white, through the processes of labelling and exclusion:

> I am put off teaching because I look at some of my fellow pupils and I think what they are doing now, how they are ruined because of their school, because the teacher didn't teach them and they didn't try to get past the barriers which the pupils were putting up. The teachers just sent them to sit in the hall for an hour's detention. I don't want to do that. I want to think that I have given all the kids an equal chance, whether or not they decide to reject it, but it will not be because of my fault. It is just labelling and it can have a really great impact and can affect you for the rest of your life. If you get a label I think you are finished, unless you really try.
>
> (Naomi)

In a study of Asian and white sixth-formers attitudes to teaching as a career, Singh *et al.* (1988) found that a major deterrent for Asian students was a concern about the racism that they would be likely to face as teachers. The sixth-formers in this study did not tend to see racism as a barrier to teaching as a career, arguing that they were likely to face racism in any walk of life and that the important thing was to develop personal strategies to protect yourself, as far as possible, from some of its damaging effects. Moreover, while some argued that 'race' and colour were irrelevant in identifying what constitutes a good teacher, a number of them believed that black and ethnic minority teachers had a special role to play. Some suggested that they were able to relate to these teachers in a way that was not possible with white teachers. Nevertheless, their judgements of the problems such teachers may face correlate closely with the experiences of black teachers in this study.

> The Asian teacher at my primary school was given quite a lot of stick by the parents because she put a lot more discipline in her lessons. I think she was a very good teacher; she taught my sister and my sister did very well in that class, but I think it was just the parents who were white who had the objections to her. They were basically racist objections, because parents usually like strictness.
>
> (Nazir)

> Asian and black teachers have particular difficulties that don't apply to white teachers, like disciplining the children, the white kids. They don't give them as much respect as they would a white teacher.
>
> (Godfrey)

> Black teachers may face a harder time, all teachers get it from kids dossing around, but black teachers may get it from the staff, if they were more junior, or from the headmaster.
>
> (Arun)

One group of students argued that their school's attempt to recruit more white pupils from the local area gave out a strong message to both themselves and the minority of white pupils at the school that black and Asian children were inferior, and that this was likely to have an impact on their relationships with their white teachers:

> At the moment the school is trying to recruit more white people to join the first year. I think that gives some insight into how the school and many teachers view children who are non-white. They think they won't achieve as much, so the school will go down because they won't be getting the grades.
>
> (Satnam)

Nevertheless, certain schools, concerned about their position in league tables, may consider themselves under pressure to attract and recruit more white pupils or more middle-class pupils or whoever they perceive will enhance their image, regardless of the messages this gives to existing pupils and parents. A number argued that it was for white teachers to recognise where their experiences actually differed from their black pupils:

> The teacher can know as much as there is to know about racism, but if they are a white teacher then no matter how much they say they understand it I can't really relate to them. It is something very personal and unless you have experienced it first hand, at the end of the day they can't do anything for me.
>
> (Nazir)

> Teachers who try to be really understanding and helpful, a lot of the time for me, it feels like they are sort of mocking me. I would rather have a teacher who would say, 'I don't understand how it feels, but I can do this or that for you instead.'
>
> (Satnam)

Finally, one student wanted to remind his fellow students of the power and responsibility which teachers carry, regardless of where they are situated:

> I think a teacher is one of the most important jobs in the country, especially in a Third World country. I have been moving about a lot and I have been in about fifteen different schools. I have been in this country for three years. I am able to look at teachers from a different point of view. They can create a whole different community, a society we are all looking for. And if the teacher is not meant to be a teacher, he or she can do a lot of harm.
>
> (Ahmed)

Preparing to teach: BEd and PGCE students

Introduction

Teaching has been described as a hazardous profession and the narratives of experienced teachers, examined in Chapters 5–8, reveal some of the particular challenges faced by teachers from black and ethnic minority communities. This chapter draws on the narratives of 25 PGCE and BEd students preparing to become teachers in primary and secondary schools. It begins by focusing on students' perceptions of teaching as a career before going on to examine their own schooling and its impact on their understanding of their role as teachers. Student teachers are in a process of transition from student to teacher; this chapter reviews their experiences of their courses, college cultures, student–tutor relationships, teaching practice and education for racial equality.

Teaching as a career

A CRE survey (1988a) recorded that only 2.6 per cent of teacher education students were from minority groups, although black and ethnic minorities formed 4.4 per cent of the population. The 1991 Census indicated that 7.2 per cent of the 15–24-year-old British population was from black and ethnic minority communities. Their underrepresentation in teaching remained a cause for official concern in the early 1990s, when the Higher Education Funding Council for England (HEFCE) set aside £500 000 for special projects to encourage ethnic minority participation in teacher training. HEFCE recognised that 'the successful encouragement of students from ethnic minorities in this area would have a significant benefit to both the education system in general and to the ethnic minority communities in particular' (HEFCE 1995: 5). A total of 17 projects involving 19 teacher education institutions were consequently funded from 1993 to 1994.

Although black and ethnic minority teachers can be found in all types of school, a disproportionate number of black and bilingual teachers have taken up posts funded under Section 11. Section 11-funded posts have generally been viewed as being of low status; Newham Asian Teachers' Association (1985) reported that about one-third of the borough's Asian teachers were employed under Section 11 and that there was a tendency for these teachers 'to be marginalised and not seen as an integral part of the school'. Richardson (1996a) characterises Section 11 teachers as 'often located in rather power-less and marginal places' but notes that they 'nevertheless include some of the most committed, energetic and expert teachers . . . marvellously influ-ential over the years in speaking up for black and ethnic minority pupils'. Changes in the administrative rules have left such teachers with low job security as contracts are issued for a fixed term in line with specific fixed term projects. As a consequence of employment patterns, a disproportionate number of black and bilingual teachers are likely to be affected by these changes. The available evidence suggests that black teachers are seen as a cheap commodity by their employers (Blair 1994), more likely to be employed at lower pay levels and to be on temporary contracts.

In a small-scale survey of students' perceptions of teaching (Singh *et al.* 1988) there was generally a marked similarity between the views of South Asian and white respondents, with discipline problems and poor promotion prospects emerging as common concerns, but the presence of racism among pupils and teachers featuring as the only significant point of difference. Asian respondents identified it as among the least attractive aspects of teach-ing. Although racism was a theme running through most of the present sample of students' stories, and many recounted incidents in their own schooling which had been particularly painful, it was not always an issue that was explicitly developed in students' accounts; most often it was taken as given, a routine experience and one of the realities of daily life. The assumption was invariably made that the researcher, as a black person, had a shared understanding and experience. Some students expressed a concern that racism might hinder their progress in teaching, but most were deter-mined that they would overcome such difficulties, and to a number teach-ing seemed less likely to hold such barriers than other professions:

> Teaching struck me as having more equal opportunities than many other professions; it struck me as the most reasonable one. I did have the perception that if you watch TV you do see black headteachers, again more in America than here.
>
> (Simon)

For a small number of students, the recognition of the inadequacies of their own schooling was the primary motivating factor in choosing teaching as a career:

> I think the main thing was that pupils like me could have something that I didn't have – that encouragement that I think black pupils do need within a school or within the education system. I think that I

could offer that encouragement and give black kids the aspiration to
go on.

(Claudette)

What led me into teaching? Having a bad education myself . . . it was a
profound sense of powerlessness, that's what I remember at school, and
I started to think if others are less aware of what is happening to them
then maybe I had a valuable contribution.

(Kwame)

Black and ethnic minority students presented a wide range of reasons
for choosing teaching as a career. Like the sixth-form students, few seemed
to have benefited from formal careers advice and some found their initial
choice of occupation disappointing or unsatisfying; a number of these were
then encouraged to consider teaching by family and friends. The stories of
Ravinder and Huma were quite typical:

There are several reasons why I have actually come into teaching. One
of the main reasons is probably the influence of relatives in teaching.
I have got two cousins who started teaching last year . . . Before teaching I worked in industry for a couple of years . . . I probably looked
down upon teaching compared with the commercial jobs. I didn't enjoy
the job I was doing in commercial management so I left there of my
own accord and went abroad to Canada for a few months . . . Family
were an influence. My dad does part-time teaching at a Saturday school;
he teaches languages and he could obviously tell me quite a bit, and his
friends were an influence as well.

(Ravinder)

My family, my parents and my older sisters, were actually teachers and
I thought I don't want to go into teaching just because it's the expected
thing. So I did work in industry for about six or seven months and I
wasn't happy . . . that's when I realised that this is the sort of thing I'd
like to do with my future, helping people to overcome problems which
they think they cannot overcome, and helping them achieve things that
they might not necessarily achieve.

(Huma)

While some students knew that they had always wanted to teach, others
had simply pursued their education for its own sake and had made a recent
career decision. For Feroza, acting as an interpreter at her local primary
school had made her curious about teaching and she had volunteered as a
classroom helper; Asif had enjoyed the A level tutoring he had taken on
while working as an television engineer and Farah had found that training
others to do her work as a laboratory technician was, for her, the most
rewarding aspect of her job.

Black and ethnic minority students' career choices and life chances are
nevertheless restricted by experiences which are determined by 'race' and

skin colour. Ali was working in local government and had a substantial amount of experience teaching karate and other sports in his spare time; he had also been involved in a Section 11 project helping black children with mathematics. He had felt for some time that he would like to take up teaching as a career, but he still could not see himself, as a black person, working as a 'real' teacher:

> I asked him [a teacher friend]: 'Do you actually think I'd make a good teacher?' And he said: 'You're already a good teacher.' I said: 'No, I mean proper teaching, in a classroom.' And he told me: 'Yeah, you seem to have the character for it and you get on with the kids. You've got a very good chance of becoming a very good teacher.' I still wasn't convinced . . . well, teaching is good but when I was at school you didn't see many black teachers, and getting a good job was quite difficult for black people. I'd already got established in my council work because I was a shop steward there and I think I was going places but going into teaching was like starting off afresh and I didn't know what obstacles I was going to get.
>
> (Ali)

While a lack of black role models had led Ali to doubt whether he could become a 'proper' teacher in a state school, another student, Jonathan, had begun to question whether the state sector could offer him the opportunities he was looking for. He wanted to work with black students in an inner-city school but had some doubts as to whether he could be true to himself or whether he would be expected to compromise his own identity:

> 'I don't really believe that I will take the traditional route as a teacher. It sounds a separatist thing to say but I would like to see a black school. Black teachers, black kids, black culture.'
>
> (Jonathan)

Jonathan was one of just two students in this sample who advocated 'separate' schools. The other, Muna, who had herself attended a Muslim school for a short period, was considering the possibility of working in a Muslim school, partly as a result of her teaching practice experiences, where she had observed Muslim students' needs neglected.

Teaching in schools was not the final goal for all these students. One hoped eventually to work in further education and two had academic careers in mind. Only one student saw teaching as a second best; she had always wanted to train as a doctor.

Primary teaching – a suitable career for a girl?

Two female BEd students reported that their motivation to teach in primary school was confirmed by their experiences in the family:

I am the eldest out of my family, and not just my own family but out of all my cousins . . . so I look after them quite a lot. And I find I can manage them and I can take on the role of a responsible person.

(Kalsoon)

Despite the fact that her mother had been a teacher in Pakistan, Kalsoon was careful to stress that it had been her own decision to teach:

My mum's a teacher so I had the basis, but it wasn't because of her. I thought I could make a good job of this. And because of the practical side to it, I didn't want to go into anything too academic.

(Kalsoon)

Parveen enjoyed mathematics, and as well as wanting to use this subject in her work, sought a qualification and profession which would be recognised in Pakistan and would thus give her some flexibility and geographical mobility in the future. Her mother has been instrumental in her decision-making and sees teaching as a suitable career for a woman, which will fit in with family responsibilities. Nevertheless, she wishes her daughter to be economically independent and achieve more than she has:

I want to eventually go back to live in Pakistan and I wanted to choose something where I can get the qualifications here, but I can use it [here] and get work in Pakistan as well. I was born in England but . . . I have been on visits and I really like the place . . . [My mum tells us:] 'I don't want you to get married at a young age. I don't want you to be dependent on your husband. If anything does happen you have got your own career. I want you to be able to look after yourself in life; I don't want you to be dependent on your in-laws.'

(Parveen)

Parveen stressed her career as the most important feature of her future life, although she saw it as inevitable that she would marry.

The attitudes of both young women are consistent with those of the Asian girls and young women that Brah (1988) studied: both placed considerable emphasis on obtaining educational qualifications and assumed that they would be economically independent. Indeed it would seem that Parveen's mother has emphasised this issue in the upbringing of her daughters. A study of Muslim mothers' expectations of their daughters' education suggests that most see it as a means of achieving independence in adult life; those who are themselves economically dependent nevertheless expect their daughters to be in a position to establish economic independence should the need arise (Osler and Hussain 1995). The approach which Kalsoon and Parveen adopt towards their future careers differs somewhat from that of some of the Asian women teachers in this study, who entered colleges of education in the 1970s specifically to avoid an early marriage; their expectations of a future career are much stronger.

Kalsoon felt there was little immediate chance of attracting South Asian men into primary school teaching because of the status attached to teaching and the way in which it is viewed by many within the Asian communities as a female occupation:

> You can go to any other university department and you would find that the intake of Asian men is quite high. But teaching – it is mocked. If you go to Pakistan and you ask people their opinion, no matter how educated they are they would laugh, you know, male primary teacher, Asian male primary teacher, what sort of joke is that? Here, even if my brother wanted to I don't think he would say it because of his friends.
>
> (Parveen)

Parveen emphasied that it was only primary teaching which would be viewed in such a way; it is seen in a very different light from secondary or higher education:

> Primary teaching is supposed to be a low status type of thing. 'So you teach primary children, what exactly do you teach then? What exactly do you do?' They think there is no work in it . . . It is women's job, it is part of what they do anyway.
>
> (Parveen)

Deborah, a mature student, blamed the low numbers of black people in teaching on a school system which has largely failed them, but noted how few black men appeared to be entering the profession:

> The three [African Caribbean] female students that are here are all mature students. I think that has a lot to do with the fact that for a lot of us, we have left school without full qualifications. I have just completed an access course; fortunately we did all succeed, and fortunately there were a lot of black men there . . . I really don't know why there aren't any in teaching; maybe it is not seen as an academic job, like you say [it's seen as] just an extension of the role of women, and a caring position.
>
> (Deborah)

Like some of the experienced teachers in the study, Deborah hopes that she might one day be a headteacher. Recognising that structural racism may operate to frustrate this ambition she has, like others, considered the possibility of opening her own school as one means to achieve this goal. She chose primary teaching on the assumption that it was at this stage that she could be most influential in black children's lives, before they encountered difficulties at secondary school. Despite this desire to meet black children's needs within the British school system, Deborah thought that she too might eventually choose to work abroad, perhaps for a short while in an African country, and then in the Caribbean, arguing that teachers are undervalued in Britain:

I do want to work with black children, but like Parveen, I hope to go elsewhere. I don't intend to work in this country, mainly because I don't feel the government values the teachers, whether they are black or white.

(Deborah)

The impact of black students' own schooling

The student teachers in this study were, on the whole, those who had managed to achieve examination results which gave them direct access to higher education. A smaller number had left school without the necessary formal qualifications and had entered higher education as mature students by circuitous routes. I consider the impact of these school experiences on their professional priorities and values.

Of those students who had been educated largely or wholly in Britain about one-third talked about their schooling in generally positive terms, focusing on their successes, on the fun they had had, and the friendships they had enjoyed. Some spoke of the particular support of an individual teacher. Nevertheless, on reflection, all had some strong reservations about their schooling and these generally related to specific cultural or religious misunderstandings between pupils and their teachers and criticisms of a narrow anglocentric curriculum.

Muna felt her school was sensitive to the cultural and religious needs of Muslim pupils and her father had advised the school on such matters. Despite this she felt it was a 'typical white schooling':

In English you'd get the typical books with white people in and history I always hated because we were always doing history of either Britain or some white people – the kings and queens of England – and I didn't see any point . . . My favourite subject at school was RE [religious education]. That was taught by a black teacher and . . . I became really close to her. She was one of the people who influenced me to continue.

(Muna)

A small-scale study of African Caribbean women students in higher education found that most of these women also felt they received encouragement from a particular teacher (Tomlinson 1983). Muna in turn gave special encouragement to Asian girls. She saw herself as a strong role model:

It gives them encouragement to want to do either the same thing or to feel maybe they can be successful in other fields. I know that when I was at school if I had seen any Asian teachers, especially women, dressed like me, that would really have encouraged me a lot.

(Muna)

Her sister Huma was also on the course, preparing to be a science teacher: 'When I went into teaching I thought to myself I'm going to be myself, I'm going to be a Muslim and I'm going to be a teacher as well.' She was not prepared to sacrifice her values, for although generally she had been happy at school she had felt humiliated by a physical education teacher who had insisted on communal showering:

> When I look back I think, why didn't she respect my religion and respect the difference in culture rather than enforcing her own ideas upon people and making you look as though your way of thinking is a very backward and sick way of thinking?
>
> (Huma)

Deborah's motivation to teach lay in the inadequacies of her own schooling. Although she stressed her strong personal desire to work with black children she felt that many black teachers had little real choice since they were acutely aware of the inadequacies of the education system and the failure of many white teachers to meet the needs of black children. Deborah had suffered at high school from the overt racist attitudes of a number of teachers:

> There was so much that went on at high school. Once I was in a maths lesson and there was no chair where I was going to sit down, so I went and I was dragging a chair . . . The teacher turned round and said, 'Stop acting like a nigger in the wood, come and sit down and be civil.' . . . It was the first time I had heard that expression – I was 14 at the time – and I said, 'You can't make racist comments like that.' I . . . told my mum and the head of year said, 'Oh, it is just a saying. OK it was a bit out of touch, but it is nothing really.'
>
> (Deborah)

Peter, who was also training to be a primary school teacher, was particularly concerned about the narrowness of the National Curriculum and of the ways in which this might inhibit opprtunities to develop a curriculum which gave all children a sense of pride and genuinely promoted equity and social justice. He arrived in London from Uganda at the age of 8 years and felt his own education had never addressed these issues:

> The school was a multiracial school. At the time there was a lot of racism from the children. You would get called names, I don't know why but I used to get offended being called 'Blackie' . . . You understood it was meant to be an insult rather than turning it round and saying, 'Yeah I am, black and proud.' I enjoyed the school and I never sensed any kind of animosity from the teachers. One of my friends . . . one day he got serious with me and said, 'Pete, tell me this, what have black people done?' I think about that, he was saying that when he looks at the news and all the books we used to have in those days – we were only 9 or 10 years old – but we still realised that black people were always portrayed as not having a history . . . Where's the ancient history, where are the pyramids and where are the great glorified

buildings in Africa and other parts of the world? What have they invented? What have they contributed to the modern world? And I didn't know, I just didn't know.

(Peter)

Those who had largely negative recollections of their own schooling tended to focus on teachers' poor expectations of black children. This was most strongly felt by all the African Caribbean students and by the South Asian women. Language was an area where a number of students, particularly as recent migrants, had been made to feel inadequate. In these cases it was not difficulties in understanding that the student teacher recalled as the problem but the attitude of the teacher.

Claudette was educated in Handsworth, Birmingham, but from an early age recalls how there were misunderstandings between her and her primary school teacher as she spoke Creole at home and sometimes used vocabulary which was unfamiliar to her teacher. The teacher's attitude left her with a feeling of inadequacy and inability to express herself which remained with her throughout her schooling and during her A-level studies. Such experiences caused these students to place a heavy emphasis on the quality of student–teacher relationships in their own work. They had high expectations of children and saw student achievement in school as the critical measure of their success as teachers. Student teachers' and teachers' understandings and perceptions of their own schooling as bilingual learners and the influence of these on their practice as teachers are developed in more detail elsewhere (Osler 1994c).

Those who had been educated overseas in India, Pakistan, Iraq, Malaysia and Singapore, brought a different perspective to the classroom. They reflected on whether they would have been able to succeed as children in British schools given the racism they have encountered here. Difficulties in trying to enter the British education system as adults, the struggles of part-time study and the lack of recognition of their overseas qualifications meant that these student teachers were particularly sensitive to the ways in which the education system at all levels can operate to limit black people's life chances. Salman arrived in Britain aged 18 years, from India where he had lived as a refugee after fleeing Burma. Lack of residents' qualifications meant that he was unable to obtain a study grant and so he had taken a job in a factory, studied part time, and eventually graduated while working for the health service. His decision to become a teacher in his forties arose out of his interest in education generally, and particularly in the education of his own children as Muslims in Britain. Acutely aware of racism through his experiences in employment and in the education system, his priority was the education of Muslim children and the sensitisation of teachers to their religious and cultural needs.

Regardless of their own experiences of schooling, the vast majority of students felt a special commitment to the education of black and ethnic

minority children, and to the education of all children who were disadvantaged in the system. Women students, regardless of their own social background, also emphasised the damaging effects of sexism and the particular
ways in which it operates to restrict opportunities for black girls.

College culture: BEd students' experiences

The college where the BEd students were studying specialises in primary
education and the vast majority of students are women. It is situated in an
urban area where black and ethnic minority communities represent more
than 20 per cent of the overall population but, as a Catholic college, has
a tradition of attracting students from schools of the same denomination.
Although no accurate figures were available concerning the percentage of
black and ethnic minority students on the course, tutors reported that there
were very few.

The majority of students at the college are resident and for this reason the
college culture is of particular interest; it tends to have a greater impact on
individuals than it would if the students were part of a much larger institution. Deborah was a mature entrant in her early thirties, and Kalsoon and
Parveen had come straight to college after completing their A levels. The
students reported that the handful of black and ethnic minority students in
their intake were all women. All three students felt isolated as black women
within a predominantly white college: Parveen noted she tended only to discuss college work with other students, what she referred to as the 'safe' topics
of conversation. She argued that when Asian women began to express
something about their cultural identity it was likely to be disbelieved, or
regarded as exceptional by white students. White women were likely to take
an issue such as arranged marriage and discuss it in isolation, without reference to marriage in general or any understanding of Asian family patterns.
If an individual Asian woman argued that it was not necessarily oppressive,
her view would be discounted as atypical. Similarly, Kalsoon observed that
when she and another South Asian woman choose to speak Urdu in the
students' common room among the other students 'some people smiled and
some gave me a funny look'. She felt frustrated that what was normal
behaviour should be met by discomfort or condescension. She saw their
response as an effective challenge to her rights. She observed that while
her teaching experience school seemed to value her bilingual skills, college
tutors did not acknowledge this or know which languages she could speak:

> I particularly want to work with bilingual children. At home I practice
> my linguistic skills in Urdu a lot. I am doing English as my main subject,
> so I am constantly in touch with two languages. And I think there is
> a need for something like that in schools, even in secondary schools . . . I
> don't think the tutors here are aware of my languages.
>
> (Kalsoon)

Deborah, unlike the other two, was resident in college and felt a need to assert her own political and cultural identity in a very conscious way and challenge white students' preconceptions:

> In my room it is pure blackness. I've got my Malcolm X poster up, consciously I have black pictures up. I want people to know that I am aware of my blackness. Nobody has actually come in and said, 'Who is that on the wall? Why does it say, *by any means necessary*? Why has he got a gun in his hand?' When I first came here a very close friend of mine, an Asian friend, she got married and I was like her escort at her wedding . . . I came back and I'd got all the pictures, and a girl next door was saying, 'Well, most of these Asian ladies they are not really happy and it is quite a primitive thing.' And I like jumped on her and I said, 'Primitive? What do you mean by primitive? . . . Are you going out and judging people in the schools that you are working with?'
>
> (Deborah)

Teaching experience and the subsequent discussions that took place in college had highlighted fellow students' stereotyped attitudes towards black and ethnic minority people. Kalsoon described how the class teacher had responded to her, arguing that she displayed a form of unconscious racism:

> I was in an inner-city largely Asian school and the teachers were generally supportive . . . [but] the teacher just couldn't see me as a teacher in the beginning. She said, 'Well, what if you went to an English school with a largely white population?' It was because I managed to learn all of their names . . . I think she was quite taken aback by that. And so she said, 'Well, if you were in an English school would you remember things like Richard and Clyde?' And I was really shocked. In the sixth form I spent two years at [a predominantly white school], I was with English girls all of the time . . . I thought that was a great insult although I know she didn't mean any harm.
>
> (Kalsoon)

The teacher's initial difficulties in recognising Kalsoon as a potential teacher of white children able to cope with aspects of their culture is one which is particularly disturbing since a class teacher in a primary school is likely to have considerable power over a student teacher in her classroom. The question arises of how such a teacher might assess the teaching practice of a student she finds so difficult to accept (Crozier and Menter 1993; Osler 1994b). A PGCE student interviewed for this study described how she was mocked by teachers for fasting during a teaching practice which took place during the month of Ramadan, and of how a teacher demanded to know how a Muslim could be a religious education teacher.

Parveen observed how she was welcomed by the staff in a largely white primary school and how the children, who were initially curious about her traditional Asian clothes, also quickly accepted her. Nevertheless, she was concerned about the way in which the only African Caribbean child in the class was allowed to be placed in a group working at a level far below his potential, and about the narrowness of the curriculum:

> In my own experience of primary school we learnt about other cultures and everything. One thing I noticed at St Mary's was that they were only concerned with the one culture, even though they had other cultures inside their school. . . . They were very Roman Catholic. I asked once if they did other religions, did they study Judaism or Islam or anything like that? They replied, 'No, because this is a Roman Catholic place we just stick to the Roman Catholicism.' It was coming up to Christmas time and it was Divali. I mentioned it once and they said, 'No you shouldn't, because we just stick to the policy we are given.' They were all shocked, like, 'What's she talking about?' They didn't know anything about other cultures and I think they should have.
>
> (Parveen)

At the school where Deborah was placed there was some attempt to include a range of cultural experiences by giving each a mention during a morning assembly, but the school avoided prayers or any form of collective worship. She was particularly concerned about the attitude of another student who was placed in the same school, which went unchallenged by their tutor:

> In our feed-back session the other day, one of the girls who was placed in my school said, 'Oh these children were really bad because it was a multicultural school.' And she just said it. Just like that.
>
> (Deborah)

The three women described how the college had invited a black headteacher to talk to the students immediately before going on teaching practice, but although the initial response among students had been quite positive, this was not reflected in the way they described the schools in which they had been placed:

> He was here to say, this is what is happening in the urban schools: 'Remember this is what is happening when you pick up the papers and you read about the inner cities, these are the children you are reading about.' . . . a lot of people were placed in areas where there were predominantly black and Asian children, and they came back and said, 'Oh it was such a rough area, these kids you can't pronounce their names. They don't speak any English and the parents were all split up, and all these black families are here, and these women are all by themselves and they are all on income support and yet they are all dressed nice.'
>
> (Deborah)

Clearly, the attitudes of students and the ways in which they exhibit these in their conversation and behaviour is likely to have a direct impact on their pupils. Tutors' responses, or lack of response, to ignorant, uninformed or even racist attitudes expressed by student teachers towards their pupils or teaching practice schools play an important part in establishing a college culture which either promotes racial equality or reinforces the racism of the wider society.

In the cases from the 1960s and 1970s described by headteachers in Chapter 7, colleges were so insensitive to the needs of black students that when they encountered racism and were unable to find lodgings in the private sector, they were unable to offer any alternative provision within college. While discrimination in housing is now clearly unlawful, the question remains of whether the white staff in initial teacher education have become more sensitive to the experiences and needs of their black students or have made sufficient progress in responding to those needs so as to guarantee equitable treatment.

It would seem critical that in developing initiatives designed to attract black people into teaching (HEFCE, 1995) colleges and universities not only produce videos and promotional materials, but consider equality issues within these courses, particularly how they are going to meet the needs of a culturally diverse student intake in the context of a racist society. Promotional materials aimed at black students' colleges might provide information on the support systems available, the types of placements that can be offered, and the percentages of black and ethnic minority students entering and completing their courses. It is clear that all students need to understand structural racism, and that white students need to consider their own behaviour in this context. Careers counselling and the encouragement of black students to enter teacher education needs to be matched by efforts to address potentially discriminatory practices within institutions. One priority must be the training and preparation of various categories of college staff, including teacher educators and administrators, to work with black students, to fulfil their requirements under the Race Relations Act 1976 and to prepare all student teachers to do the same.

Initial teacher education: PGCE students

The two university departments of education (UDEs) from which the PGCE students are drawn are very different in structure and in the focus of their work: the first, where the majority of students were studying, is in a traditional university where initial teacher education (ITE) is restricted to a secondary PGCE course and where there are substantial numbers of overseas students following advanced courses. The proportion of black and ethnic minority students on the PGCE course was 11 per cent. The second UDE is in a new university (former polytechnic) and focuses largely on ITE courses for primary and secondary teachers. The majority of students were following four-year BEd degrees, with smaller numbers following the one-year PGCE. Black and ethnic minority students made up 13 per cent of course members on the first year of the BEd and about 6 per cent of PGCE students. Of the 22 PGCE students interviewed there were 12 men and 10 women; 16 were of South Asian descent, three African Caribbean, two African, and one was from Iraq. Seventeen of the students had completed their secondary schooling either largely or wholly in Britain. Both institutions had taken steps to promote equal opportunities with some staff development and policy development.

Of the 22 PGCE students 15 had some experience of other employment before entering teaching. Among the secondary students, who make up the bulk of the sample, six (four women and two men) were preparing to teach humanities subjects and 14 (six women and eight men) were preparing to teach mathematics and sciences. A study of Asian teachers found that those who migrated to Britain in the 1960s and 1970s, tended to find jobs in the shortage subjects of mathematics and science, in community languages or EAL. Among teachers classified as 'second generation', two out of three were teaching either science or mathematics (Ghuman 1995). It would seem that a large proportion of black and ethnic minority teachers are still concentrated in these subject areas or in religious education; of the 11 experienced secondary teachers in this study, six were specialists in mathematics or science, three taught religious education, and the remaining two English and social sciences.

Student–tutor relationships

The process of developing from a student to a teacher, which begins during a PGCE course, requires a high level of trust between student and tutor; students need to know that in discussing their strengths and weaknesses and debriefing their teaching experiences with their tutor that the process is going to be a genuinely diagnostic tool used to enable them to overcome any difficulties. Most students following ITE courses are likely to be very conscious of the fact that they are being assessed, and, however good the personal relationship is between tutor and student, and however innovative the form of assessment, will be aware of the power dynamics that inevitably operate in such situations. ITE courses provide a new type of challenge, since to succeed students need to develop a new set of professional skills beyond those academic skills and qualities already learned. Teacher educators, both consciously and unconsciously, begin making judgements about students from the earliest stages of their course.

Black and ethnic minority ITE students are likely to come from a broad variety of educational backgrounds and are likely to bring a wide variety of perspectives, some highly critical, to their teacher education courses. The students in this study raised a number of issues which are likely to have an impact on student–tutor relationships. Student teachers, like pupils in school, are unlikely to include on their record of achievement skills or experiences which they judge the institution not to value. A large proportion of the students in the sample had experience, often current, of working in supplementary schools, usually teaching basic skills or community languages; many were also experienced in interpretation and translation. Most neglected to include such experience on their record of achievement, arguing that the form was not designed to encourage such information or that the tutor might not see the relevance, coming from a particular subject specialism.

Many raised the question of whether a white tutor could genuinely understand their experiences. They felt that it was the responsibility of the tutor and not the student to raise issues of 'race' and that even with tutors for whom they had considerable respect and liking, it was not easy to raise 'race' issues since there was no guarantee of a sympathetic understanding, either from the tutor or from fellow students.

Teaching practice

Student teachers need to understand structural inequality and be prepared to deal with equality issues in schools in order to meet the needs of their pupils (Barton *et al.* 1992). Black students and women students also need to consider how they will respond to racism and/or sexism at a personal level and its potential impact on their professional practice. Research suggests that school practice may provide the worst experience of racial discrimination for many black student teachers (Siraj-Blatchford 1991; Robbins 1995). Current developments towards school-based training make students' school experiences more significant than ever and a number of concerns have been raised about the potential impact of these developments on education for racial equality and social justice (ARTEN 1992, 1996; Crozier and Menter 1993).

One area where black and ethnic minority students would have liked more say was in relation to their teaching experience placements. While this is likely to be a concern of any student, many of these students were worried that they might be placed in schools in areas known for their high levels of racist activity. Interviews revealed that this was not an issue which students had felt able to raise with their tutors on an individual basis, though those who were organised in a support group did bring it to their equal opportunities committee. Clay *et al.* (1991) question a system in which the allocation of teaching practice placements and supervisors lie 'within the gift of individuals' and where assessment remains 'imprecise and impressionistic'.

A number of the students in this study observed the impact of 'race' on the professional practice of black teachers and considered the implications for ITE:

> Discipline is very, very different for a black teacher, because a white teacher walking into a school – I'm talking now from my own experiences of teaching practice – you can walk into a classroom, you are

expected to be there because you are white, you are a teacher. But a black teacher walking into a classroom is different. Now, you're looked at first of all as: 'Why are you there? You couldn't possibly be a teacher. But you're not dressed like the handyman. I suppose you have to be a teacher.' And I think in some communities the same thing applies to a female teacher, especially if she's black or Asian. Like, she can't be a teacher, because tradition says: 'Well, we don't listen to what women say.'

(Ali)

Only a small minority of the students in the sample undertook teaching experience in a school where there was a black headteacher or senior staff member. Some found themselves as the first black professional within a school and they often brought a very different perspective:

There was this generalised view that we're working in a school in a deprived area, people coming from a deprived background. But I don't care about that. If the child's got the potential as far as I'm concerned they should have the opportunity to do well.

(Claudette)

Students who expressed alternative viewpoints felt that this was likely to damage their chances of a favourable assessment. Muna, for example, reported that her tutor advised her that she would have to make more of an effort to 'fit in' to a staff room where she had encountered hostility to her religion:

My tutor said: 'If you want to succeed on this course you'll have to compromise your values because you're too formal [with teachers].' I found that quite offensive. Why should I compromise my values to become a teacher? He said: 'You're not fitting into the norm of a teacher . . .' When he said, 'You don't follow the norm,' he obviously meant, 'You don't follow the norm of a white person.'

(Muna)

In this case the student felt that the tutor accepted the school's judgements, but was unable to recount to the tutor the full extent of the hostile climate she encountered. As a Muslim woman brought up in Britain she was experienced in challenging racist and sexist stereotypes, but she had no experience of doing this within a professional context.

The implications of the inequalities of power between tutor, teacher and student are discussed by Crozier and Menter (1993: 98–100). Research suggests that even on courses where there is a strong commitment to equality issues, this rarely leads to their effective treatment within the triad (Menter 1989). With the development of school-based training, the teacher-mentor plays an increasingly important role and may have the strongest influence over the student. This suggests that effective, fair assessment for all is only likely to be achieved if mentors are encouraged to explore the complex implications of structural inequality as an integral part of their training.

Black students and teacher education for racial equality

In both university education departments equity issues were addressed directly through a Professional Studies course, and consisted of a series of classes aimed at all students; additionally each tutor was responsible for incorporating 'race' and gender issues into subject-based courses. Students were divided as to whether there had been sufficient depth and raised concerns about whether white colleagues had necessarily benefited:

> I think this course has basically got to grips with the issues [of racism], but I feel it's a bit too late really. They [fellow students] know what they have got to say, they will say it in the assessment, maybe even in discussions they'll participate and then – adults are no different from kids – they'll go out and they'll have the same set beliefs. It's got to start from primary school, secondary school and then it can be effective . . . some of them haven't got a clue. They seem to think it's completely irrelevant.
>
> (Shazia)

One primary PGCE student felt his course had failed altogether to address the issues and argued that some fellow students' and tutors' responses indicated a superficial understanding:

> They're hearing stuff from uninformed people teaching uninformed people. People, I think, are still backward – I'm not trying to be offensive – but backward in their analysis in that they think you're only racist if you're in the National Front, or you're only sexist if you come in and you say to your wife: 'Make sure my dinner's on the table' . . . they're not self-critical enough to look at how they are contributing to sexism, to racism.
>
> (Kwame)

An HMI report, *Responses to Ethnic Diversity in Teacher Training,* in response to the 'great concern' about the 'under-representation of ethnic minorities in the teaching profession' expressed in the Swann Report, suggested that the presence of ethnic minority students 'is helpful in raising awareness of diversity and in establishing the normality of that diversity. They can make a particular contribution in seminars and workshops' (DES 1989b: 19). One danger of this approach is that it may lead to black student teachers being seen as experts on all aspects of 'black culture', rather than as individuals with a full range of experience and knowledge. One student provides an example of this on a preliminary visit to his teaching experience school with a white student:

He turned to me and said: 'I think you're going to be all right Ali, you'll
have no problem here.' I kept playing with that idea in my mind. I
mean, we're here being trained as teachers; now if we had gone to a
white school I wouldn't have said to my partner, 'You'll be all right
here,' just looking at the type of children in the corridor. How was
I supposed to be all right with a group of Asian children and a few
Afro-Caribbean? I was from Sierra Leone, West Africa. People living
in Birmingham have a different way of life from London where I was
living or even Coventry, but I'm supposed to be all right because I'm
in a category 'black'?

(Ali)

Another difficulty with the HMI approach is that the institution may feel
relieved of the responsibility to recruit black staff since the presence of
black students and one or two staff gives it a multicultural image. Students
in this study highlighted the need for more black and ethnic minority tutors,
but acknowledged that black staff, like black students, may be placed in
an invidious position or forced to compromise their identity. A number
expressed the view that the course tended to address issues of 'race' and
multiculturalism largely from a white perspective and only to meet the
needs of white students; for example, students did not have the opportunity to discuss how they would handle racist incidents if they encountered
racism directed at themselves as teachers. Moreover, some were reluctant
to express their opinions to tutors for fear of being seen as extreme or as
trouble-makers.

Education for racial equality and participation requires tutors to review
the content and structure of courses and reflect on their own teaching
styles. This may demand personal development as well as professional change,
and is therefore a much more complex process than many equal opportunities policies and staff development training programmes acknowledge.
Two women students recalled incidents involving staff and students in
which entrenched attitudes served to undermine initiatives to broaden the
curriculum:

It was the last session before Christmas. Some students stood up to make
a presentation on how you could make Christmas more multicultural . . .
It was completely racist and degrading – not only racist but sexist. There
were a lot of sexist jokes, they'd come up with some sort of Christmas
rhyme. All I can remember is being really offended. The other students
there were offended as well but they didn't say anything . . . the tutors
. . . just laughed at the jokes, they supported it.

(Shazia)

I found one of the tutors extremely patronising towards Asians and
blacks. He didn't mean to be and that is the worst thing about it. He
said: 'I had a student a few years ago, a particularly striking black

woman who was extremely pretty and she was teaching a group of mediocre looking white students.' . . . He was teaching us about multi-cultural education and the sort of books we could use in the school, and I don't see the relevance.

(Ferdous)

The two universities from which the PGCE students are drawn had both gone some way towards involving students in decisions about equity issues through their respective equal opportunities committees. The comments above suggest that, even when the courses had given the issues quite explicit coverage, black students doubted their effectiveness in relation to changing the attitudes or behaviour of their white colleagues.

Summary

Many British ITE institutions claim they wish to recruit a larger proportion of students from ethnic minority backgrounds. Clearly there is a need for more black and ethnic minority teachers and the students in this study demonstrate the wealth of talent and experience that such recruits bring into teaching. It is not enough merely to attract such students onto courses, universities and colleges need to review their practices to ensure that black and ethnic minority students are given full and equal opportunities to develop their skills and talents.

Education for racial equality demands that students are able to actively participate in their education and teacher educators must therefore be aware of the ways in which racism may act as a barrier to effective participation. Not only does the institution need to review its structures, well-intentioned individuals also need to acknowledge that good intentions are not a guarantee of good practice; well-intentioned behaviour can still lead to discriminatory outcomes.

Education for racial equality must be seen as essential in teacher education if students are to develop into effective teachers capable of promoting equality and justice in schools. A full and explicit examination of issues of equity and social justice is important, but students also need to develop skills which enable them to be self-critical and to look critically at their own education; they need to be encouraged to explore their own values and to share responsibility with their tutors in identifying their needs.

It is important that these issues are addressed in a way which acknowledges the racially structured nature of society and the ways in which gender and class intersect with 'race'. Students had experienced courses which had adopted both a direct model of teaching for equality through their professional studies courses and a permeation model through their subject studies. They saw the need for both, since they identified differences in the level of commitment to equality issues among their university subject tutors.

The current developments in teacher education towards a school-based train-ing have significant implications for equality issues since students are no longer likely to have direct teaching on these issues from tutors with expert-ise in this field. All tutors and teacher-mentors now need to address these issues and evaluate their own practice if they are to ensure that black stu-dents are not assessed by racial criteria.

Part four ─────────────

Changing the future

Eleven

Education, racism and black teachers: structure and response

Introduction

Part One of this book set out to examine the nature of racism and the ways in which policies and practices have developed in response to the presence of black and ethnic minority communities in post-war Britain. The ways in which schools reflect and reproduce the racism of society have been explored in some detail, as have the contribution of multicultural and anti-racist approaches in challenging racism both within and beyond schools.

Educational approaches which seek to modify the curriculum of schools and make it more inclusive have sometimes presented racism as an indi-vidual, psychological problem which can be simply remedied by cultural pluralism. Such approaches have come under attack by writers such as Sarup (1982) who point out that issues such as immigration and the loca-tion of black and ethnic minority people in the economy have not generally been seen as part of multicultural education programmes. Such responses to racism fail to acknowledge its structural nature.

Here we are concerned with exploring how black teachers respond to racism in schools and in society, how they interpret the contexts in which they work and, more importantly, how racism can be effectively challenged. While schools can take initiatives, such as those highlighted in Chapter 2, to review policies and practices to ensure that they are not reinforcing racism, such initiatives may be inadequate if we fail to explore the day-to-day realities of black people in schools and in the education system more broadly.

Structural theories offer an explanation of racism at a societal level but do not explain how those who experience racism live or work within this context. More significantly, they do not adequately explain how individuals are able to negotiate or effectively challenge racism or how they are able to develop strategies to minimise its impact on their lives and on the lives of their fellow teachers and students, while at the same time often recognis-ing its structural and all-pervasive nature. In this chapter I draw upon the experiences of black and ethnic minority students and teachers to develop an understanding of racism which not only recognises its structural nature but which also considers the differing ways in which individuals experience and manage it. I consider the strategies which individuals adopt to minimise the impact of racism on their lives and on the lives of their students. It is an attempt to explore the relationship between structural racism and individual agency.

Through an examination of the complexities of the lived experiences of black and ethnic minority people, we may be able to identify ways in which racism can be effectively challenged by individuals or groups and change can be effected. My intention is to reflect on the experiences of the black students and teachers in this study and the meanings they attach to events in their lives, setting these within the broader political framework in which they are operating. It is an attempt to rework some difficult problems, recognising that the overall social context is both complex and dynamic.

Complexity and diversity of experience

It is important to emphasise that racism, as experienced by the teachers and students who participated in this study, was felt in many different ways. As the interviewer, I did not raise the issue or ask people how they had 'coped' with racism; the subject of racism was always introduced by the interviewee yet it featured in every interview, without exception. Sometimes it was treated as one of the inevitable features of life and referred to almost in a casual way; its existence and damaging effects were recognised in the much the same way that schooling is usually acknowledged as a part of childhood. On other occasions individuals would express their hurt or anger at particular occurrences or situations. Some teachers, such as Hazel, felt it had had a huge impact on their lives: 'I am one of those people who have actually experienced what racism is all the way through my education.' Hazel went on to explain that, although she had regularly come top of her primary school class, a decision, taken while she was still at primary school, to send her to a secondary modern school, had an impact on her access to public examinations at 16 years old. Her secondary school offered a very limited number of subjects at O level, and mathematics, a general entry requirement for teacher education courses, was not among them. It was only at her parents' insistence that she took O levels, passing eight. Low expectations of teachers and of careers officers were to be a continuing feature of her education, right through until her graduation from teacher training college.

Hazel's story is not exceptional; a number of students and teachers recounted similar experiences and many more observed similar patterns among the children at the schools they attended:

> In secondary school there were a lot of Asian girls, it was a five-streamed
> school, but all the Asian girls were in what we used to call the 'cookery

class'. It was the bottom stream and they were called the 'bottom stream' and they spent the day cleaning cookers, this was their job. I was just shocked. West Indian girls weren't allowed in that school, it was a real stereotype. It was a fact of 'If we get them at 11 we kick them out at 12.' . . . And sure enough, this girl was gone by 12, and I couldn't believe it, I had never been in the same class as a West Indian child before, but I had no reason to believe they would be treated in any different way. But I saw it, my God I saw it. It is one of the most vivid memories I have. Cookery class wasn't good enough for this one. In assembly she would only twitch and she was out. Prayers, we all had to bow our heads but she wouldn't, she would look round, but don't we all, she would be the first one to be picked on.

(Salma)

In schools where there were very few black pupils, a number of teachers tended to judge the institution as non-racist, although this did not necessarily mean that either individual pupils or staff would not act in what was seen to be a racist fashion:

There wasn't any [racism]; I must be honest in saying there wasn't any. There was one teacher who we always felt was racist, and that was one of our geography teachers and I think it was in lessons where maybe we would be talking about places like India or Bangladesh and he would keep looking at us, me and the other Asian girl, sneering almost, and saying, 'Can these people live?' and 'Aren't you better off here?' It was just him and his attitude towards certain pupils and we always felt that Asian pupils and black pupils were worse off than anyone else with him.

(Balbir)

Whether racism was perceived to be structural or the result of individual prejudice, all participants had examples from their own schooling, and teachers and student teachers were able to identify similar and continuing patterns in their professional lives. It was often through the determined effort of their parents that these teachers were able to achieve their ambitions, and overcome the low expectations of their own teachers, although the struggle to do so was often painful.

A recognition of the diversity and complexity of experience also leads individuals to recognise that identity itself is multiple and complex. As teachers present the narratives of their lives they discuss the influences and expectations placed upon them by family, colleagues, their students and the wider community which help shape and reshape their personal and professional identities. While Modood (1988, 1992) rejects the notion of an inclusive black identity as meaningless, his criticisms fail to acknowledge that personal and professional identities are likely to be multiple and hybrid. He tends to emphasise Muslim or 'Asian' identity as paramount, but teachers' own narratives reveal that it is possible, for example, to assert an Asian identity in one context and a black identity in another. Similarly, some teachers and students who emphasise their Muslim identity when explaining certain aspects of their experiences and understandings also apply the term black to themselves when wishing to express another aspect of their experience or to express solidarity with others who do not share their religion or culture but who share an experience of racism. He adopts an 'either/or' model of identity rather than a 'both/and' model. Teachers' recognition of a 'both/and' model is critical if we accept that 'education is essentially a process whereby we are enabled to acquire additional identities and identify with wider communities' (Osler and Starkey 1996: 75).

Black educators' responses to racism in schools

In Table 11.1 I identify six broad orientations or responses to racism in schools, drawn from the evidence provided by the students and teachers in this study. The intention is not to suggest that there are six clear-cut perspectives, or types of people; it is likely that an individual might be able to place themselves in more than one orientation at any time, indeed, throughout an individual's career she or he may have responded in many, if not all, of the broad orientations.

The first orientation identified in Table 11.1 is the *rejecting orientation*. Perhaps not surprisingly, this was not an orientation which any of the educators in this study adopted since the research focused on those who are trying to work within the education system. To explore this orientation more fully it would be necessary to conduct a study of black and ethnic minority teachers who have withdrawn from teaching or from state-run schools. Nevertheless, this category has been included because there was some evidence from interviewing sixth-formers, that a number felt that for them, as black people, a career as a teacher was not feasible. Similarly, among the PGCE students there were two students, an African Caribbean man and an Asian Muslim woman, who felt that their experiences while following their teacher education course confirmed a belief that to be a teacher within the state system might be, for them, untenable. They would be required to collude with a system which they believed was not serving the interests of black and ethnic minority students in general or which was disadvantaging a particular group. Since the PGCE and BEd students have not, as yet, been traced from university to work, it is not clear whether they have adopted such a position. A study of those teachers working full-time in black-run schools outside of the state system might also throw some light on this question. Given the scarcity of well-funded privately run black schools, it is probable that many teachers leaving the profession, who might be said to come within this orientation, are in fact finding work in different, possibly related, fields.

Of those who might be perceived to be within the *conforming orientation*, they were more likely to be student teachers, or teachers with very little experience. This was the case with some individuals who had not experienced direct or overt discrimination before entering teaching. Sometimes a short teaching practice caused an individual to question this orientation. None of the senior educators in the study can be placed within this orientation, although a number of them have been within it at an earlier stage in their careers. This is not to suggest that it would be impossible for a senior black educator to take up such a position.

One difficulty for a black person adopting this position would be in the area of student/community response. While an individual black teacher might argue that all students should be treated the same, and adopt this position in the classroom, problems might arise if the individual was subject to personal abuse of a racist nature. While abuse from students might be interpreted as a discipline issue, and dealt with in this fashion, a conforming response would become more difficult to sustain if a teacher faced a staffroom culture in which racist comments, 'jokes' or behaviour were accepted. It would seem that among many of those teachers in the study who began their careers from within this orientation, it was the behaviour of colleagues, either to black and ethnic minority teachers, or more usually students, which led them to adopt a different orientation or perspective.

Many of the parents of teachers in this study adopted a conforming position early on in their child's schooling, either believing that schools would not discriminate in their treatment of their children, or that things would improve in time, and the injustices which they experienced as immigrants would not be repeated in the lives of their children. The evidence presented by the teachers and student teachers would suggest that this is an orientation which was probably far more common in the 1960s than it is today.

A *reforming orientation* was more likely to be the career starting point of educators within this study. We have seen how a number of black and ethnic minority teachers entered the profession hoping to improve the system and provide children with a better education than they themselves had had. This perspective assumes a theoretical position which explains racial inequality in terms of individual prejudice or behaviour. Consequently, any change or improvement of schools or society will be possible through increased knowledge and interpersonal contact between prejudiced individuals and ethnic minority communities. Disadvantage can be corrected through the promotion of positive images of black and ethnic minority people which will lead to greater self-esteem within minority communities and particularly among youth. The responses to students and community are designed as remedial measures to better inform parents about the British school system and enable students to cross a culture gap between home and school. Within this orientation there is no acknowledgement that students might be able to operate successfully in more than one culture, that of the home and that of the school or that they might adopt

Table 11.1 Strategies adopted by black educators in response to racism in schools

Orientation	Diagnosis of problem	Curriculum response	Student/community response	Career focus
Rejecting	White-run schools are the problem	Disengage: to remain a teacher is to compromise black identity/politics	Expect that black students will reject/sabotage the system	Leave teaching Join black community school
Conforming	No problem and/or need to be accepted	Transmit accepted body of knowledge	Treat all students the same Things will improve in time	Seek recognition of own curriculum expertise Expect to compete on equal terms with white colleagues
Reforming	Black people devalued or invisible in the curriculum	Recognise difficulties within existing curriculum models Promote positive images of black people/multiculturalism	Provide a positive role model Mediate between school and parents Assist with supplementary schools	Adopt home-school liaison, ESL roles Acknowledge problems within schools, but avoid confrontation and work within school's designations Prejudice can be overcome by personal contact
Affirming	Black perspectives are missing	Add on black perspectives to existing curriculum Introduce Black Studies Enable students to explore own history and values Emphasise black identities	Promote and support black voluntary schools Offer special support and encouragement to black students Work in parallel to system rather than seek to reform it	Act as advocate of black students Network and support other black teachers

Challenging	Black people's experiences of schooling are highlighting widespread inequalities in the education system	Challenge and test existing paradigms Recognise 'race' as a category of analysis Begin to integrate black experiences into the curriculum	Encourage collaboration between students and teacher, and between students Support black parents/communities in making their expectations of schools known	Question narrow designations assigned black people/black educators Use positions of influence to encourage school community to be self-critical
Transforming	Injustice and racism Structures and attitudes inherited from the past	Transform the paradigms Inclusive and interdependent vision of human experience – not based on generalisation but acknowledging diversity/hybridity and promoting multiple identities Curriculum reconceptualised as a consequence of inclusion of black perspectives How do class and gender intersect with 'race'?	Empowerment of all students and communities through participation in decision-making of school Explore the potential of education for liberation	Work alongside parents to act on community priorities Continual self-critical development to transform old attitudes and establish new power relations

multiple or hybrid identities; nor is there any understanding of structural racism.

While a disproportionate number of black and ethnic minority teachers have found work as ESL or home–school liaison teachers, the intention is not to suggest that all working in these areas are of a reforming orientation. While a number might have taken on such roles in order to reform the system, this kind of work is likely, as we have seen, to act as a means of politicisation, what one teacher referred to as her 'development as a black person'. Moreover, many older teachers may have taken up such work because as immigrants to Britain they were unable to find jobs within their subject specialism (Ghuman 1995). Within the sample of teachers from this study, who tended to be younger and mostly educated in Britain, there were a significant number for whom it was the only way they could achieve promotion. For others, the expansion of Section 11 projects and multicultural support services in the mid-1980s offered them opportunities to develop their skills and challenge racism in education which they could not find in 'mainstream' education or within the confines of a single school.

Both the conforming and reforming orientations may imply the acceptance of racist designations to a certain degree. Racist behaviour and stereotyping can have a more serious and widespread damaging effect on those sections of the black communities who end up either accepting the stereotyped image of themselves or lowering their expectations of what can be achieved in a racist society. We have seen how a number of teachers, and senior educators in particular, have highlighted the fact that they cannot always count on the unconditional support of the black and ethnic minority communities. In some cases this may be a question of convincing the communities that the educator and the community share the same goal. Blackness is not equated with skin colour; individual educators may need to prove to the communities they serve that they have their interests at heart and have not 'sold out' in order to achieve their own personal or professional goals.

A more difficult problem to overcome may be the acceptance by certain individuals or groups of black and ethnic minority people of racist designations of themselves. For example, we have found some headteachers in this study who suggest that some black parents may have less faith in a black-led school, or who may prefer to send their children to a white-run school, believing that it must be superior, or believing that a school with a majority of black and ethnic minority children must necessarily be an inferior school. Similarly some teachers, although they have had the support of their families, have found that within the wider black community there were some who were not ready to accept a black person as a teacher. In Hazel's case, some black people made it clear that she was chasing an impossible dream:

This may sound contradictory, but some of my friends and relatives kept saying, 'You are black you will never make it as a teacher.' They had to justify me being a teacher, 'Oh, you are tall, you will like it.' It wasn't for academic reasons, ever.

(Hazel)

Such attitudes can work against black people in professional positions, particularly those in positions of power and authority.

This concern about the undervaluing of black professionals from within the black communities echoes the concerns that have been voiced by those engaged in liberation struggles in Africa and elsewhere over what has been termed 'mental colonisation' (Frederikse 1982). Part of the legacy of colonialism may be that at the same time as they assert their own value and worth, some of those who have been subjected to colonisation and racism may fail to challenge part of the racist ideology: this may lead to an internalisation of the concepts of black-as-other and white as superior. Such attitudes may be traced directly to colonial systems of education, which have been described by some as miseducation (Mugomba and Nyaggah 1980).

Black and ethnic minority teachers may find they need to invest energy in asserting their professional skills and leadership in a way that white teachers need not do. They may need to convince local communities that they have a particular personal and professional contribution to make to the education of black children and persuade some parents to overcome the feeling that black teachers are a poor second to their white counterparts or that schools with a majority of black and ethnic minority children must inevitably be second-rate schools.

Some students reported that their reason for not entering teaching was because black and minority perspectives are missing from the curriculum, and within education more broadly. Nevertheless, for many black educators an awareness that black perspectives are missing was their starting point. The *affirming orientation* includes those who are trying to work in parallel to the system, often through black community organisations, or through supporting individual black students. This orientation is in some ways similar to the reforming orientation; indeed, aspects of both the reforming and the affirming orientations might be held simultaneously. With the introduction of a National Curriculum, which largely determines curriculum content, it is possible to see how black and ethnic minority perspectives might be added on to the curriculum of schools within the affirming orientation, although less likely perhaps that they can be fully integrated into the curriculum, as within the challenging orientation. Nevertheless, within the affirming orientation, it is possible for black teachers to rid themselves of racist designations; even if an individual teacher does not challenge racist designations of herself or himself, she or he may act as an advocate on behalf of black pupils.

While some aspects of an affirming orientation, such as the introduction of black studies, might be rejected by some black educators as a step away from a more central goal of ensuring the achievement of black and ethnic minority pupils, other aspects, such as enabling students to explore their own history and values; offering special support to black and ethnic minority students; and acting as an advocate on their behalf were central to the work of many of the more experienced teachers in the study, and particularly possible for those in a position of influence and power in schools. For those, like advisers and inspectors, whose influence in schools must now be more indirect, networking and supporting black teachers, particularly those who are isolated or in junior positions, is clearly part of this perspective. An affirming orientation would recognise the value of supplementary schools in terms of their cultural or religious contribution, as much as any role they might have in supplementing an education which is deficient in terms of black and ethnic minority children's achievement.

The *challenging orientation* implies not only a mature understanding of education but may well also normally require an individual to be in a position of some security, independence or power. That few PGCE students came within this designation might also reflect a relatively uncritical approach to education within the limitations of short initial teacher education courses. Indeed, it might also reflect recent changes in the organisation of teacher education, with greater emphasis placed on the acquisition of specific technical 'competencies'. There is less opportunity for reflection as much of the programme is passed to schools and teachers who are already overloaded and who may not be in a position to support student teachers in examining broader questions concerning the purposes of schooling. Increasingly, teacher education courses are not meant to be critical. Such difficulties are reinforced by the nature of the National Curriculum; an exploration of recently published geography and history textbooks, for example, reveals that there is little support for this type of approach either among textbook writers or within National Curriculum guidelines (Hopkin 1994; Osler 1994b). Within the individual classroom it may be possible to go some way towards encouraging collaboration between students and teacher and between teachers, but less established teachers in particular may feel vulnerable if they adopt such a position within a school which does not endorse such an approach.

Another difficulty is that a challenging position is a potentially controversial one. While this type of approach might be difficult for any teacher, it is likely to be more difficult for a black teacher working in isolation, given that anything a black teacher may do may be perceived as controversial by the very fact of the teacher's blackness. There is certainly some evidence from the teachers in this study, particularly from the senior educators, that black teachers are more likely than white to attract attention and that black senior educators are particularly 'visible'. Senior black educators certainly perceived themselves to be more 'visible' than their white colleagues, and sometimes attracted a hostile press reaction for behaviours which might well have gone unnoticed in a white senior educator.

Achieving change within a challenging orientation might well depend on the cooperation of the wider community. It has been seen that black educators cannot automatically depend on the support of black and ethnic minority communities; such support may depend both on the individual's local reputation and on the various constituencies in the communities rejecting racist designations and recognising that black people can be effective leaders. Black educators must also be able to persuade white communities that the changes they are proposing are in their best interests also. Given that black educators felt more comfortable within black or multiracial environments and given that some had experienced direct racial abuse and harassment from white communities and, indeed white teachers, to achieve the collaboration of the white communities is not likely to be an easy task. This is not to ignore the importance of working with individual white allies. Many of the black teachers in this study retained their ideals, but most were realistic about their position in schools. There is evidence that those adopting a challenging orientation would compromise in favour of an affirming or reforming position when circumstances indicated that a direct challenge was unlikely to be successful. A reading of any individual teacher's narrative indicates that they were moving from one orientation to another according to the context in which they were working as much as at different times in their careers.

The final orientation, the *transforming orientation*, is one of ideals. This is not to suggest that those working within this orientation were mere idealists. All the senior educators and a number of the teachers diagnosed the problem as one of injustice and racism, arising from structures and attitudes inherited from the past. The logical implications of such a position are to seek to transform the system. Educators within this orientation sought to implement their ideals within their professional practice. This orientation recognises the liberating potential of education and draws inspiration from Freire (1972) and others who have stressed the liberating power of education, particularly for oppressed groups. A number of the teachers in the study held the broad goal of transforming the system to meet the needs of all, but a close look at the detailed implications of such an approach raise a number of political and practical problems.

The National Curriculum in place in schools does not encompass such an inclusive and interdependent vision of human experience as would be required to genuinely bring about curriculum change of the type suggested within a transforming orientation. Nevertheless it is important, as some of the senior educators pointed out, to be aware of one's ideals in day-to-day efforts to improve the system and make it work for all children. One senior educator, who spoke of his 'sense of betrayal' at recent educational changes, still quite clearly held a vision of better and transformed future, which made it easier to deal with immediate difficulties but also had the practical purpose of a measuring stick against which current developments could be judged. Another, a headteacher, looked forward to a future in which she would leave her headship and work with and on behalf of the community to realise her hopes for black people. She operated with a clear vision of the importance of engaging the black communities in the decision-making processes of schools and recognised the potential of education for liberation, through the establishment of schools as self-critical communities.

Madan Sarup (1991: 140) in his final book, *Education and the Ideologies of Racism*, also argues for the retention of a transformed vision of education:

> At one time we all had a dream of education for all. It was generally admitted that it would be expensive but it was argued that it was necessary for a democratic society. Of course, the goal of open access has always entailed struggle. The educational sphere has always been an area of class struggle and conflict. Education has always been jealously guarded because it is irredeemably subversive. It is, after all, a source of power and pleasure.

Sarup identifies the problems of working with the community to achieve such an ideal: he raises questions about cost, teacher concepts of professionalism, popular cynicism, and the danger that communities may want an education with reactionary aims. Nevertheless he concludes (Sarup 1991: 142):

> A socialist society should develop its own curricula and pedagogies, its own definition of 'really useful knowledge'. In such a society education would be redefined as a strategy for changing not only the self but the world.

Summary

This chapter has sought to explore how black teachers respond to racism in their lives and particularly within their work. While acknowledging the importance of structural racism, it has sought to explore how individuals engage with the problem of racism and challenge it. In doing so the emphasis is on individuals and their ability to bring about change. The six orientations to racism identified in Table 11.1 are intended as an aid to understanding. At the same time, it is recognised that such a model is inevitably general and does not allow for the range of diversity and difference encountered in the life histories.

There is always the danger, in examining racism in this kind of way, of imposing an artificial coherence on what is a broad range of experiences, and consequently simplifying or limiting the analysis of this experience. The lives and careers of African Caribbean, Asian and other minority community teachers, their experiences, aspirations and achievements might then be vulnerable to an interpretation which portrays them as little more than a catalogue of racist incidents. Black teachers, like white teachers, clearly enjoy a wide range of life experiences which extend beyond the experience of racism. Nevertheless, to deny racism would be to deny significant forces operating in the lives and careers of black teachers which they share with other black and ethnic minority people. Consequently, policies and practices for staff development which do not seek to tackle racism in all its complex forms, will fail to address the needs of these teachers.

Twelve

Conclusions

The narratives of teachers and student teachers presented in this book contain two contrasting but related strands: the first is a struggle against injustice in which individuals have shown considerable courage, determination and optimism in achieving their goals and ambitions through their education and careers. In this struggle they have come to recognise education as a powerful force for change. A number have found the company of other black teachers a valuable source of strength and support. Generally speaking, they chose not to work through large organisations like teacher unions or political parties but to establish networks which address the projects in which they are currently engaged. Although sometimes pessimistic about the direction of educational change, most have shown considerable optimism in the courses of action which they have taken. They have demonstrated through their personal histories that it is possible to effectively challenge racism through education; their lives and careers are a testimony to their professionalism and determination. That said, some of the earliest accounts within these narratives recall events of 40 years ago. Some readers may wonder about the relevance of these stories today, others may wonder that in some respects so little appears to have changed. I would argue that this history has an immediate relevance to our understanding of the present and in our efforts to create a more positive future.

The second strand in these narratives relates to a vision of education for today and for the future. We are often presented with a picture of a teaching force which is demoralised and disillusioned, yet despite a day-to-day pragmatic approach to their work, many of these teachers also maintain the idealism and optimism with which they entered teaching; they have an ongoing commitment to ensuring that the children in their care have access to justice, learning and achievement. They recognise the political nature of education and actively work to bring about social change through their working lives. The development of their personal and professional identities as black teachers reflects this understanding. As a teacher offers support or encouragement to an individual child, a headteacher works for the cooperation of her staff in a new initiative, or an adviser offers support to a younger colleague, each is engaged in a continuous process of personal development, growing politicisation and sometimes transformation. These black teachers are much more than role models for black children or even for all children, they are acting as advocates for any child who is disadvantaged in education.

Individuals are engaged in an ongoing struggle with structural inequality while at the same time often engaging in what is sometimes a parallel practical struggle to survive the difficulties of a particular day. Although this study has shown that individuals have adopted varied strategies to achieve their goals, these life histories can be seen as offering considerable encouragement to other educators working for social justice. The senior educators whose narratives are presented have positioned themselves within the mainstream of education, forming alliances with others who share their goals, but at the same time remaining critical campaigners for change whilst their more junior colleagues, in less influential positions, are also working with pupils and parents to promote racial justice, believing that education can change the lives of individuals. Whether a particular professional activity or goal positions an individual within an affirming, challenging or transforming orientation the process of development is one which reflects both critical and self-critical approaches.

The narratives offer us new insights into the complexity of black people's lived experience and the diversity of black identities and show the identities of individuals as being in a continual process of change and development. Black identities are not fixed or immutable but are formed and reformed as individuals encounter new situations, people and communities. Many of these educators' identities have been shaped and reshaped in a process of politicisation which has taken place as individuals have sought to negotiate their particular career paths. Professional success has been achieved despite structural barriers, whilst the discovery of alternative career routes has been closely tied to an ongoing commitment to justice in education.

The narratives raise a number of questions concerning, in particular, initial teacher education and the ongoing professional development of teachers. It has already been argued that policies and practices for staff development which do not seek to tackle racism in all its complex forms will fail to address the needs of black teachers. Similarly, it must be acknowledged that policies developed within the education service will fail to be fully effective if they are not backed up by measures designed to challenge racism in other fields – while education may be a powerful force for change, it is not the only force.

The narratives suggest a need for public debate and a general deeper understanding of the nature of the multicultural society in which we live, an examination of questions relating to 'race', identities and culture and an exploration of shared human rights and values. Schools and teacher education have key roles to play in this process. As teachers and teacher educators we have perhaps been willing to work with an understanding of identities which has sometimes been superficial. Throughout the discussion of black identity there has been the assumption that blackness is a socially constructed category which does not have fixed boundaries. It is important also to remind ourselves that whiteness is also a similarly constructed category which also needs to be explained and analysed. A genuine multicultural education will be inclusive of white identities and celebrate hybridity.

Within initial teacher education, the processes of ethnic monitoring which have begun should be developed beyond the mere collection of statistics. There is a need for individual institutions and the Teacher Training Agency to analyse the data, identify the causes of unequal opportunities and develop policies and practices which promote genuine access for all. Ideally, those measures which seek to identify quality in teacher education should include criteria which explicitly address equity issues in the curriculum and in the support systems available to students. These should include an exploration of structural racism.

The recruitment into teacher education of staff from black and ethnic minority communities would appear to be an urgent priority. This is a key area of education where black people are seriously underrepresented, yet there is some evidence to suggest that there is a strong pool of potential recruits from among black teachers, many of whom appear to be more highly qualified than their white counterparts.

ITE institutions should examine their student selection procedures to consider whether they are able to identify the particular skills and experiences which black applicants bring. All applicants should be encouraged to consider their attitudes towards equality issues at interview. Institutions should reflect on whether they are able, within the confines of existing courses, to effectively challenge the attitudes of misinformed or prejudiced applicants.

Priority areas for research within ITE might include the impact of recent changes in teacher education on black and ethnic minority students and their communities. Another important area of research would be to trace newly qualified teachers from black and ethnic minority communities and establish how they progress, particularly to establish the effectiveness of their initial teacher education.

There is a need to review when and how students at school receive information about future careers. Ideally careers education should begin at primary level, with pupils encouraged to extend their aspirations. This should continue at secondary level. Before all option or course choices, students should have access to individual careers counselling. Similarly, information about degree courses should be made available at an early stage. Those wishing to encourage young black and ethnic minority people into teaching need to address them while they are still in compulsory schooling and ensure that they do not restrict their options at undergraduate level by choosing an inappropriate degree course.

The research has a number of implications for the continuing professional development of teachers and for school management. Headteachers, governors and others involved in the selection of teaching staff should be made aware of their responsibilities under the Race Relations Act 1976, whilst 'race' equality issues should be incorporated into management training programmes. Headteachers have a special responsibility for ensuring that the formal and informal processes of staff development, including the opportunity to gain 'on the job' experiences which might enhance promotion prospects should be available to all their teaching staff. Included in this should be an examination of the formal and informal ways in which mentoring takes place within their institutions.

The research suggests an urgent need for all schools to review their policies relating to equality and ensure that they have in place specific measures to address racial harassment; these should take into consideration staff needs as well as those of students. Those responsible for the support and supervision of student teachers and newly qualified teachers should be encouraged to explore 'race' equality issues as part of their training, which should include an examination of the structural nature of racism and the experiences of people from minority groups.

On a practical level, all teachers and teacher educators should be encouraged to understand their rights and responsibilities under the Race Relations Act 1976 which seeks to protect individuals against racial discrimination. As teachers, and especially as teacher educators, we have a particular responsibility to inform our students about these rights and responsibilities and encourage critical debate about the strengths and limitations of existing legislation. Policies, training and the development of effective laws all have a part to play in promoting a more just society but we have seen that, to date, they have not secured such a society. Much more can, no doubt, be achieved with greater political will, but within schools and teacher education there is a need for students to examine the moral arguments which support racial justice, rather than depend solely on laws and policies. These laws and policies will only be effective where they attract broad consensus and understanding.

LEAs should explore ways of supporting and encouraging black teachers' networks which can be crucial to the personal and professional development of many isolated teachers. This book has addressed the experiences of black teachers in urban areas where there are established black and ethnic minority communities. In the absence of national ethnic monitoring of the teaching force, the collection of data at LEA level would support those concerned to promote equality in employment. This could be followed by target-setting to encourage the development of a teaching force which more closely reflects the ethnic make-up of the pupil population and the employment of black and ethnic minority teachers at all levels within schools. There is need for further research which examines the experiences of black and ethnic minority teachers working in more isolated environments.

In teaching and in other professions, a few black and ethnic minority people have achieved successful careers, and this success deserves to be celebrated. Nevertheless, it has taken place in a context where black and ethnic minority people still experience widespread racism in employment, particularly when they move outside those sectors which are recognised as traditional areas of black and ethnic minority employment. Levels of unemployment, particularly amongst African Caribbeans, Bangladeshis and Pakistanis, remain much higher than those of white people. Progress in some areas does not cancel out disadvantage, discrimination and regression in others. While many middle-class white people may now find themselves working alongside people from black and ethnic communities, we need to remind ourselves that regressive forces still remain. Black teachers such as those whose life histories are presented here have a key role to play in the continuing struggle for racial justice, but this will only be achieved within education in alliance with white colleagues who share their goals.

Bibliography

Abbott, D. (1989) Young, gifted and black, in S. MccGwire (ed.) *Transforming Moments*. London: Virago.

Adia, E. (1996) *Higher Education: The ethnic minority student experience*. Leeds: Higher Education Information Services Trust.

Adler, S., Laney, J. and Packer, M. (1993) *Managing Women*. Buckingham: Open University Press.

Alexander, C. (1996) *The Art of Being Black: The creation of black British youth identities*. Oxford: Oxford University Press.

Amin, K. and Richardson, R. (1994) *Multi-Ethnic Britain: Facts and trends*. London: The Runnymede Trust.

Apple, M. (1986) *Teachers and Texts: A political economy of class and gender relations in education*. London: Routledge and Kegan Paul.

Arnot, M., David, M. and Weiner, G. (1996) *Educational Reform and Gender Equality in Schools*. EOC Research Discussion Series, 17. Manchester: Equal Opportunities Commission.

ARTEN (Anti-Racist Teacher Education Network) (1992) *ARTEN's Response to Kenneth Clarke's Speech for the Reform of Initial Teacher Training* (a consultation document).

ARTEN (Anti-Racist Teacher Education Network) (1996) *ARTEN's Concerns and Recommendations with Respect to Teacher Education*.

Ball, S. J. (1987) *The Micropolitics of the School: Towards a theory of school organisation*. London: Methuen/Routledge.

Ball, S. and Goodson, I. (eds) (1985) *Teachers' Lives and Careers*. Lewes: Falmer.

Bangar, S. and McDermott, J. (1989) Black women speak, in H. de Lyon and F. Widdowson Migniuolo (eds) *Women Teachers: Issues and experiences*. Milton Keynes: Open University Press.

Bansal, R. (1990) A Sikh by night, *The Times Educational Supplement*, 20 July.

Barton, L., Pollard, A., and Whitty, G. (1992) Experiencing CATE: the impact of accreditation upon initial training institutions in England. *Journal of Education for Teaching*, 18: 41–57.

Ben-Tovim, G., Gabriel, J., Law, I. and Stredder, K. (1986) *The Local Politics of Race*. London: Macmillan.

Bhachu, P. (1991) Ethnicity constructed and reconstructed: the role of Sikh women in cultural elaboration and educational decision-making in Britain. *Gender and Education*, 3(1): 45–60.

Birmingham City Council (n.d.) *Constituency and Ward Profiles: 1991 Census topic reports.* Birmingham: Birmingham City Council.

Birmingham City Council (1996) *Report of the Chief Education Officer to Education Committee: Education Service Equal Opportunities Statement,* 12 November.

Blair, M. (1994) Black teachers, black students and education markets. *Cambridge Journal of Education*, 24: 277–91.

Blair, M. and Maylor, U. (1993) Issues and concerns for black women teachers in training, in I. Siraj-Blatchford (ed.) *'Race', Gender and the Education of Teachers.* Buckingham: Open University Press.

Bourne, J., Bridges, L. and Searle, C. (1994) *Outcast England: How schools exclude black children.* London: Institute of Race Relations.

Brah, A. (1988) Black struggles, equality and education. *Critical Social Policy*, 24: 83–90.

Brah, A. and Shaw, S. (1992) *Working Choices: South Asian young Muslim women and the labour market.* Research Paper 91. London: Department of Employment.

Brar, H. S. (1991a) Teaching, professionalism and home-school links. *Multicultural Teaching*, 9(3): 32–5.

Brar, H. S. (1991b) Unequal opportunities: the recruitment, selection and promotion prospects for black teachers. *Evaluation and Research in Education*, 5: 35–47.

Brennan, J. and McGeevor, P. (1990) *Ethnic Minorities and the Graduate Labour Market.* London: Commission for Racial Equality.

Brenner, M. (1981) Patterns of social structure in the research interview, in M. Brenner (ed.) *Social Method and Social Life.* London: Academic Press.

Bryan, B., Dadzie, S. and Scafe, S. (1985) *The Heart of the Race: Black women's lives in Britain.* London, Virago.

Burton, L. and Weiner, G. (1993) From rhetoric to reality: strategies for developing a social justice approach to educational decision making, in I. Siraj-Blatchford (ed.) *'Race', Gender and the Education of Teachers.* Buckingham: Open University Press.

Carby, H. (1982) Schooling in Babylon, in Centre for Contemporary Cultural Studies, *The Empire Strikes Back.* London and Birmingham: Hutchinson.

Casey, K. (1993) *I Answer With My Life: Life histories of women teachers working for social change.* London and New York: Routledge.

Chevannes, M. and Reeves, F. (1987) The black voluntary school movement: definition, context and prospects, in B. Troyna (ed.) *Racial Inequality in Education.* London: Tavistock.

Clay, J., Gadia, S. and Wilkins, C. (1991) Racism and institutional inertia: a 3-D perspective of initial teacher education (disillusionment, disaffection and despair). *Multicultural Teaching*, 9(3): 26–31.

Coard, B. (1971) *How the West Indian Child is made Educationally Subnormal in the British School System.* London: New Beacon Books.

Cohen, L. and Manion, L. (1989) *Research Methods in Education.* London: Routledge.

Commission for Racial Equality (1987) *Living in Terror.* London: CRE.

Commission for Racial Equality (1988a) *Ethnic Minority School Teachers: A survey in eight local education authorities.* London: CRE.

Commission for Racial Equality (1988b) *St George's Medical School. Report of a formal investigation.* London: CRE.

Commission for Racial Equality (1992a) *Response to DES Consultation on Proposals for Reform of Initial Teacher Training*. London: CRE.

Commission for Racial Equality (1992b) *Second Review of the Race Relations Act 1976*. London: CRE.

Commission for Racial Equality (1992c) *Secondary Schools Admission Report of a Formal Investigation into Hertfordshire County Council*. London: CRE.

Connell, R. (1985) *Teachers' Work*. Sydney: George Allen and Unwin.

Connolly, P. (1995) Racism, masculine peer-group relations and the schooling of African/ Caribbean infant boys. *British Journal of Sociology of Education*, 16(1): 75–92.

Cooper, P., Upton, G. and Smith, C. (1991) Ethnic minority and gender distribution among staff and pupils with emotional and behavioural difficulties in England and Wales. *British Journal of Sociology of Education*, 12: 77–94.

Cross, M. (1978) *Ethnic Minorities in the Inner City*. London: Commission for Racial Equality.

Cross, M., Wrench, J. and Barnett, S. (1990) *Ethnic Minorities and the Careers service: An investigation into processes of assessment and placement*. Department of Employment Research Papers. Series No. 73.

Crozier, G. and Menter, I. (1993) The heart of the matter? Student teachers' experiences in school, in I. Siraj-Blatchford (ed.) *'Race', Gender and the Education of Teachers*. Buckingham: Open University Press.

Daniels, C. and Aldred, M. (1986) The responsibility of black parents and teachers to the black student, in A. S. Saakana and A. Pearse (eds) *Towards the Decolonisation of the British Educational System*. London: Karnak House.

David, M. (1993) *Parents, Gender and Educational Reform*. Cambridge: Polity Press.

Davies, A. M., Holland, J. and Minhas, R. (1990) *Equal Opportunities in the New ERA*, Hillcole Group, paper 2. London: Tufnell Press.

Davis, A. (1982) *Women, Race and Class*. London: Women's Press.

Deem, R. (1989) The new school governing bodies: are gender and race on the agenda? *Gender and Education*, 1(3): 247–61.

Deem, R., Brehony, K. and Hemmings, S. (1992) Social justice, social divisions and the governing of schools, in D. Gill, B. Mayor and M. Blair (eds) *Racism and Education*. London: Sage.

Delsol, S. (1984) *The New Black Teacher: Part one*. London: Gresham Supplementary School.

de Lyon, H. and Migniuolo, F. W. (eds) (1989) *Women Teachers: issues and experiences*. Milton Keynes: Open University Press.

Department for Education (1993) A new deal for 'out of school' pupils. *DfE News*, 126/93, 23 April.

Department for Education (1994) *Statistical Bulletin. Students in Higher Education in England 1991 and 1992*. 17/94 November. London: DfE.

Department of Education and Science (1981) *West Indian Children in Our Schools*. The Rampton Report. London: HMSO.

Department of Education and Science (1985) *Education for All: The report of the committee of enquiry into the education of children from ethnic minority groups*. The Swann Report. London: HMSO, Cmnd 9453.

Department of Education and Science (1989) *National Curriculum: From policy to practice*. London: HMSO.

Department of Education and Science (1989b) *Responses to Ethnic Diversity in Teacher Training*. Circular 117/89. London: HMSO.

Department of Education and Science (1991) *School Teacher Appraisal,* Circular 12/91. London: HMSO.

Deshpande, P. and Rashid, N. (1993) Developing equality through local education authority INSET, in I. Siraj-Blatchford (ed.) *'Race', Gender and the Education of Teachers.* Buckingham: Open University Press.

Dixon, R. (1977) *Catching Them Young.* London: Pluto.

Doe, B. (1996) LEAs return to exclusion zone. *The Times Educational Supplement,* 15 November.

Drew, D. (1995) *'Race', Education and Work: The statistics of inequality.* Avebury: Aldershot.

Drew, D. and Gray, J. (1991) The black–white gap in examination results: a statistical critique of a decade's research. *New Community,* 17(2): 159–72.

Driver, G. (1977) Cultural competence, social power and school achievement: West Indian secondary pupils in the West Midlands. *New Community,* 5(4): 353–9.

Driver, G. (1979) Classroom stress and school achievement: West Indian adolescents and their teachers, in V. Saifullah Khan (ed.) *Minority Families in Britain: Support and stress.* London: Macmillan.

Dummett, A. (1973) *A Portrait of English Racism.* Harmondsworth: Penguin.

Dyer, R. (1988) 'White'. *Screen,* 29(4): 44–65.

Ealing, London Borough of (1988) *Ealing's Dilemma: Implementing race equality in education. A summary of the Inquiry's findings and the Council's response.* London: Race Equality Unit, London Borough of Ealing.

Eggleston, J., Dunn, D. K. and Anjai, M. (1986) *Education for Some: The educational and vocational experiences of 15–18-year-old members of minority ethnic groups.* Stoke-on-Trent: Trentham Books.

Epstein, D. (1993) *Changing Classroom Cultures: Anti-racism, politics and schools.* Stoke-on-Trent: Trentham.

Evetts, J. (1988) Married women and career: career history accounts of primary headteachers. *Qualitative Studies in Education,* 2(2): 89–105.

Evetts, J. (1989) The internal labour market for primary teachers, in S. Acker (ed.) *Teachers, Gender and Careers.* Lewes: Falmer.

Figueroa, P. (1991) *Education and the Social Construction of 'Race'.* London: Routledge.

Forbes, A. (1990) The Open University: The OU my great hope. *Multicultural Teaching,* 8(3): 36–7.

Frederikse, J. (1982) *None But Ourselves: Masses vs. media in the making of Zimbabwe.* Harare: Zimbabwe Publishing House.

Freire, P. (1972) *Pedagogy of the Oppressed.* Harmondsworth: Penguin.

Fryer, P. (1984) *Staying Power: The history of black people in Britain.* London: Pluto.

Fuller, M. (1980) Black girls in a London comprehensive school, in R. Deem (ed.) *Schooling for Women's Work.* London: Routledge and Kegan Paul.

Galtung, J. (1967) *Theory and Methods of Social Research.* London: Allen and Unwin.

Ghuman, P. (1980a) Bhattra Sikhs in Cardiff – family and kinship organisation. *New Community,* 8(3): 309–16.

Ghuman, P. (1980b) Punjabi parents and English education. *Educational Research,* 22(2): 121–30.

Ghuman, P. A. Singh (1995) *Asian Teachers in British Schools.* Clevedon: Multilingual Matters.

Ghuman, P. and Gallop, R. (1981) Educational attitudes of Bengali families in Cardiff. *Journal of Multi-cultural and Multi-lingual Development,* 2(2): 127–44.

Gibbes, N. (1980) *West Indian Teachers Speak Out their Experiences in some of London's Schools.* London: Caribbean Teachers' Association/ Lewisham Council for Community Relations.

Gibson, D. (1987) Hearing and listening: a case study of the 'consultation' process undertaken by a local education department and black groups, in B. Troyna (ed.) *Racial Inequality in Education.* London: Tavistock.

Gillborn, D. (1988) Ethnicity and educational opportunity: a case study of West Indian male–white teacher relationships. *British Journal of Sociology of Education,* 9: 371–85.

Gillborn, D. (1990) *'Race', Ethnicity and Education: Teaching and learning in multi-ethnic schools.* London: Unwin Hyman.

Gillborn, D. and Gipps, C. (1996) *Recent Research on the Achievements of Ethnic Minority Pupils.* London: HMSO.

Gilroy, B. (1976) *Black Teacher.* London: Cassell.

Goode, W. J. and Hatt, P. K. (1952) *Methods in Social Research.* New York: McGraw Hill.

Gordon, P. (1986) *Racial Violence and Harassment.* Runnymede Research Report. London: The Runnymede Trust.

Gordon, P. and Rosenberg, D. (1989) *The Press and Black People in Britain.* London: The Runnymede Trust.

Graduate Teacher Training Registry (1992) *Annual Statistical Report: Autumn 1992 Entry.* Cheltenham: GTTR.

Griffin, C. (1985) *Typical Girls? Young women from school to the labour market.* London: Routledge and Kegan Paul.

Gupta, Y. (1977) The educational and vocational aspirations of Asian immigrants and English school leavers: a comparative study. *British Journal of Sociology,* 28(2): 185–98.

Hall, S. (1981) The whites of their eyes: racist ideologies and the media, in G. Bridges and R. Brunt (eds) *Silver Linings: Some strategies for the eighties.* London: Lawrence and Wishart.

Hall, S. *et al.* (1978) *Policing the Crisis.* London: Macmillan.

Hargreaves, A. (1994) *Changing Teachers, Changing Times: Teachers' work and culture in the postmodern age.* London: Cassell.

Her Majesty's Inspectorate (1988) *Secondary Schools: An appraisal by HMI.* London: HMSO.

Henry, D. (1991) *Thirty Blacks in British Education: Hopes, frustrations, achievements.* Crawley: Rabbit Press.

Higher Education Funding Council for England (1995) *Special Initiative to Encourage Widening Participation of Students from Ethnic Minorities in Teacher Training.* Bristol: HEFCE.

Hofkins, D. (1994) Bid to prevent pupils losing the lead in skills. *The Times Educational Supplement,* 9 December.

Hopkin, J. (1994) Geography and development education, in A. Osler (ed.) *Development Education: Global perspectives in the curriculum.* London: Cassell.

Howson, J. (1996) Equal opportunities and initial teacher training. *Education Review,* 10(1): 36–40.

Jeffcoate, R. (1979) *Positive Image: Towards a multiracial curriculum.* London: Readers and Writers Publishing Co-operative.

Jones, T. (1993) *Britain's Ethnic Minorities: An analysis of the Labour Force Survey.* London: Policy Studies Institute.

Kitwood, T. and Borrell, C. (1980) The significance of schooling for an ethnic minority. *Oxford Review of Education*, 6(3): 241–53.

Klein, G. (1985) *Reading into Racism: Bias in children's literature and learning materials.* London: Routledge and Kegan Paul.

Klein, G. (1993) *Education towards Race Equality.* London: Cassell.

Klein, R. (1995) Where prejudice still flares into violence. *The Times Educational Supplement*, 6 January.

Mac an Ghaill, M. (1988) *Young, Gifted and Black: Student–teacher relations in the schooling of black youth.* Milton Keynes: Open University Press.

Mac an Ghaill, M. (1989) Coming of age in 1980s England: reconceptualizing black students' schooling experience. *British Journal of Sociology of Education*, 10(3): 273–86.

Macdonald, I., Bhavnani, R., Khan, L. and John, G. (1989) *Murder in the Playground: The report of the Macdonald Inquiry into racism and racial violence in Manchester schools.* The Burnage Report. London: Longsight.

McGurk, H. (ed.) (1987) *What Next?* London: Economic and Social Research Council.

McKellar, B. (1989) Only the fittest of the fittest will survive: black women and education, in S. Acker (ed.) *Teachers, Gender and Careers.* Lewes: Falmer.

McKenzie-Mavinga, I. and Perkins, T. (1991) *In Search of Mr McKenzie.* London: Women's Press.

Maginnis, E. (1993) *An inter-agency response to children with special needs – the Lothian experience – a Scottish perspective.* Paper presented at National Children's Bureau Conference, Exclusions from School: bridging the gap between policy and practice, London, 13 July.

Menter, I. (1989) Teaching practice stasis: racism, sexism and school experience in initial teacher education. *British Journal of Sociology of Education*, 10(4): 459–73.

Milner, D. (1983) *Children and Race: Ten years on.* London: Ward Lock Educational.

Milner, D. (1975) *Children and Race.* Harmondsworth: Penguin.

Mirza, H. S. (1992) *Young, Female and Black.* London: Routledge.

Mortimore, P. (1991) The front page or yesterday's news: the reception of educational research, in G. Walford (ed.) *Doing Educational Research.* London: Routledge.

Modood, T. (1988) 'Black', racial equality and Asian identity. *New Community*, 14(3): 396–404.

Modood, T. (1992) *Not Easy Being British: colour, culture and citizenship.* Stoke-on-Trent: Trentham.

Modood, T. and Shiner, M. (1994) *Ethnic Minorities and Higher Education: Why are there differential rates of entry?* London: Policy Studies Institute.

Mugomba, A. T. and Nyaggah, M. (1980) *Independence Without Freedom: the political economy of colonial education in Southern Africa.* Oxford: Clio Press.

Mullard, C. (1982) Multiracial education in Britain: from assimilation to cultural pluralism, in J. Tierney (ed.) *Race, Migration and Schooling.* London: Holt, Rinehart and Winston.

Murray, P. (1987) *Song in a Weary Throat: An American pilgrimage.* New York: Harper and Row.

National Union of Teachers (1990) *Memorandum of the Executive on Black Teachers: Annual Conference 1990.* London: National Union of Teachers.

Newham Afro-Caribbean Teachers Association (1985) *A Report on the Working Conditions and Status of African-Caribbean Teachers in Newham.* London: Newham Afro-Caribbean Teachers Association.

Newham Asian Teachers' Association (1985) *Racial Discrimination in Education*. London: Newham Asian Teachers' Association.

Nias, J. (1989) *Primary Teachers Talking: A study of teaching as work*. London: Routledge.

Oakley, A. (1981) Interviewing women: a contradiction in terms, in H. Roberts (ed.) *Doing Feminist Research*. London: Routledge and Kegan Paul.

Ofsted (1995) *The Ofsted Handbooks: Guidance on the inspection of schools* (nursery and primary, secondary and special). London: HMSO.

O'Keeffe, D. (ed.) (1986) *The Wayward curriculum: A cause for parents' concern?* London: Social Affairs Unit.

Osler, A. (1989) *Speaking Out: Black girls in Britain*. London: Virago.

Osler, A. (1994a) An equal start? Black students and assessment practices in initial teacher education, in S. Butterfield (ed.) *Qualifying Teachers: Assessing professional work*. Birmingham: Educational Review Publications.

Osler, A. (1994b) Still hidden from history? The representation of women in recently published history textbooks. *Oxford Review of Education*, 20(2): 219–35.

Osler, A. (1994c) 'The flavour of the moment'? Bilingual teachers' experiences of teaching and learning, in A. Blackledge (ed.) *Teaching Bilingual Children*. Stoke-on Trent: Trentham Books.

Osler, A. (1994d) The UN Convention on the Rights of the Child: some implications for teacher education. *Educational Review*, Special Issue 26, Teacher Education and Equal Rights, 46(2): 141–50.

Osler, A. and Hussain, Z. (1995) Parental choice and schooling: some factors influencing Muslim mothers' decisions about the education of their daughters. *Cambridge Journal of Education*, 25(3): 327–47.

Osler, A. and Starkey, H. (1996) *Teacher Education and Human Rights*. London: David Fulton.

Owen, D. (1994) *Black people in Great Britain: Social and economic circumstances*. 1991 Census Statistical Paper No. 6. Warwick: Centre for Research in Ethnic Relations.

Ozga, J. (ed.) (1988) *Schoolwork: Approaches to the labour processes of teaching*. Milton Keynes: Open University Press.

Ozga, J. (1993) Introduction: in a different mode, in J. Ozga (ed.) *Women in Educational Management*. Buckingham: Open University Press.

Parekh, B. (1991) Law torn. *New Statesman and Society*, 14 June.

Parekh, B. (1994) *Racial Violence: A separate offence? A discussion paper*. The All-Party Group on Race and Community, Houses of Parliament Session 1993–94. London: Charter Mede Associate Company.

Parsons, C. (1995) *Final Report to the Department of Education: national survey of local education authorities' policies and procedures for the identification of, and provision for, children who are out of school by reason of exclusion or otherwise*. London: DfE.

Partington, G. (1986) History: re-written to ideological fashion, in D. O'Keeffe (ed.) *The Wayward Curriculum: A cause for parents' concern?* London: Social Affairs Unit.

Peters, M. (1996) Today's race for equality. *The Times Educational Supplement*, 8 November.

Powney, J. and Watts, M. (1987) *Interviewing in Educational Research*. London: Routledge and Kegan Paul.

Preiswerk, R. (ed.) (1980) *The Slant of the Pen: Racism in children's books*. Geneva: World Council of Churches.

Rai, H. K. (1990) Asian children with special needs: parental concerns. *Multicultural Teaching*, 9(1): 11–12.

Richardson, R. (1992) Rottweilers and racism – notes and stories towards ethical resistance, in M. Leicester and M. Taylor (eds) *Ethics, Ethnicity and Education*. London: Kogan Page.

Richardson, R. (1996a) Funding and race equality – the need for a new system. *Education Review*, 10(3): 46–51.

Richardson, R. (1996b) The terrestrial teacher, in M. Steiner (ed.) *Developing the Global Teacher: Theory and practice in initial teacher education*. Stoke-on-Trent: Trentham.

Robbins, M. M. (1995) Black students in teacher education. *Multicultural Teaching*, 14(1): 15–22.

Ross, K. (1992) *Television in Black and White: Ethnic stereotypes and popular television*. Research Paper in Ethnic Relations No. 19. Warwick: Centre for Research in Ethnic Relations.

Runnymede Trust (1993) *Equality Assurance in Schools: Quality, identity, society*. Stoke-on-Trent: Trentham Books with The Runnymede Trust.

Sarup, M. (1982) *Education, State and Crisis: A Marxist perspective*. London: Routledge and Kegan Paul.

Sarup, M. (1991) *Education and the Ideologies of Racism*. Stoke-on-Trent: Trentham Books.

Scott, S. (1985) Feminist research and qualitative methods: a discussion of some of the issues, in R. Burgess (ed.) *Issues in Educational Research: Qualitative methods*. Lewes: Falmer.

Selltiz, C., Jahoda, M., Deutsch, M. and Cook, S. W. (1965) *Research Methods in Social Relations*. London: Methuen.

Shepherd, D. (1987) The accomplishment of divergence. *British Journal of Sociology of Education*, 8(3): 263–76.

Sikes, P., Measor, L. and Woods, P. (1985) *Teacher Careers: Crises and continuities*. Lewes: Falmer.

Singh, R. (1988) *Asian and White Perceptions of the Teaching Profession*. Bradford and Ilkley Community College.

Singh, R., Brown, T. and Darr, A. (1988) *Ethnic Minority Young People and Entry to Teacher Education: A survey of perceptions of the teaching profession of South Asian and white students in Bradford schools and Bradford and Ilkley Community College*. Bradford and Ilkley Community College.

Siraj-Blatchford, I. (1991) A study of black students' perceptions of racism in initial teacher education. *British Educational Research Journal*, 17(1): 35–50.

Sivanandan, A. (1982) *A Different Hunger*. London: Pluto.

Skellington, R. and Morris, P. (1992) *'Race' in Britain Today*. London: Sage.

Smith, D. and Tomlinson, S. (1989) *The School Effect: A study of multi-racial comprehensives*. London: Policy Studies Group.

Solomos, J. (1988) *Black Youth, Racism and the State: The politics of ideology and policy*. Cambridge: Cambridge University Press.

Stanley, L. and Wise, S. (1993) *Breaking Out Again*. London: Routledge.

Stinton, J. (1979) *Racism and Sexism in Children's Books*. London: Writers and Readers.

Stirling, M. (1996) Government policy and disadvantaged children, in E. Blyth and J. Milner (eds) *Exclusions from School: Inter-professional issues for policy and practice*. London: Routledge.

Stone, M. (1981) *The Education of the Black Child in Britain: The myth of multiracial education*. London: Fontana Press.

Taylor, M. (1981) *Caught Between: A review of research into the education of pupils of West Indian origin*. Windsor: NFER/Nelson.

Thomas, D. (ed.) (1995) *Teachers' Stories*. Buckingham: Open University Press.

Tomlinson, S. (1983) Black women in higher education: case studies of university women in Britain, in L. Barton and S. Walker (eds) *Race, Class and Education*. London: Croom Helm.

Tomlinson, S. (1984) *Home and School in Multicultural Britain*. London: Batsford.

Tomlinson, S. (1987) *Ethnic Minorities in British Schools: A review of the literature 1960–1982*. Aldershot: Gower.

Tomlinson, S. (1992) Disadvantaging the disadvantaged: Bangladeshis and education in Tower Hamlets. *British Journal of Sociology of Education*, 13(4): 437–46.

Tomlinson, S. (1993) The multicultural task group: the group that never was, in: A. King and M. Reiss (eds) *The Multicultural Dimension of the National Curriculum*. London: Falmer.

Troyna, B. (1982) The ideological and policy response to black pupils in British schools, in A. Hartnett (ed.) *The Social Sciences in Educational Studies*. London: Heinemann.

Troyna, B. (1984) Fact or artefact? The 'educational underachievement' of black pupils. *British Journal of Sociology of Education*, 5(2): 153–60.

Troyna, B. (1994) The 'everyday world' of teachers? Deracialised discourses in the sociology of teachers and the teaching profession. *British Journal of Sociology of Education*, 15(3): 325–39.

Troyna, B. and Williams, J. (1986) *Racism, Education and the State*. Beckenham: Croom Helm.

Troyna, B. and Siraj-Blatchford, I. (1993) Providing support or denying access? The experiences of students designated as 'ESL' and 'SN' in a multi-ethnic secondary school. *Educational Review*, 45(1): 3–11.

Twitchin, J. (1990) *The Black and White Media Book: Handbook for the study of racism and television*. Stoke-on-Trent: Trentham Books.

Virdee, S. (1995) *Racial Violence and Harassment*. London: Policy Studies Institute.

Walker, C. (1993) Black women in educational management, in J. Ozga (ed.) *Women in Educational Management*. Buckingham: Open University Press.

Willis, P. (1977) *Learning to Labour*. Farnborough: Saxon House.

Woods, P. (1986) *Inside Schools: Ethnography in Educational Research: Life histories*. London: Routledge and Kegan Paul.

Wright, C. (1986) School processes – an ethnographic study, in J. Eggleston, D. Dunn and M. Anjali (eds) *Education for Some: The educational and vocational experiences of 15–18-year-old members of ethnic minority groups*. Stoke-on-Trent: Trentham.

Wright, C. (1992) *Race Relations in the Primary School*. London: David Fulton.

Young, S. (1993) Asians join push for parents' rights. *The Times Educational Supplement*, 27 August.

Zimet, S. G. (1976) *Print and Prejudice*. London: Hodder and Stoughton.

Index